HUNGARY

First Edition
1991

TABLE OF CONTENTS

LIST OF MAPS

HUNGARY

0   30km

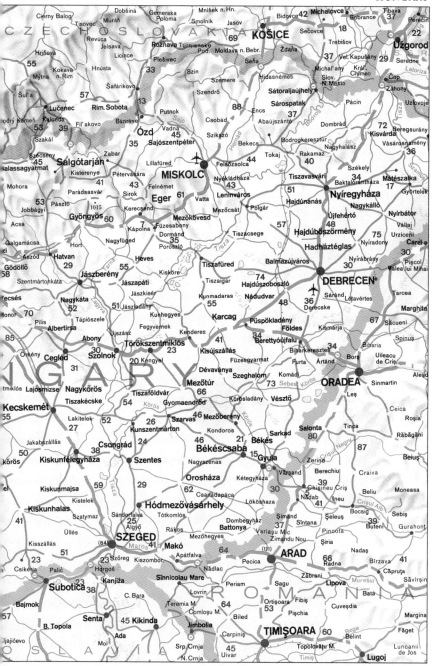

THE HISTORY
OF
HUNGARY

THE NATION'S BIRTH

Stuck between its master for over forty years the Soviet Union and the temptations of Western capitalism, Hungary at the end of the 1980s attracted world-wide attention and admiration for its diplomatic skills in steering a course in dangerous waters. In March, 1989, it broadcast an interview with the deposed leader of the Prag Spring Alexander Dubcek which naturally reached Czechoslovakia; it closed its borders to the two-stroke Trabants and Wartburgs from then East Germany but in September it opened them to thousands of East Germans fleeing westward. Hungary also applied for membership in the European Council and has dreamed aloud about one day becoming a member of the EEC.

Given the history of the Hungarians, none of these moves are in fact surprising. Dealing greater forces than themselves, vassals of nomadic overlords, bosom pals of such expansionist dynasties as the Habsburgs and the Third Reich, has made them masters of sitting on several chairs at once.

Starting east of the Urals some 6000 years ago, Magyar tribes began heading west across the great Russian steppes in search of living and grazing space, pressed in the rear by other tribal migrations. Reconstructing the millenia-long trip was the task of linguists and archeologists of the past two centuries who researched everything from morphology and syntax of isolated tribes to ancient

Preceding pages: A florid costume at the Debrecen flower festival. Hungary's future. Music – a part of Hungarian life. The parliament building in Budapest. Left: An early Hungarian chronicle.

graveyards. By the 7th century, seven Magyar tribes had reached the Black Sea region between the Danube and the Don rivers. There they served as an elite cavalry to the Kagan, the leader of the powerful Khazar people. For some reason though, when asked to suppress a rebellion, they not only refused but even granted refugees asylum. Perhaps the Magyar military leaders (known as *gyulas*) felt the Khazars were weak, perhaps they had a strong sense of nomadic justice which prevented them from suppressing an already oppressed people. Two things they knew for certain: The Kagan would seek revenge and, secondly, from their military excursions west, they knew of a stretch of land beyond the Carpathian mountains where the tribes might find both fertile grounds and security. When the Pecheneg tribe emerged in the east cutting a breach through the Khazar empire, Árpád, the most powerful Magyar *gyula*, led his tribe to safety. The last members crossed the Verecke-pass (today in the Soviet Union) in late 896.

Hungarian historiographers have two euphemistic descriptions for the next few decades: *Honfoglalás* and *kalandozás*: the "land-taking" and the "time of adventures". The first suggests occupation of a barren stretch of territory. In fact the Carpathian basin was thinly populated with a colorful mixtures of Slavs, Germans, leftover Avars and the likes. While the Magyars were still trudgeing across the Russian steppes, Celtic and Avar cultures had flourished on these fertile grounds. The Romans made Pannonia (Transdanubia) one of their provinces in 14 B.C. and held on to it right until the 4th century. The nomadic Huns, whom popular wisdom still confuses with the Hungarians, also spent some time along the Danube.

As for the "adventure" the Hungarians enjoyed, it was definitely at the expense of Bavarians and Northern Italians. With a sense of mission the Magyar riders,

13

fearless, efficient and extremely cruel according to the chronicles, rode through these regions picking up booty and leaving death and destruction in their trail. At this time they were mixed up with an earlier horseback scourge known as the Onogurs, which resulted in the peculiar linguistic fact that Magyars are called *Hungarians* (Hongrois in French, Ungarn in German, Ongarese in Italian, etc.).

The fun and games ended abruptly in 955 when emperor Otto I, thereafter named "the Great," dealt the Magyars a stunning blow in the battle of Lechfeld near Augsburg in today's Germany. Christian medicine, above all its heavily armed knights, had proven more powerful and the next leader, Géza, a descendant of Árpád realized it was time to sign treaties. Sensing the growing rivalry between the eastern and western churches, wily Géza played a little hard to get with both sides in order to hammer out the best

Above: The Roman settlement of Aquincum in Budapest. Right: Magyar tribal leaders.

deal for his tribes. When Otto, who after all had defeated the Magyars, invited eastern European kings and princes to Quedlinburg in 973 to pledge their allegiance to the Holy Roman Empire, Géza sent representatives instead of appearing in person. The message was clear: The Magyars were willing allies but refused to become vassals of the West. This political objective, as well as a Western (especially Germanic) eagerness to swallow Hungary, has dominated their history since then.

Christianity

Géza converted and promptly set about zealously converting his fellow countrymen. Bent furthermore on insuring his dynasty's position at the head of the Magyars, he officially declared his son István, a dyed-in-the-wool Christian and pupil of the great Adalbert, Bishop of Prag, heir. In 997 he succeeded Géza as leader and maintained his father's westerly foreign policy with securities in the

east. He married Gisela, the sister of Heinrich, Duke of Bavaria and future Holy Roman emperor. In 1000 he dispatched envoys to Pope Sylvester II and Emperor Otto III to seek apostolic and political blessings. A year later he received the crown, mantle and insignia that went along with the royal title Gran Esztergom served as his capital. István also further established his rule over the Magyars by sallying forth against Koppány, a distant cousin, potential rival and heathen who ruled the region south of the Balaton. With the help of Bavarian knights he quickly defeated him in 997 and had him quartered. The head he sent to his uncle Gyula, the ruler of Transylvania and just for good measure – and perhaps for the gold and salt they produced – he confiscated his lands. István's last major internal enemy was Prince Ajtony who ruled the area between the Danube, Tisza and Maros rivers. In spite of his rapprochement to the Eastern Church, Ajtony remained an unrepentant, polygamous heathen. When he started

taxing the gold and salt being shipped up from Transylvania, István sent his general Csanád on a successful punitive expedition.

Besides solving sybling rivalries, István also created a functional state. The country was divided into districts – that have remained in existence to this date – each headed by an *ispán* chosen by the king directly to look after the administration and finances (such as collection of taxes) and two royal representatives who concerned themselves exclusively with judicial matters. They ruled out of fortresses (*vár*). The centralization of power meant that many of the old tribal leaders had to surrender their power, but the army and government now provided an opportunity for career advancement. A two-tiered aristocracy grew out of this system with a small clan of extremely wealthy land-owning magnates or barons at the top and a free but often poor class of nobles at the bottom. The bulk of the people consisted of disenfranchised, poverty-striken, overworked serfs.

15

The church played a vital role in the re-organization of society. Every ten villages were ordered to have one church and a priest, Veszprém, Györ, Pécs, Vác, Eger among others became bishoprics, Esztergom and Kalocsa were even elevated to the rank of an archbishopric. Monasteries and cloisters mushroomed and holy men flocked to the land. Among them was Gellért, later the bishop of Csanád, whom heathens cast into the Danube, enclosed in a bespiked barrel in 1046 from the cliff in Buda.

István's most important works though were of a literary and legal nature. His lists of crimes and punishments bridged the gap between a budding Christian society and the nomadic common law. Further, his *Admonitions* to his son provided vital guidelines to anyone trying to run a modern state. For example, they warn strongly against irritating state ser-

Above: The intricately carved battle horn allegedly used by the Magyar chieftain Lehel at the battle of Lechfeld.

vants, and suggest that inviting foreigners to settle in Hungary would be of great benefit to the country as they "bring with them various values, customs, weapons and science that make the court richer and more splendid and scare enemies."

István's efforts to maintain peace and order ultimately failed. For the first three decades of his reign he could still count on the support of the Holy Roman emperors. Between 1014 and 1018 he decisively ended the Bulgarian threat on his southeastern borders. Then in 1030 the new emperor Konrad II tried to incorporate Hungary into the Holy Roman Empire. István's armies lured the knights into a swampy region and defeated them using guerilla tactics. In 1031, however, István's only son Imre was killed in a hunting accident throwing open the ticklish issue of succession. The legal heir was his cousin Vásoly, but the king suspected him of paganism and opted for his nephew Peter, the son from the marriage between his sister and Peter Orseolo, the Doge of Venice. To make sure Vásoly would make no claims to power, he had him blinded, deafened and sent his three sons into exile to Russia.

After István's death in 1038 the country fell prey to chaos. Peter proved ineffective and was additionally despised for being a foreigner. A powerful chieftain from the Mátra region, Samuel Aba, a brother-in-law of Istvàn usurped power for a while until Peter retook his throne, albeit with the help of the troups of the Emperor Henry III who could not wait to bind Hungary. The sons of Vásoly grew up and returned to lay their claims to the throne with the eager help of Byzantium. To top it all off heathens began rebelling and population migrations pushed fresh tribes onto Hungary's shores.

László I (1087-1095) became king at a propicious time: The emperor was too busy with the investiture struggle, the popes, in turn, needed all the support they could get and were willing to woo the Hungarians. István was officially canonized along with Gellért. László I also married a daughter, Piroska by name, to the Byzantine emperor thus securing all his borders. The Venetians, now at the height of their mercantile power were threatening Dalmatia which willy-nilly accepted the protective, annexing hand of Hungary. Croatia also became a Hungarian province at this time.

Intrigue and Murder

László I, who was also canonized, was succeeded by Kálmán I (1095-1116), a sly, rational hunchback who had at first opted for the priesthood. His great learning earned him the title "the book-lover" (*könyves*). His first deed was to have his younger brother and his son blinded to avoid any family competition. He followed up this unsavory business with a wise rule. Hungary received a new set of laws some of which were remarkably modern considering the cruelty of Christian laws of the time. Many of the cruel and unusual punishments prescribed by other monarchs especially for petty crimes were eliminated. He patterned his foreign policy on that of László I, marrying off a cousin to the Byzantine heir, himself marrying into the Sicilian royal family, and finally annexing Bosnia and further sections of Dalmatia.

Thanks to László I and Kálmán I, Hungary in the first half of the 12th century was safe, solid and relatively prosperous. A crisis with an unusual twist at the end did, however, grow out of the Byzantine connection. A son named Manuel born to Piroska (László's daughter) became emperor in Constantinople and envisioned Hungary as part of the Byzantine empire. With that in mind he kidnapped the youngest son of the then ruling King Géza II (1141-1162), Béla, whose lands, Croatia, Dalmatia and Syrmia, became part of the eastern Empire. In 1172 Béla returned to rightfully claim the Hungarian throne, and not only did he restore the lost provinces, but he proved to be one of Hungary's best kings. Byzantium had given him a fine education and a sense of both money and luxury. He introduced a monetary system which enabled Hungary to benefit greatly from being an important trade center between east south and west. A refined tax system and growing prosperity insured proper revenues for the country. Settlers were invited from the west and granted rights to found towns. Agriculture improved considerably. He also built a palace renowned for its luxurious furnishings and life in Esztergom. Béla III's conjugal links inclined toward the west: Anne of Chatillon and Margaret Capet were both French and had ties to the Holy Roman emperor and the British throne respectively. By upbringing he maintained good relations with Byzantium, at least for a while. He concentrated his efforts on the Balkans, specifically on the Dalmatian coast.

Béla III's successor, András II (1205-1235) demonstrated the reverse side of

economic wisdom by plundering the royal coffers to feed his expensive, expansionist foreign policy. He fought with Russia, embarked on a fruitless crusade costing him a part of Dalmatia which he ceded to Venice in exchange for aid. He lived lavishly at home pursuing the pipe dreams of some eastern monarch. He pawned off the royal lands and priviledges to barons and those who had enough cash on hand just to remain solvent while the nobles, freemen in the army and churchmen, who owed their allegiance to the king became increasingly poor. In 1222 they rebelled and forced András II to sign a document, the Golden Bull, that established and secured the rights of the aristocracy against the magnates and the king: They no longer had to engage in foreign wars if they were deemed pointless, and they were allowed to rebel against the king if his policies were threatening the country.

Above: The royal insignia of Hungary. Right: The mysterious chronicler Anonymous.

The Golden Bull put an end to András' overspending, but his son Béla IV (1235-1270), a serious fellow with honest concern for his country, had no time to prepare Hungary for the next danger. For some time already Cuman and other nomads streaming in from the east had been bearing reports of some horrendous scourge, an army of wild, cruel, murderous riders: the Tatars. Béla IV scrambled to organize defenses. He encouraged the Cumans, courageous albeit heathen warriors, to settle in Hungary and participate in the country's military history. (The prefix *kun* recalls the places where they settled: for example, the Kiskunság and Nagykunság regions east and southeast of Budapest and such towns as Kiskunfélegyháza and Kunszentmiklós). He pleeded for help from the Holy Roman Empire and from the Pope, but both were involved in their own little tug-of-war. in addition at the 11th hour the Cuman alliance also fell apart. On April 11, 1241, in Muhi near the juncture of the rivers Sajó and Hernád, the Tatars led by the great

Batu Khan totally annihilated the Hungarian army.

While the Tatars continued their westward campaign annihilating any settlement they rode through, Béla IV hid, for as long as he lived the nation still existed. In 1242 the Tatars crossed the Danube, and suddenly, as if by magic they disappeared: A succession dispute had broken out in Mongolia and Batu Khan had to go back home.

Béla IV spent the rest of his reign preparing for a renewed Tatar assault which never materialized. He married off three daughters to eastern princes, his son István married a Cuman – much to his disliking, as the Cumans had never shaken off heathenism. Having noticed that the Tatars had no proper siege strategy he feverishly encouraged the magnates to build fortresses, Diosgyör, Füzer, Sümeg and others. Settlers, mainly Germans and Romanians, arrived to repopulate the devastated areas.

The reconstruction of Hungary went fast but cost both money and some of the king's clout vis-á-vis the magnates on whom he depended for political and military support. His most severe opposition came from his own family: István, his own flesh and blood, became the pawn in the magnates' power game.

In addition to the internal problems, Austria and Bohemia started speculating on Hungary's weakness, and the unscrupulous magnates went along with them. The Árpád dynasty, however, was thinning out. Béla's son István ruled for a mere two years, before his grandson László V took over. He was a colorful ruler at best, slightly deranged, extravagant at worst. He did not hide his attraction for the Cuman traditions and customs of his mother including paganism. At first he might have been searching for support against the magnates but with time it became an obsession. He was finally murdered, and no one asked who did the job. A distant cousin, András III occupied the Hungarian throne from 1290 to 1301. When he died without issue the Árpáds came to an end.

THE ELECTORIAL MONARCHY

A violent wringing for the throne through the female line of the Árpáds, with both foreign dynasties and the magnates competing for the title, foreshadowed difficult times. Ultimately, in 1307, Charles Robert of Anjou prevailed and set about demonstrating to the cantankerous magnates that he had little intention of submitting to their every whim. In a struggle lasting 14 years he re-established royal authority at the cost of his foreign ventures. He practically abolished the Diet of nobles, raised new taxes to enrich the royal coffers and thereby give the king more power. He let the magnates foot the bill for their own armies while the king commanded one of his own. Trade too picked up considerably especially after agreements were reached on trade routes to western Europe through Poland and Bohemia, thus circumventing the dangerous and expensive Viennese crossroad. Last but not least the mining of precious metals gave the economy a much-needed boost and Hungarian agriculture earned itself an international reputation.

Charles Robert's long reign was followed by the long reign of another strong monarch, Lajos I, "the Great", as he was nicknamed for his ambitious, military escapades. He fought in Italy for the Neapolitan throne; he continued to pressure Dalmatia and Bosnia and he even accepted the Polish crown. Barring the sempiternal wars and internal strife, it was a blooming epoch in Hungarian history, one which attracted not only merceneries and pioneer farmers, but also artists and intellectuals to the country. Much of the great architecture of the period has since been destroyed by the Turks and the Habsburgs, but not such institutions as the University of Pécs.

Left: The Turks – a Hungarian trauma for over 200 years.

The third great monarch in succession was Sigismund of Luxemburg who, with a little luck and some political finagling, succeeded in taking the reigns in 1396. As with the two previous kings, Sigismund maintained the policy of an iron hand in a steel glove with respect to power in Hungary. He slithered his way out of palatial intrigues on behalf of other dynasties and he brutally crushed a peasant rebellion in Transylvania that had grown from the peasants' poverty coupled with the rhetoric urging of the refractory Hussites, the anti-church followers of the religious rebel Jan Hus.

Sigismund also became deeply involved in European politics after becoming Holy Roman emperor in 1310. For Hungary it was prestigious and for his enemies, who were free to conspire during his long absences from the country, a boon. Meanwhile another danger was creeping up through the Balkans, the highly organized Turkish army. Lajos I had already fought them in 1377. In 1396 a large international force met a solid defeat at their hands at Nicopolis. By 1418 the Turks had reached the southern border of Transylvania. In 1428 they defeated a Hungarian force at Galambóc. Albert V, who ruled for two years after Sigismund, understood the imminence of the Turkish threat but could do little against it. Before dying he ordered a loyal commander named Hunyadi János to take over the defence of the country.

For Hunyadi chasing Turks out of Hungary became an obsession. In 1442 he led a campaign against the army of Bey Mezid who was killed in the encounter. Another successful campaign in 1443 followed, and yet another in 1444 which, however, ended in defeat at Varna where the young King Wladislav was also killed. Hunyadi used merceneries whom he paid out of his own pocket, and the king in turn paid him in land. As a result of this barter, Hunyadi became Hungary's largest land-owner ever.

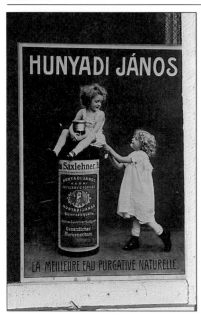

With intrigue in his back Hunyadi nevertheless continued striking at the Turks militarily and diplomatically. Keeping an upper hand proved difficult especially since the smaller countries in the Balkans such as Wallachia leaned easily toward the Ottoman empire. In 1456 Hunyadi, demoted to mere commander general ever since László V had taken power, led his last campaign, this time to free Belgrade. With the help of the plague he not only raised the siege but set back a potential Turkish invasion of Hungary by many decades. The Pope ordered all bells to be tolled at midday to celebrate this victory, a practice that continues to this very day throughout the whole Christendom.

But the plague also carried off Hunyadi 11 days after the battle. A miniature civil war broke out in Hungary: László V egged on by Cilli had László Hunyadi murdered and Mátyás Hunyadi taken into custody in Prag. A year later László V, the hope of the Habsburg faction, died in turn – apparently of natural causes. With no other adequate ruler in sight the magnates gathered ransom money for Mátyás (Corvinus from the crow on this coat-of-arms) and chose him to be Hungary's next king.

He quickly established himself as "the boss", trusting no one outside himself and his friend and teacher János Vitéz. His maternal uncle Michael Szilagy tried in vain to act as regent, but the 17-year old king was tougher than anyone expected. He moved quickly and efficiently against refractory magnates, especially the Garai family. With a revamped system of taxation he was able to project a solid image for himself and Hungary and like his father, he could pay for a substantial army of mercenaries (the Black Army) with which he underscored his foreign political aims.

Hungary in the meantime had entered one of its most critical and complex phases. In 1440 the Diet, with a lower house for the nobility and an upper house for the magnates, was reconstituted to elect a king, as Albert had died leaving only a pregnant wife. The lower house opted for Wladislav Jagiello while a baronial faction, with the Austrian count Cilli hovering in the wings, wished to see the unborn child crowned. The former won technically, but Elizabeth, Albert's remarkably brazen wife, gave birth to a boy László, had the royal insignia stolen and had her 12 week old son crowned! When Wladislaw died at Varna, the lower house elected Hunyadi as regent of Hungary until László came of age. The fact that Hunyadi himself had two children, László and Mátyás, further complicated matters as the magnates and their cohorts were apprehensive of potential rivals.

Above: Purgative waters were named after Hunyadi, the great Turk hunter. Right: The grave of Gül Baba in Budapest.

Barring skirmishes along the border, relations with the Turks remained by and large peaceful. In 1464 Mátyás responded swiftly to an incursion into Bosnia.

Most of the time, however, he spent locking horns with the Habsburg emperor Frederic III, who had been himself crowned King of Hungary in 1459 by the anti-Hunyadist barons. He possessed the royal insignia only returning them after Mátyás agreed to pay a ransom and sign a treaty stipulating that, should he die heirless, a Habsburg would succeed him.

Mátyás' grand design seemed to have been the creation of a powerful nation with neighbors Poland and Bohemia as allies to fend off attacks from both the Habsburgs and the Turks. At the height of his reign, in 1485, he held Moravia and Silesia, had pushed Frederic's army out of Lower Austria and Styria, had reached the gates of Salzburg, and after a short siege had occupied Vienna. He was fortunate in having excellent military commanders such as Pál Kinizsi, István Báthori, Tobias Cernahora and János Zápolya, the Voivode of Transylvania.

Hungary under Mátyás Corvinus bathed in a blaze of glory. The Italian renaissance, which had already started refreshing the weightier gothic style at the beginning of the century, found fertile and above all well-financed soil. Mátyás' third marriage to Beatrix of Ara gon, daughter of the King of Naples, had something to do with this.

The End of a Golden Era

All of Mátyás' efforts, the entire Golden Age he created vanished with his passing in 1490. His only major failure, having been unable to produce a proper heir, in the end brought his carefully constructed house down. Johannes Corvinus, his only son, was the product of a morganatic marriage, and European crowned heads refused to have their daughters marry a lower noble. The magnates quickly elected the Wladislav II Jagiello to succeed, a gentle but malleable fellow. They also undermined royal power by no longer supporting the royal army. The nobles meanwhile agitated for a Hungarian king, specifically the above-mentioned Zápolya of Transylvania. The

23

court palatin and Archbishop of Eszter-gom, Bakócz, finally hammered out a compromise stating that should Wla-dislav II die without an heir, Zapolya would take power.

In the meantime, political degradation was reflecting on the country's economy and in turn on the condition of the peasants and townspeople. In 1514 they rebelled, led by a lesser Transylvanian noble, György Dózsa. Zápolya crushed the revolt at about the time the court jurist István Verböczy – a spokesman for the Zápolya cause – was concluding the *Tri-partium*, a set of laws establishing the equal rights of the magnates and nobles and reconfirming serfdom for the pea-sants on the occasion of the Dózsa revolt.

The Tragedy of Mohács

The son of Wladislav Jagiello, Louis II, as well as his sister Anna both married Habsburgs which only further irritated the nobles who were seeking a national king. To top it off, the Reformation, that had already given Dózsa some impetus, was now making political headway as a means of rebellion against the rapacious Habsburgs and their Hungarian sup-porters. Not only Hungary but Europe it-self was falling apart under the weight of intrigue and Machiavellian diplomacy. In 1521 the Turks occupied Belgrade and in 1526 they began a major offensive against Hungary. Neither the Pope, nor the self-professed Catholic Habsburgs, nor the Catholic king of France Francis I cared to help. The latter even sided with the Turks as they kept the Habsburgs busy while he satisfied his own lust for territories in Italy. Louis II, in the manner of an inexperienced 20-year old, led an army of ca. 25.000, so the history goes, that virtually disintegrated against a four times larger Turkish force near Mohács on August 29, 1526. Louis II drowned while fleeing. The Turks, convinced that the Hungarian force had been a diversion,

decided to wait before continuing their advance. Little did they know, that was about all the Hungarians could come up with in a manner of soldiers that season.

Mohács served as a lesson to no one. The nobles elected Zápolya to be king while in the west the magnates chose Archduke Ferdinand of Habsburg. Stra-tegically both kings could help, the first by his familial ties to the powerful Polish kingdom, the second because of ties to Charles V., the Holy Roman emperor. But both chose to fight for power while the Turks inexorably continued their march into Europe. Only winter prevented them from starving Vienna into submission in 1529. By 1543 they had occupied a wedge encompassing Esztergom in the North, Buda, Kecskemét, Pécs, Szé-kesfehérvár. Royal Hungary, that western slivver of land along the Austrian border had become nothing more than a buffer zone for the Habsburgs while Zápolya for his part, in order to maintain the balance of power against them, accepted help from the Sultan.

János Zsigmond, Zápolya's son, was an infant when his father died in 1540. The bishop of Transylvania, George Mar-tinuzzi, assumed the regency and procee-ded to conduct a brilliant tightrope dip-lomacy between Royal Hungary, Turkey and Transylvania to maintain peace until Austria and Hungary could jointly purge Europe of the Turks. The theory had me-rit, the practice, however, as the fol-lowing centuries were to demonstrate, failed owing to the Habsburgs' insatiable thirst for land and addiction to absolutist rule. In 1551, for example, they sent an expedionary force into Transylvania, pro-voking the Turks into action. When Mar-tinuzzi tried to appease the Sultan to gain time, the Austrian general Castaldo, sus-pecting foul play, had him executed. The Ottoman army promptly took Transyl-vania and moved as far north as Eger which successfully held out a 39 day siege. In 1556 they installed János Zsig-

Moravia

Poland

H A B S B U R G

Hungary

○ *Košice*

Danube

Vienna ○ ○ *Bratislava* *of*

○ *Miskolc*

Győr ○

D O M A I N S *Buda* ○○ *Pest*

○ *Debrecen*

Moldavia

Kingdom

Drava

Balaton

V O I V O D S H I P

O F

T U R K I S H *Tisza*

Pécs ○ *Szeged*

T R A N S Y L V A N I A

○ *Zagreb*

Brașov ○

D O M A I N S

Sava

○ *Beograd*

Danube

ADRIATIC
SEA ○

TRIPARTIUM 1541

0   250 km

mond on the throne and Transylvania became another Turkish protectrate.

It was clear to all that neither side had enough power to make a decisive military move. The Turks were overstretched, the Habsburgs had too much internal trouble to fully concentrate on their eastern border. They kept the Turks at arm's length until the 1590s. What Transylvania lacked in military power it compensated for in diplomacy, gradually growing into a great powerbroker of sorts. István Báthory, who succeeded János Zsigmond in 1572, even became king of Poland where he distinguished himself by leading a campaign against the aggressive Russian Czar Ivan IV, "the Terrible". Also, barring rebellions in particular by the Szeklers, an ancient Hungarian tribe, religious tolerance provided for a relatively solid social fabric. The army in times of continuous war, provided good opportunities for getting ahead in life.

Unification with or under the Habsburgs was however an inevitable fact of *Realpolitik*. János Zsigmond even recognized them as legitimate kings while maintaining his voivodship. Of course offering the Habsburgs a finger was like a lamb offering a starving wolf a helping paw.... In 1591 the Turks resumed their attacks. The Transylvanian army, a ragged mass of Szeklers and Hayducks, originally cattle watchers – literally cowboys – freed and inducted, under the command of István Bocskai succeeded in liberating large parts of Transylvania and the Great Plain. Seeing the tide turning, Zsigmond Báthory, István's not so competent son, literally turned the country over to the Habsburgs. The Austrian general Basta, however, arrived with his army not as a liberator but as an enemy, laying the country to waste, looting, burning and recatholicizing refractory townships with a vengeance. Most Transylvanian leaders went into exile in Turkey. Bocskai consolidated the valiant Hayducks, threw out the Austrians and rightfully clambered up onto the Transylvanian throne. The Hayducks were gran-

ted extensive privileges including freedom from taxation *in perpetuo* as long as they pledged themselves to always serve as warriors. The prefix *Hajdu-* of many towns on the Great Plain recalls where this soldierly clan settled.

The 17th century opened auspiciously. In Vienna Rudolf II had been replaced by his brother Matthias, thanks to support from the Austrian, Moravian and Hungarian aristocracy. The latter, feeling largely ignored by the emperor, had turned increasingly to Protestantism. The trend was now reversed by the tender care of bishop Pázmány who gave Catholicism in royal Hungary a humane face.

Transylvanian Greatness

East of the Turkish wedge, Transylvania blossomed again under Gábor Bethlen who ruled with a luxurious, solid but fair hand. Trade increased after a war-

Above: In honor of the Hussars, the backbone of the Hungarian army for centuries.

time hiatus, arts and crafts received important support and religious freedom persisted. Even the Jews were granted certain rights. With one hand Bethlen held the Turks at bay, while with the other he fought off the Habsburgs partly by enrolling the help of the French, who under Louis XIII and later Louis XIV were particularly covetous of Habsburg lands, and partly by sending armies into the fray of the 30 Years War. György Rákóczi followed in Bethlen's footsteps with less success. Internal problems stymied his anti-Habsburg activities: In electing him the nobles had by-passed Bethlen's younger brother István who tried in vain to take power with Turkish help.

In spite of its external appearance though, Transylvania's power rested upon dissension within the ranks of its real and perceived enemies. György II Rákóczi (1648-1660) overestimated his ressources. In 1656 he attacked Poland without consulting the Sultan, who sent a division of Tatars to put an end to the expedition. Shortly thereafter Rákóczi himself died in battle. In the twinkling of an eye Transylvania had crossed the barrier between riches and rags. Austria, self-satisfied and huge, smiled glibly. Royal Hungary, firmly in its hand, was the last hope for liberation from the Turks.

The star of the Ottoman empire had been sinking very gradually ever since the death of Suleiman II in 1566. A century later though the Turks still had enough military clout to launch dangerous campaigns although Vienna always eluded them.

The 1663 campaign first encountered Hungarian resistance under the leadership of the viceroy of Croatia, Miklós Zrínyi. In 1664 General Montecuccuoli routed the Turks at Szentgotthárd. The Habsburgs however, too involved with the War of Spanish Succession with France, made concessions to them in order to maintain peace on the eastern front. Enraged Hungarian nobles conspired to overthrow Leopold, but they were unmasked, most were exececuted and Royal Hungary subjected to a Habsburg-chosen governor who let the heavy hand of Catholicism fall on the country.

One young count named Thököly, whose father had died in the war against Habsburg repression, made it his duty to take revenge. With help from France and Turkey he led a veritable crusade against the Austrians at the head of his so-called *kuruc* – a name deriving from the Latin *crux* or "cross"; the pro-Habsburg soldiers were called the *labanc*. The rebellion lasted a full three years until the Austrian government was forced to concede a Hungarian constitution and freedom of religion.

Thököly however let power climb to his head and, not trusting Austria, he allowed himself to be made king of Hungary by the Turks. He probably assumed that Turkish might still played an important role in southeast Europe. Indeed in 1683 they launched what was to be their final offensive against Vienna. Com-

mander Jan Sobieski, however, stopped them at the gates of the city. In the following year Pope Innocent XI or ganized a kind of crusade against the Ottomans. Thököly's *kuruc*, feeling the wind had changed direction, conveniently changed sides. In 1686 Buda was retaken and by 1699 the bulk of Hungarian territory had been liberated.

Liberated? The Habsburgs entered a land morally and physically devastated by 150 years of occupation and war, a land they hovered over like a stray dog over a juicy bone. Hungary, supine, exhausted, in ruins, hardly seemed ready to resist becoming a vassal. Governor Caraffa let the Austrian armies live high on the hog, Germans and Serbs were invited to settle in Hungary not only to re-populate some parts but also to dissolve the population and create a Habsburg-faithful stratum. Once again rebellion was in the air, this time under the leadership of Ferenc II Rákóczi whose father Ferenc I Rákóczi had been a member of the anti- Habsburg conspiracy of 1664. After he died, his wife Illona Zrinyi (daughter of Miklos Zrinyi) married Thököly and commanded the last *kuruc* outpost in the Munkacsi fortress (today in the USSR).

The Hungarian War of Independence started well for the rebels but soon began stagnating. It was bloody and long. Ferenc II Rákóczi, a talented commander and successful diplomat, kept it alive sometimes with last minute support in the form of money and soldiers. In 1711 he was in Moscow to gain the support of Peter the Great. His deputy, Count Károlyi, took the opportunity to sign the peace of Szatmár to bring an end to the bloodshed. No one had lost and no one had won. Rákóczi himself never accepted the treaty. He went into exile in Turkey where he died in 1735 having tried several times to rekindle the war. It was to no avail: The Hungarians no longer had any blood to spare.

THE HABSBURG ERA

The end of the war of independence finally brought peace to Hungary. Rákóczi loyalists tried in vain to fire up a new rebellion during the flushing of the Turks from Transylvania but the will was simply lacking. The country-side had been bled dry and accordingly agriculture had ground to a halt. In addition to the man-made catastrophes, plagues at the end of the 17th and beginning of the 18th centuries made heavy dents in the population. Another factor in Hungary's recumbency was undoubtedly the conciliatory reign of the Austrian emperor Charles IV and the charismatic qualities of general Eugene of Savoy who led the Austrian armies (reinforced with Hungarian divisions) to victory against the Porte.

For the 18th century was Austrian. Vienna promoted resettlement in Hungary from its crowded western provinces, Tirol, Styria, Franconia, Swabia and others. They arrived on the Danube, were thereafter arbitrarily referred to as Danube Swabians and their main goal, southern Hungary, became known as "Swabian Turkey". Throughout the century Austrian-trained artists wandered through the western half of the country in particular, redesigning churches and houses in Baroque, Rococo and the sober Zopf and Classical styles. Catholics received preference, which did cause discontent amongst Hungarians.

Thanks to the Pragmatic Sanction, a policy signed in 1722 by Charles IV allowing female succession in the event of an emperor dying without male issue, no succession disputes emerged on the political horizon. Maria Theresia duly became empress and "king" of Hungary in 1740. Of all the Habsburgs who ruled Hungary, she was probably the most honest, direct and kind (in spite of an ob-

Left: Revering the Virgin Mary, the kinder face of Habsburg brand Catholicism.

sessive dislike for Protestants). In 1741, when Bavaria, Bohemia and Tirol turned on Austria in its war against Prussia, Maria Theresia went before the Hungarian Diet in the capital Pozsony (today: Bratislava, Czechslovakia) to plead for assistance which, barring a few eastern votes, she received. In exchange for their loyalty the magnates were by and large left alone. The old feudal structures stayed in place, while reforms only affected the administration. Government became increasingly centralized and bureaucratized and Hungarian nobles turned to Vienna to make a career for themselves. Gently cradled by the empress, Hungary slowly fell asleep while Austria, Russia and the upstart Prussia redrew the European map.

Sleeping beauty awoke with a jolt. Prince Charming came in the guise of the Joseph II in 1780, an enlightened despot in the best of traditions, filled with the social precepts of Rousseau, Voltaire, Quesnay and Diderot. He wore austere, military clothing, refused to be crowned king of Hungary, had the royal paraphenalia packed away as the relic of some ridiculously pompous past, abolished serfdom – to the horror of the magnates –, abolished all monasteries and cloisters that failed to either educate or care for the poor, the old and the sick, and had guidelines drawn up for building and redesigning of churches. His Edict of Tolerance of 1781 gave civil rights to Protestants, Jews and other second-class citizens. The bureaucracy grew and to help its workings, German replaced Latin as the official language. Gradually the laws and regulations penetrated every aspect of life, regulating such things as the holy mass, the cracking of whips and yodeling. On his death bed, in 1790, before the entire realm broke into revolution, Joseph II retracted some of his promulgations.

His brother Leopold II, who reigned for a mere two years let himself be

crowned king of Hungary, restored Latin as the official language and hastily convened the Hungarian Diet. In the meantime the Enlightenment, that had appeared so attractive to the 18th century rulers, had given way to the French Revolution and the Jacobin terror. Europe's equanimity swayed between new and old thought and no one wanted revolutions occuring in their frontyards. Franz I (1792-1835) kept a tight rein on dissent at home and made sure the European clock did not move too fast. Hungarian nobles, fearing for their feudal rights, towed the line. Only a small group led by a somewhat bizarre figure, brother Ignatius Martinovics, tried to lead the Hungarians into rebellion, but most of the instigators were executed in Buda on a patch of ground since named *Vérmezö*, Field of Blood.

The Congress of Vienna (1815), held under the aegis of the conservative

Above: Docile magnates honoring Emperor Leopold II. Right: Lajos Kossuth, Hungary's fiercest advocate of freedom.

Austrian foreign minister Prince Metternich, brought the tumultuous events of the revolution to a close, but the sense of nation had been irretrievably sown. In Hungary the long-neglected language came alive again under the pens of Ferenc Kazinczy, a survivor of the Martinovics conspiracy, Mihály Csokonai Vitéz, József Katona and the poets Mihály Vörösmarty, Ferenc Kölcsey (who wrote the Hungarian national anthem) and finally Sándor Petöfi, the national poet. At the same time the country sprouted several great figures.

István Széchenyi, the son of a magnate who had founded the Hungarian National museum in 1802, understood that a new era had arrived in Europe and that, if Hungary was to become a competitive nation, it could no longer hang on to some archaic system. He saw the future in economic liberalism and industry. He helped found the Science Academy, he had docks built in Obuda, designed the chain-link bridge (*lánchíd*) named after him, had tracks laid, ships for the Balaton built and planned the regulation of the Tisza and Danube.

Széchenyi's political equivalent was the journalist and lawyer Lajos Kossuth who advocated changes in the status quo of the Austrian empire allowing Hungary more autonomy. His inflammatory tone landed him a three year prison sentence which did nothing to cool his temper. And there were others who had historic roles to play, Count Batthyányi, the lawyer Ferenc Deák, Count Eötvös.

Elusive Independence

The pressure for change mounted rapidly during the first half of the 19th century especially after the mild Ferdinand I became emperor in 1835. In 1844 Hungarian was introduced as an official administrative language. Then, in 1848, revolution broke out in Paris again and rapidly spread across the continent finally offering the budding opposition in Hungary a chance to push its program through, including the ticklish issue of freeing the serfs. By March 15, Kossuth was in Vienna clamoring for power. King Ferdinand agreed to let the Hungarians form their own government under Batthyány and to give his blessings to the laws promulgated by the Hungarian Diet. Kossuth took over the Ministry of Finances, Széchenyi was in Public Works and Transportation, Deák Justice and Eötvös Religion and Education. Meanwhile in Pest's Café Pilvax a group of young revolutionaries kindled by the inflammatory words of Petöfi wrote out twelve demands including for freedom of expression and abolition of censorship.

Within a few days the Diet in Pozsony had liberated the serfs (compensating the landowners), had created a national army (*honvéd*), and had declared equality for all before the law. The revolution took Viennese hardliners by surprise, because its quasi-legal character made it difficult to oppose. Still the first resistance came

mostly from within the Hungarian dominions themselves. The ex-serfs were not all that sure their new status was better, Hungary's nationalities also felt left out of the picture and the course the revolution had embarked on seemed inevitably headed toward total independence from the Habsburgs. Serbs and Croats in particular feared changes in the staus quo. As the year wore on Imperial forces succeeded in extinguishing rebellions in Italy and Prague. In August Batthyány decided it was time to find some compromise with Vienna but apparently the conservatives felt strong enough to reject his proposals. It was the time the loyal Ban of Croatia, Jelacic, chose to invade Hungary. Batthyány's cabinet resigned and Kossuth was chosen to head a government of national defence. He immediately mobilized the country for war. Jelacic, was expelled from Hungarian territory and the *honvéd* started its march on Vienna where it planned to give support to the Austrian rebels. It was stopped at the city gates at Schwechat on October

31, allowing General Windischgraetz to restore order in the seething capital. A period of stalemate ensued during which the Viennese government regrouped: New conservatives such as Justice Minister Alexander Bach and Interior Minister Franz Stadion appeared in government under the leadership of Prince Schwarzenberg; and on December 2, the 18 year old Franz-Joseph I replaced his incapable uncle on the throne.

Franz-Joseph I

Recapturing Hungary now began in earnest. Windischgraetz led his troups into the unrepentent nation, initially taking Buda, Pest and parts of Transylvania. In March, convinced of quick and easy victory, Schwarzenberg declared that Hungary's status would be that of a mere crown colony. This coincided with a powerful *honvéd* offensive under Artur Görgey which in one fell swoup pushed the Austrians all the way to Komárom. From the new capital Debrecen on the Great Plain, on April 14, 1849, Kossuth prematurely proclaimed Hungary's independence. Franz-Joseph I secured the alliance of the ultra-conservative Russian Czar Nicholas I whose army quickly tipped the scales in favor of the Austrians. After a few wild cavalcades – one of which allegedly cost the life of Petöfi –, Görgey decided that further bloodletting would be pointless. On August 13 he surrendered with his army at Világos. Many went into exile, Kossuth to Turkey and Széchenyi ended up in an insane asylum near Vienna where he ultimately committed suicide.

The repression that followed under the new Austrian General von Haynau was meant to be exemplary but hardly served to reconcile the Hungarians with the empire. 13 generals were executed – though not Görgey – as was Count Batthyány. They were succeeded by more executions, heavy prison sentences, dispossessions and other punitive measures. Hungary was divided into five administrative districts and its constitution suspended. Franz-Joseph I took his absolutism seriously: In 1850, on the heels of Haynau, came the so-called "Bach-Hussars", mainly foreign civil servants sent by Alexander Bach to run the country.

The opposition was divided. From abroad Kossuth tried repeatedly to fire up the spirit of 1849. Deák, on the other hand, a placid, brilliant, patient lawyer who had left the revolutionary government when it became too radical, tended more towards the more constitutional spirit of 1848. Eventually his quiet diplomacy carried the day but not without a little help from Chance.

For one, the young and pretty Bavarian princess Elizabeth (Sissi) who had married Franz-Joseph I, was a rabid hungarophile and luck would have it she had learned Hungarian from Deák. Secondly, the Viennese cabinet had become more moderate. Thirdly, the emperor had engaged in some rather unsuccessful foreign ventures especially with France and Italy in 1859 that increasingly required stability at home. The military districts in Hungary were quietly dissolved and the former order reinstated. In the October Diploma of 1860, Franz-Joseph made certain concessions to the old federal status of Hungary, but failed either to go far enough or include the detached dominions of Transylvania, Croatia and Serbia. Then, in 1861 the parliament reconvened and Deák in his opening statement reminded the emperor of his historic constitutional duties towards Hungary: "The yoke of absolute royal power, however, and constitutionality are contradictions that cannot exist together even in thought. If the sovereign is allowed to consider the laws sanctioned by his pre-

Right: The free-wheeling days of capitalism during the much-lauded days of the K. and K. monarchy.

Klotild-paloták. Klotilden Palais. BUDAPEST.

decessors as not binding to his own person, what will become of our constitution, of the legal freedom of the country, of the laws passed and to be passed?" It was of course a good rhetorical question, but apparently the emperor was not yet ready for a compromise.

Under King and Kaiser

Prussia sounded the knell of Austrian absolutism in 1866 by its victory over the Austrian armies at Sadowa. Within a few months Franz-Joseph agreed to a new status quo; on June 8, 1867 he was crowned king of Hungary in a pompous celebration at the Mátyás Church in Buda. It was the beginning of a by and large golden era known as "K. and K.", (from *Kaiser und König*), that is Emperor and King. Practically it meant a complex redesigning of the entire governmental and financial system of both countries. Austria and Hungary were each represented by an upper and a lower house whose decisions were to be considered

and discussed by two committees of 60 delegates (20 from the upper house and 40 from the lower) before being sanctioned by the Emperor. The ministries of Finances, of War and of Foreign Affairs came under dual control and Hungary was given 30 percent of the monarchy's financial burden. The country's internal affairs were its own business insofar as they did not threaten the constitution.

Hungary, it is often thought, fared even better than Austria under the terms of the so-called Compromise, for it enjoyed not only proximity to the ephemeral prestige of Viennese court and artistic life, but could also rely on mother Austria to foot the greater part of the bill. The industrialization once sought by Széchenyi, finally flowered in the machine and food industries. The numbers tell one side of the story: Between 1867 and 1914 Hungary's road network grew 1000 percent, it developed an entire railway system, whereby the country not only laid its own tracks but also produced them, the locomotives and the coaches. By 1910 the

33

number of agricultural workers had reached 60%, down from 75% in 1870. In 1872 the three cities of Pest, Buda and Óbuda were unified under the single name Budapest. As a capital it attracted people from all corners of the Empire, which in turn attracted more investors. This accounts for its great number of architectural delights.

But beyond the range of the twinkling lights of Budapest's chandeliers, far from the wheeling and dealing of financiers and big time industrialists, lived thousands of exploited, displaced people, working for a pittance under hard conditions. They lived in break-down shacks or hastily erected tenements without proper sanitation, without any insurance and without much hope for the future. The Angyalföld district in Pest was one of these. Its name, literally "angel's field", derives from the fact that infant

Above: Hungarian Secession, an expression of national self- consciousness in the pre-World War One days.

mortality was so high there. In the provinces a similar shift took place, with impoverished peasants forced to seek survival along the railroads, in the mines or along the rivers where they hired themselves out as day laborers. Museums in Csongrád and Szeged recall the stringent lives of the *kubikus,* men who tramped around the country doing the work of modern bulldozers, with a spade, a small wheel-barrow and a harness.

This polarization of Hungarian society, or rather shift from a feudal system to a kind of industrial feudalism spawned a labor movement. Early attempts to set up unions were stifled in the panic of conservatism following the Paris Commune. In 1880 Leo Frankel, a Hungarian who had participated in the Commune, founded the General Workers' Party that later became the Social Democratic Party, albeit as a party it had little chance of growing in light of government opposition. As the century wore on, strikes multiplied, many with a high blood toll. Politically, the K. and K. period opened promisingly, with

Count Andrássy heading a liberally-minded cabinet. Deák, wise as usual, retired before the quibbling began. Count Lonyay, who succeeded Andrássy, was not only ineffective but after his forced resignation in 1873, the country's coffers were found to be empty. A kind of opposition had already formed meanwhile, the so-called Left of Center Party headed by Kálmán Tisza, a foxy old '48er who had supported the Compromise without fully approving of its practical manifestations. In 1875 he led his party into a coalition with the government and steered Hungary successfully in and out of crisis for the next 15 years.

Vienna looked with increasing sourness upon Hungary's liberal policies coupled with growing demands for general franchise and greater social and political freedom. After Kálmán Tisza's fall in 1890, tensions increased further, in spite of temporary measures to stabilize the economy by the Weckerle cabinet (1890-1892) and the passing diversion of the bombastic millenial celebrations of the Hungarian state in 1896. Hungary was definitely pulling away from the Empire, and furthermore its entire internal political organism was also falling apart. The great coalition that had ruled Hungary for 30 years went down in flames in the 1905 elections after the government under Tisza's son István simply fell apart on the basic issue of the Compromise. In February 1906, the Emperor even sent in troups to restore order and loyalty, an action that failed to elicit response from the Hungarian people and therefore successfully stymied nationalist opposition.

The Road to the Great War

Other cracks, however, were also showing: poor versus rich, worker versus employer, strife amongst the magnates and other noble strata. But most disturbing of all was the nationalities question which successive governments failed to take into consideration, and which in the end caused Hungary enormous grief. Though considered equal under the law, each of Hungary's ethnic or national minorities – including the Romanians, Croats, Ruthenians, Slovaks and more – sought greater autonomy, recognition, rights. Unfortunately the Hungarians' own nationalist strivings coupled with a program of magyarization – teaching Hungarian in schools, using Hungarian as an official language and promoting Magyar culture – only served to irritate the minorities.

In August 1914 the Great War began. Politicians thought it would be a quick little success that would raise everyone's spirits and close all ranks. But no heroic cavalcades brightened up the endless fields of mud and barbed wire, the impersonal murder of machine guns and heavy artillery. The muck and the mire soon wore down the initial enthusiasm and any sense of unity. In 1916 Franz-Joseph died leaving the throne to Charles I who was promptly swamped by the events. The nationalities issue re-emerged in all its virulence, with Czechs clamoring for independence and Romanians trying to occupy Transylvania while Hungary was busy on the eastern front. Food shortages prompted discontent especially among the poorer classes. The Left made considerable gains during this period: On May 1, 1917, it organized large-scale demonstrations. It received moral impetus from the Russian Revolution later that year, and by 1918 was organizing strikes. On October 17, 1918, after large-scale mutinies, Prime Minister István Tisza conceded that the war was lost. 14 days later Romanians, Czechs and Croats declared their independence. The Empire had disintegrated of its own accord and all Hungary could hope for was that the 14 points promulgated by the American President Woodrow Wilson would apply to her as well, especially where the integrity of national boundaries was concerned.

THE 20TH CENTURY

World War One was ending, and the man of the hour, one of Hungary's few magnates blessed with a sense of decency, was Mihály Károlyi. On October 25 he founded a National Council which the king appointed to take the reigns and lead Hungary into peace. A cease-fire was signed on November 3 and on the 16th Károlyi proclaimed a republic with a progressive constitution guaranteeing freedom of speech and franchise for men and women over the age of 21. Together with the brilliant journalist Oszkar Jászi he revived plans for a Danube federation, a kind of eastern Switzerland that would have allowed all the nationalities in the area to live in peace, and might have been strong enough later to resist both pressure from Nazi Germany and the Soviet Union. Unfortunately time was not ripe for Károlyi's idealism: The nationalities had only territorial gains in mind; the victorious powers, in particular the French, acted as irresponsible arbiters in handing out Hungary's erstwhile dominions, and bitter Hungarian landowners foiled Károlyi's efforts whenever they could.

Economic and social chaos exacerbated political problems: Production was at a standstill, there was high unemployment and a refugee problem, all of which served the purposes of the growing Communist movement. When the French requested that the Hungarians vacate certain areas in the east, thus allowing the Romanians to move into the Great Plain, Károlyi – on March 4, 1919 – turned the reigns over to the Social Democrats, who in turn allied themselves with the Communists led from prison by the journalist Béla Kun. Kun took over the foreign ministry and within a short time had assumed dictatorial powers. His so-called

Left: Count Mihály Károlyi who formulated brilliant policies at a time when no one was interested.

"Lenin Boys" took care of policing the streets, collectives were created and all land and industries nationalized. Child labor was abolished and women were given equal rights.

At first the new ideas and the firm leadership enjoyed a wave of popularity. On the other hand, capital fled the country and reactionary forces quickly gathered in Vienna and Szeged. As for the Entente, it hoped that Czech and Romanian campaigns into Hungary could deal with this nuisance, but the hastily mobilized Hungarian Red Army fought successfully against the intruders. On June 7 Hungary was promised a hearing if it moved back to the demarcation lines of 1918. The Romanians, however, refused to budge until the Hungarians had been disarmed, at which point Kun resumed hostilities. The momentum had been broken, though, and furthermore the forced collectivization and various shortages had eroded much Communist support in the countryside. Militarily the Romanians gained the upper hand and by August 3 Kun was in Vienna and they had entered Budapest.

The governments that followed the Soviet until the elections in January 1920 had little meaning. The real leader of Hungary was Admiral Horthy and his general Gyula Gömbös, who led a counterrevolutionary army that took over Budapest when the Romanians left (taking as much booty as they could). Right-wing repression, the so-called *white terror*, swept through the country, dwarfing anything Kun's Lenin Boys had done not only in volume but in style as well. Anti-semitism played an important role in the selection of victims.

After the elections the country was essentially led by the right wing, 40 percent of the vote having gone to the newly founded Smallholders' Party and about 35 percent to a coalition called the Christian National Union. The Social Democrats decided to boycott the election because of the white terror that made free ballotting virtually impossible. Among the earliest laws passed were some restricting the electorate, thus insuring the succession of right-wing cabinets. The king was also once and for all officially deposed and Horthy installed as regent on the throne. An attempt by Charles I to recapture his crown militarily failed miserably on the outskirts of Budapest.

The government's main task was to sign the peace treaty of Trianon, whereby the country was left with less than a third of its original territory and about a third of its pre-war population. All of Transylvania went to Romania, Czechoslovakia swallowed a large portion, and Croatia was incorporated into Yugoslavia. Even Austria, whose expansionism in the Balkans had sparked the war, was granted a little piece of Hungary, though this decision was reversed in a local plebiscite.

Opposition to Trianon had a certain unifying effect on Hungary. Count István Bethlen, a fine specimen of a Transylvanian diplomat, had the difficult task of steering the country through the 1920s. He recruited support from the Hungarian workers by agreement with the Social Democrats. Under a conservative regime, and with a relatively docile proletariat, Hungary once again became attractive to foreign investors. In 1923 Bethlen manoeuvered the country into the League of Nations and in 1924 secured a 250 million guilders loan that set the economy in motion. It took several years for the standard of living to reach pre-war levels, but people seemed ready to wait. Strikes and demonstrations in 1927 protesting continued economic hardships were easily suppressed by a combination of force and lack of support.

Fascist Rise

The Wall Street crash in 1929 and the ensuing world-wide depression ended Hungary's economic growth. Unemploy-

ment and poverty grew, while attempts to revise Trianon and the illusion of unity it had conjured swiftly faded. The liberal-conservative alliance weakened in favor of the anti-democratic right wing, where a nationalist racist movement had been festering under the leadership of Horthy's one-time general Gyula Gömbös. In 1932 Horthy appointed him to be prime minister. Though Gömbös failed to straighten out the forever wobbly economy, he was able to rally people to his side, gain the support of the army and administration and, by the time of his death in 1936, secure strong economic ties with Nazi Germany. In fact it was Gömbös who first coined the term "axis", suggesting a coalition of Central Europe's fascist powers to resist both western liberalism and eastern bolshevism.

As the '30s wore on, Hungary became increasingly dependent on the German market, and Hitler's own success at thumbing his nose with impudence at the Entente powers kept hopes of abrogating Trianon alive. By 1939 it had a fairly powerful Nazi party of its own, complete with para-military units, flags and rituals, the Arrow-Cross (*Nyilas*) movement led by Ferenc Szálasi. Hitler, for his part, courted the Hungarians, granting them their old territories in Slovakia and Ruthenia after consultations in Vienna in November 1938. In February 1939 Hungary joined the anti-Comintern pact.

The more moderate conservative forces that controled Hungary after the Gömbös interlude also saw the advantage of maintaining relations with Hitler, but were reluctant to sever contacts with western powers. It was a dangerous political game that was in the end to have quite real results. Anti-Jewish legislation was passed in part to satisfy the thirst of the extreme right, while at the same time the German Wehrmacht was prohibited from using Hungarian territory to reach Poland at the onset of World War II. Prime Minister Teleki even allowed the

Moravia

POLAND

○ *L'vov*

U . S . S . R .

Brno ○   ○ Zilina
C Z E C H O S L O V A K I A

S l o v a k i a
○ Košice

Danube   VIENNA ○   Bratislava   Miskolc ○   Chust ○
Debrecen ○

Győr ○   BUDAPEST ○   Tisza

AUSTRIA
○ Graz

H U N G A R Y

T r a n s y l v a n i a

Balaton   ○ Cluj

Drava

Szeged ○   R O M A N I A

Slovenija   Pécs ○   Oradea ○   ○ Sibiu

○ Zagreb
Trieste   *C r o a t i a*

Sava   Danube   *W a l l a c h i a*

ADRIATIC
SEA   Y U G O S L A V I A   Beograd ○

Kingdom of Hungary until 1918
Hungary in 1920 and after 1945/47

TREATY OF TRIANON 1920
0   250 km

Polish army to retreat onto Hungarian territory. In 1940 Hitler bought more of Hungarian public opinion by handing Northern Transylvania back to Hungary. The West meanwhile continued playing hard to get and Teleki found it increasingly difficult to hold the balance of powers. In despair over the failure of his policies, unable to conclude some kind of alliance with the British and under pressure from the army, he committed suicide on April 2, 1941. On April 11 Hungary joined the German army in invading Yugoslavia. On June 27 using the somewhat flimsy excuse of an alleged Russian bombing of the town of Kassa (today Kosice in CSFR), Hungary sent a first contingent into the Soviet Union to fight alongside the Nazis. The country was now committed to the axis powers.

The end of 1941 brought the first consequences: The Americans entered the war and the German army faced the Russian winter dressed in summer clothes. By early 1942 the Nazis were demanding greater Hungarian participation in what was looking suspiciously like a lost war. In winter 1943 a Hungarian army disappeared into the deep-frozen Voronezh front, shortages began plaguing the nation, inflation ravaged the economy and Nazi Germany was unable or unwilling to pay its debts.

Throughout those hard years Hungary maintained a certain independence from Germany. Prime Minister Miklós Kállay tried in vain to re-open ties with the West. On March 19, 1944, unsure of Hungarian loyalty toward the Reich, the Nazis took over the country and installed a more tractable government under Döme Sztojay. Adolf Eichmann then made it his duty to eradicate the last intact Jewish community in Europe. The exposed Jews in the countryside were quickly disposed of, but in Budapest Eichmann met his match in a Swedish attaché named Raoul Wallenberg, who issued protective passes for the Jews; and since Sweden was both neutral and an important source of iron for the Reich, for a while the ploy worked. R. Wallenberg later disappeared

39

behind Soviet lines after saving any-where up to 100.000 lives.

Inexorably the Red Army approached Hungary. On August 23, 1944, the Romanians who had fought beside the Nazis suddenly declared war on them. By September the first Soviet units had crossed into Hungarian territory. On October 15 Horthy announced the end of the war. But the Nazis captured his son and ordered him to appoint Ferenc Szálasi and the Arrow-Cross movement to run Hungary. It was Horthy's last move before being taken into custody to Germany.

The final months of the war for Hungary were marked by the wholesale slaughter of the Jews by the Nyilas, by the bloody siege of Budapest, with a contingent of SS holding out in the citadel until February 1945, by hunger and destruction as the Soviet army slowly moved across the country.

Above: Béla Kun, revered as a prophet by the new Communist leaders. Right: Stalin's sphinx smiles.

Apocalyptic Rebirth

While the Soviets had been moving in Hungary's political life had already started coming to life again. A National Assembly gathered in Szeged on December 2, 1944. Social Democrats and Smallholders reemerged from the woodwork, as well as a well-trained core of Communists including Rákosi, László Rajk, Ernö Gerö and Imre Nagy who returned from exile in Moscow. In spite of the overwhelming presence of Soviet troups, though, it was the rather conservative Smallholders who captured the absolute majority of the votes (57 percent) in the elections held in November, 1945. Social Democrats and Communists got about 17 percent apiece making them ideal candidates for a coalition. The latter did however receive the most important cabinet post, the interior ministry which controled the newly created secret police force, the AVO (later called AVH). This allowed them to slowly tie up the opposition, hence the name "salami tactic".

The war had divided the nation, killed many, remains of Nyilas units were still at large terrorizing people, industry hardly existed (the Wehrmacht had destroyed what they could from railroad tracks to bridges and the Soviet Union had taken what was left), agriculture was in similar shape and inflation raged until the forint was introduced on August 1, 1946. Under the circumstances it seemed perfectly reasonable to place banks and industry under supervision of the government, a Communist notion.

In spite of strong propaganda holding of vital offices, aid from the Soviet army of occupation and such crude tactics as ballot-box stuffing, the 1947 elections hardly gave the Communists better results than in 1945. The main difference lay in the atomization of the rest of the political spectrum into a myriad of small parties. Even the Social Democrats faced a philosophical dilemma, which in 1948 ultimately pushed them into a lethal coalition with the Communists. The move was followed by the elimination of the liberal and conservative opposition, the purging of "right-wing" social democrats and finally, in 1949, the purging of the Communist Party itself, notably of those members who had spent the '20s and '30s in Hungary.

Left alone, the Muscovite wing of the party under the beastly Rákosi went full steam ahead with collectivizing the land and imposing Stalinist rule with all its egregious trappings on the Hungarians. For anyone failing to stay the course, there was a small but efficient gulag waiting. By force and without the slightest consideration for human needs, the Communists attempted to turn the country into an industrial power. Stalin's death in 1953 brought some relief: Imre Nagy, a friendly and popular figure, introduced limited reforms, from reduction of the secret police force to shifting production to an emphasis on consumer goods. In 1955 when the thaw seemed to have

ended in the USSR, Nagy was expelled from the party and Rákosi resumed his old seat. But a year later, Khrushchov's speech at the 20th Party Congress denouncing Stalin and his methods fell like a bomb in the Communist world. In Hungary the clamor for reforms, embodied in part by Imre Nagy, became louder and clearer. A workers' revolt in Poland and the defiant independence of Yugoslavia further heated the atmosphere.

The Trauma of 1956

On October 23 a great crowd gathered to demand reforms. It was met by a volley of bullets from the secret police, bringing about a spontaneous revolution. The armed forces under Pál Maléter and the regular police force sided with the people, and all the Party could do was to recall Imre Nagy. The Soviet tanks that had started advancing on Budapest, center of the revolution, retreated, and for a while it looked as if the Hungarians had

won. Nagy, however, in a speech on October 31, promised a multi- party system within the socialist complex and an independent foreign policy. The danger of seeing their entire empire in eastern Europe unraveling was too great for the USSR. After a powerful anti-Nagy propaganda barrage the tanks returned and this time, after a 10 day battle that left thousands dead and numerous buildings in flames, they put an end to the revolution. 200.000 Hungarians fled the country. Nagy and his accolytes, along with a few hundred or thousand participants, were executed and their bodies dumped in parcel 301 of the Kozma street cemetery Thousands were shipped off to prison. The man who presided over the legal mopping up had been a friend of Nagy, and it was his anti-Stalinist past that made him apt for this rather distasteful task. János Kádár, Moscow's yes-man,

Above: The Hungarian flag freed from Communist insignia – a symbol of the 1956 revolution.

was to lead Hungary for over thiry years and in spite of his initial actions, he can to a certain extent be credited with steering the country onto an interesting course. Perhaps his conscience plagued him, for at the end of his long tenure he attempted suicide, and coincidentally, a few weeks after Nagy, Maléter and the others were re-buried with full honors, on June 16, 1989, Kádár himself was carried off to his grave.

By the early sixties many of the imprisoned '56ers had been released, though they frequently had to wait years for full rehabilitation. In 1962 Kádár borrowed a phrase from the bible to describe the future of the Party in Hungary:"Whoever is not against us is with us." This vague formulation suggested a turn away from the paranoid cold-war of Rákosi and the others, and allowed for contacts across ideological lines. In 1968 he inaugurated the New Economic Mechanism, introducing limited free enterprise, competition between state-run companies, and joint ventures with foreign, in particular

Austrian and West German companies. A by-product of these new directions was the readiness of unions to actually do something for their members rather than merely act as an extention of the Party.

Looser border policies turned Hungary into a touristic paradise. In 1970 6.3 million tourists visited Hungary, by 1981 the number had risen to 14.8 million and by 1990 it passed the 25 million mark. Many came from the West and brought much needed hard currency. Kádár reaffirmed his loyalty to Moscow simultaneously trowing bridges to the West, especially Austria, where he found the receptive chancellor Kreisky. Jokingly Hungarians referred to this period as the new K. and K. period, Kádár and Kreisky.

The Communist Debacle

The influx of consumer goods gradually pushed up Hungary's foreign debt to 7 billion dollars by the end of the 1970s and over 18 billion a decade later. Furthermore, what was considered tolerance in the '60s had not changed much by the '80s. Freedom of expression was still restricted. Among the first cracks in the façade appeared when the government embarked on an ecologically unsound project – building a dam on the Danube near Nagymaros together with the Czechs and the Austrians. The opponents quickly organized into a thinly disguised political opposition. The winds of change in the USSR also gave impetus to reformers within the party. In May 1988 Károly Grósz replaced Kádár on a platform of change.

At about the same time Hungary began agitating against the oppression of the Hungarian "minority" in Transylvania, Romania. Pressure to create a multi-party system grew stronger, and attempts to reform the old Workers party got only as far as the creation of a new Socialist Party and a sprinkling of smaller spin-offs from the old CP. A series of parties suddenly appeared on the political horizon, the Hungarian Democratic Forum (MDF), the old Social Democrats (MSZDP), the Free Democrats (SZDSZ), the hotheaded Young Democrats (Fidesz) and the Smallholders. In March, 1989 they sat down at the Round Table to discuss the future of Hungary with the powers that be.

Talks lasted long and other events had some influence on the outcome. On June 16, 1989, the MDF acted as the most visible organizer of the re-burial of Imre Nagy, an event that occupied nearly nine hours of countinuous TV time. In September, East Germans who regularly enjoyed their summer vacations in Hungary suddenly demanded to be let out across the loosest fold in the Iron Curtain, and Hungary, notably Foreign Minister Gyula Horn, arranged for their exit. Shortly after, the East German leader Erich Honecker fell and along with him, the Wall. In November a plebiscite formally expelled the CP from its leading position, disbanded the militia and set the date for presidential elections. In December 1989 the Assembly voted to disband on March 16, 1990, and to hold elections.

The election campaign was long and at times bitter accounting to a great extent for the rather low turn out. Run up elections only drew about 40 percent of the electorate. The MDF and the SZDSZ were the front runners.

Hungary now has a market economy, a rather right-wing MDF president, Joseph Antall, and a democratic form of government. The shift however has been costly: Inflation in 1990 ran at near 50 percent, a rise in the price of oil will further hurt the country and wages are low. The disappearance of East Germany has eliminated a major trading partner, and the fact that the forint remains an inconvertible currency is paralyzing the economy. Retooling the archaic industry and reigning in pollution are vital but costly tasks that lay ahead.

WESTERN HUNGARY

SOPRON

GYÖR

PANNONHALMA

PÁPA / SÜMEG

KÖRMEND / SÁRVÁR

SZOMBATHELY

Hungary's **Kisalföld** (the Little Plain), an 8403 square kilometer section in the west, includes the districts of Györ-Sopron, Vas and parts of Veszprém. Geographically it is bordered in the north by the Danube, in the west by the Sopron hills and the Hungarian Alps, and to the southeast by the foothills of the Transdanubian hills. The slopes of the Bakony hills north of the Balaton complete the circle. The region's soil is clayey and fertile, but there is also enough industry to counterbalance agriculture.

Sopron

The border town of **Sopron** is also referred to as *civitas fidelissima* (most loyal town) because its townspeople decided in favor of Hungarian citizenship in 1921. It is one of the most interesting towns in Hungary from a historical point of view, with many beautiful sights. It lies at the base of the Lövér hills, in the foothills of the Hungarian Alps. Its medieval core still exists to great extent, as it was never really destroyed. The Celts settled here, most probably on the heels of earlier settlers. They were ousted by the Romans,

Preceding pages: The omnipresent paprika. Geese on a stroll. Left: The storks are Hungary's other tourists.

who named their flourishing town *Scarbantia* and built a wall around it. Fortified in this way the town served to defend the major trade route between the Mediterranean and the Baltic. But, as archeological finds have confirmed, Sopron by no means became a ghost town when the hordes from various tribal migrations replaced the Roman occupants.

In the 10th century Sopron was taken over by Hungarian tribes. Over the next three hundred years they built a triple wall around it. The community flourished and King László IV, the Cumanian, (1272- 1290) elevated it to the status of a free royal town. The oldest street still in existence in today's horse-shoe-shaped town center is Új utca (New Street). In the Middle Ages it was called Zsidó utca (Street of the Jews). The remains of two synagogues in this street (Nos. 11 and 22), exposed during renovation work, are reminders of this former Jewish quarter. Jewish merchants from Bavaria and Austria had been coming to this town since the 13th century. Thanks both to the Sopron's geographical position and to the pro-Jewish laws enacted by Béla IV. (1235-70) they were able to conduct highly successful trade here. But after the defeat of Mohács (1526), Jews were accused of having conspired with the Turks and summarily expelled from Hungary.

Above: The pretty train station of Hidegség-Nagycenk near Sopron.

A peripheral road running parallel to the medieval town wall encircles Sopron's downtown area. Parts of the wall that have been bared again reveal fortified sections from Celtic and Roman times. Once upon a time it consisted of a series of defensive towers standing 30 meters apart, but of these only the 61 meter high **Fire Tower** still remains, the trademark of present-day Sopron. The tower comprises four stylistic features. The square base contains Roman elements, there are Romanesque parts from medieval times, the arcades and balustrades are late- Renaissance, and the clock tower, with its copper roof, is in Baroque style. The gallery provides a panoramic view of the town and the surrounding countryside. At one time guards kept watch from here for outbreaks of fire. It was also their job to signal the end of business hours with a trumpet flourish and to announce the welcome arrival in town of wares and wines, to the joy of the townspeople. The fire tower stands to the north of **Fö tér** which is surrounded by houses built between the 15th and 17th centuries. The town center stretches from the tower to Orsolya tér in the south. The whole area is under a preservation order – and rightly so, for it is filled with wonderful sights. The focal point of Fö tér is the **Statue of the Trinity**, erected in 1700. Cardinal Kollonich was it who had the statue erected, despite the Protestant majority vote on the city council. Kollonich, architect of the "re-Catholicization" of Hungary is remembered for his statement: "First I will make the Hungarians slaves, then I will make them beggars, and then I will make them Catholics". The **Storno House** (No. 8), an imposing, two-storey corner-house with a round oriel, already existed in the days of King Mátyás (1458-90). From 1698 it was owned by the Festetics counts. They had it renovated in its present form: with a Renaissance façade, an oriel and balcony. The house was then acquired by the

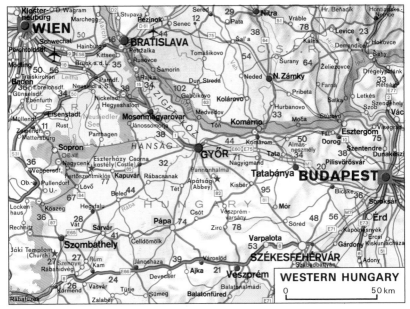

master chimney sweep, painter, restorer and art collector, Franz Storno. His extensive collection, which ranged from medieval to nineteenth-century works, was later increased by his descendents. The town of Sopron acquired the collection in reparation settlements from Storno's descendents, who were living abroad. It is now displayed in several rooms of the house, which was fully restored in 1986. The beautiful inner courtyard is also well worth seeing.

Baroque treasures

The **Fabricius House** (6, Fö tér) consists of two houses with two and three stories respectively. The first received a façade with a bay window in the 18th century, that is, it is in Baroque style. The inner courtyard of the second house is closed off by the town wall, which serves as a buttress. It is probably a patrician house from the first half of the 15th century. Its outer wall was built using roughly-hewn square blocks. Two of the four windows are arched, two are straight. Parts of the walls in the vaulted Gothic cellars are from the Romanesque period, while the foundations are Roman, and once contained a hypocaustic heating system. A Renaissance stairway takes you from the courtyard to the museum rooms on the first floor. You can also get to the museum from the promenade along the town wall.

Orsolya tér borders the southern part of the town center. It was here that Ursuline nuns (hence the name of the square) settled in the 18th century and built a neo-Gothic church, convent and school. The Fountain of Mary from the same period, like so much in Sopron, fell victim to bombs in the Second World War. But today it has been rebuilt, and now stands at the center of the square in all its former glory. The arcades of the Baroque summer house were exposed when rubble was cleared after the bombing.

If you wander down the narrow streets, made even narrower by the many tourists, you will often run into sights of both breathtaking or rather contemplative beauty. It may be Baroque and medieval houses, such as the Zichy Palace in the Kolostor utca, or it may be the treasures of Szt. György utca, such as the particularly attractive Rococo palace, with its intricate floral ornamentation. And beyond the town center there are many more monuments worth seeing. In Poysonzi út, for example, stands the **Church of St. Michael**, a Gothic hall church which dates back to the 11th century, as can be seen by its Romanesque round-arch mouldings. The 48 m tower, with its neo-Gothic steeple, was built in the 13th century. At its feet you will find the entrance portal. The building was completed in the second half of the 15 century, as can be gathered from 1485, carved in the keystone of the arch. Unfortunately the church suffered from the many, albeit well-intentioned renovations of Franz Storno, and is now neo- Gothic in character. The older chapel of **St. Jacob** in the cemetery reveals Romanesque as well as Gothic stylistic elements.

Perhaps the most beautiful and historically most interesting church is the Gothic **Church of Mary** in Templom utca. Franciscans began its construction in 1280. As with the Mátyás church in Buda, it is thought that the construction of the church was overseen by the French. The Hungarian Diet met five times here and three times it served the coronation of a king. Johannes Capistranus preached here, calling for war against the Turks in some impassioned speeches. The locals call this church "The Church of the Goat", because a goat is said to have unearthed the coins necessary to complete its construction. In gratitude, on one of the pillars of the Baroquely splendiferous interior, an angel is shown embracing a billy goat.

Right: The Hungarian Versailles, a Baroque masterpiece built in the midst of the swamplands near Sopron by Count Esterházy.

The Hungarian Versailles

When you grow tired of walking you can relax over a glass of wine in one of the little **Poncichter houses**. Vintners were called "Poncichter" because they grew beans between their rows of vines. Fortunately this did not affect the quality of the Sopron Franconian grape! A walk along the well-maintained paths of the Lövér Hills (highest elevation 350m) and their woods and chestnut groves is always pleasant, whatever the weather. If you are in search of different activities, the southern end of **Lake Fertö** (Neusiedler See in Austria) offers facilities for swimming, fishing and excursions in steam boats.

Esterházy Palace in Fertöd, only 26 kilometers south of Sopron, makes for interesting visiting, especially if one catches a concert. It is regarded as one of the masterpieces of Baroque architecture, and once belonged to Hungary's richest feudal lord. Joseph Haydn lived and worked in this Hungarian Versailles from 1760-90. **Balf** lies on the way from Sopron to Fertöd, a spa whose healing waters were already known to the Romans. The steeple of the church, built on a vineyard in the 16th century, once served as a watch tower. The church and God's acre, with its heart-shaped gravestones, are surrounded by a wall with embrasures – a last ditch defense for the final, desperate battle.

Highway 85, which runs from Sopron to Györ, forms the southern border of **Hanság**, once an almost 400 square kilometer swampland. Since the 18th century it has been extensively drained through the construction of a network of canals, and can now be farmed. Sugar beet is the main crop. The woods and waters are ideal for hunters and anglers to pursue their hobbies. The thick volutes of fog in this region can create some of the most phantastical figures. This is the cradle of many Hungarian fairytales

which tell of gnomes, water sprites and elves. But the large white shapes sometimes moving alongside the roads do not belong to the realm of fairytales. These are enormous flocks of geese fattened on the fertile meadows before eventually becoming Martinmas geese. Sheep and sometimes even pigs also graze along the roadside. As always in Hungary, one has to be prepared to avoid the odd horse or horse-driven cart suddenly swerving out on the road.

Nagycenk, 10 km south of Sopron, with its Baroque Széchenyi Palace, is well worth a visit. In **Kapuvár**, a small town described as a royal residence as far back as 1162, you can take a break at the Hotel Hanság, which you will find between the church and the castle. The castle has a nice museum displaying traditional furniture, clothing and crafts.

The Town of Four Rivers

Leaving the Austro-Hungarian border on the E5, the first sizeable town you come to is **Györ**. It has 120.000 inhabitants and is the administrative center of the district of Györ. It stands on four rivers – hence its nickname "town of four rivers". Illyrians, Celts and Romans once settled here and were successively ousted. The Turkish occupiers and Napoleonic troops burned and destroyed a great deal. However, Györ still boasts the greatest number of architectural monuments in Hungary after Budapest and Sopron. A nineteenth-century chronicler called it the crown of provincial towns. Most of its protected buildings are to be found in the historical town center. **Köztársaság tér**, with a statue of the poet Kisfaludy in its center, is a particularly beautiful square. Besides a number of old houses, it includes the erstwhile church and cloister complex of the Carmelites. House number 12 is thought to be the oldest. Its façade retains Gothic elements, but the two oriels resting on snail-shaped supports and the entrance framed in pillars are Renaissance and Baroque. The most beautiful building is the **Zichy**

53

Palace, which was built towards the end of the 18th century. It has now been completely restored. It is said that seventeen layers of paint had to be removed from the old murals before they saw the light of day again. The balcony, supported by pillars and enclosed in a wrought-iron trellis, is beautiful.

The church and cloister ensemble was built at the beginning of the 18th century, mainly from contributions made by the townspeople. The cloister has served many different purposes in its time. Under Joseph II it was the district seat, during the Napoleonic Wars and after the unsuccessful revolution of 1848-49 it served as an asylum for refugees of all sorts. Five years later it became a military prison and today it is a three star hotel. Széchenyi tér, joined to Köztársaság tér by three small streets, is surrounded by 17th and 18th century houses. A statue of Mary from the 17th century forms the

Above: Detail of the Baroque Marian column on Széchenyi Square in Györ.

focal point of the square. In earlier times popular festivals were held here, and it was the site of the town's executions. Today tourists throng to the square. Most of them visit the two-towered Benedictine Church.

The Cathedral

The cathedral on Káptalandomb, the highest geographical and perhaps even cultural point in historical Györ, is undoubtedly the most important building in town. It has borne witness to many historical events. István I (1000-1038), who made Györ an episcopal town, had a church originally built here. The Romanesque building was renovated and rebuilt many times before 1910. Today it reveals a combination of Romanesque, Gothic, Baroque and Classical stylistic features. The interior dates back to the 18th century. Franz A. Maulbertsch created the ceiling painting and the altar painting showing the Ascension of Mary. One of Hungary's great treasures is kept in the chapel, which dates from 1404. It is the Herme, a relief portraying King László I. It is a masterpiece of the Hungarian goldsmith's craft, and it is said to come from the workshop of the famous Kolozsváry brothers.

Many of the ancient buildings in Györ are prime examples of the exuberant Baroque creativity. Almost all of them were threatened by decay for many years, but have now been expertly renovated. Of the town's modern buildings, the finest is perhaps the **theater** on Czuczor utca. Victor Vasarely created the façade. It serves as home to the ballet ensemble, that became famous throughout the world under Iván Markó.

Of the museums, the **János Xantus** and the **Pharmacy Museums** on Széchenyi tér are worth both a visit, as are the **Miklós Borsos Museum** on Martinovics tér and the **Margit Kovács exhibition** on Gutenberg tér. You cannot miss the Baroque monument depicting the Ark of the Covenant on this square, designed by Fischer von Erlach.

Catholic Past

You will need half a day or more to visit the Benedictine abbey at **Pannonhalma** (21 km south of Györ), the stronghold of Hungarian Catholicism. The abbey stands like a fortress on a hill in the midst of the most wonderful countryside, at the point where the Kisalföld meets the Bakony hills. In the *Gesta Hungarorum*, the first chronicle of Hungary, it is said that Árpád climbed this hill and "was uplifted by the beauty of Pannonia". The name Pannonhalma (*halom* = hill) was coined by the Hungarian poet and language reformer Ferenc Kazinczy (1759-1831). Before him, the complex was called "Cloister on St. Martin's Hill", in honor of Bishop Martin of Tours, who was born in Szombathely in 316. Géza I (971- 997) granted St. Martin's Hill to the Benedictines. Legend has it that he laid the cornerstone of the cloister and church himself. Pannonhalma is one of the most beautiful abbeys, the Hungarian "Monte Cassino".

Nothing remains of the original buildings. From the 12th century onward much building and fortifying took place while at the same time it increased its landholdings and privileges. In 1241 the abbey withstood the storming of the Tatars, and abbot Oros was able to give King Béla IV 220 kg of silver to rebuild his ravaged country.

The complex was extended during the 18th century. Whereas the 17th century architects had resorted to Romanesque elements, the dominant style now was Baroque: splendid, grandiose, but restless. The renovations undertaken by Franz Storno in the 19th century have met with similar criticisms as those undertaken on the Church of St. Michael. The abbey's possessions include many paintings, a numismatic collection of 25.000 coins and a library with 300.000 volumes, a considerable growth rate if one considers that the first one, ordered by László I (1077-95), only had a mere 70 volumes. An expert guide can be hired to take you around the abbey.

A large number of music enthusiasts flock to the hill for the organ concerts and particurarly for the for renowned great annual Christmas concert. The boarding school next to the cloister is housed in a modern building which dates from 1940. Children from all over Hungary receive an education for life here from the Benedictines according to the principle *ora et labora*.

To the north of Györ, the **Szigetköz** stretches to the Austrian border. The Szigetköz is a 50 km by 10 km island between the Old Danube and the Moson Danube. At one time the villages were under constant threat of floods. Today they are protected by dams. It is an almost untouched natural paradise and an ideal place for avid swimmers, hunters

and hikers. Traveling down the romantic labyrinthian waterways by boat is a wonderful adventure. Panning for gold will no longer make you rich, as it did in medieval times, but it is fun nevertheless. If you have plenty of time, **Mosonmagyaróvár**, a little Baroque town fortified by a castle from the 11th to the 17th century, makes a welcome change. On the way, turn off to **Lébénymiklós** to visit one of the earliest examples of Romanesque church architecture.

On the Trace of Maulbertsch

About 50 km southwest of Györ (Highway 83), in a picturesque setting, you will find the small Baroque town of **Pápa**. It takes its name from Papo, the knight who accompanied Gisela of Bavaria to Hungary in 996 on the occasion of her marriage to István I. The thankful king gave Papo the fortress on the river Tapolca. Over the years the small town of Pápa grew into a center of trade and business. It was besieged and occupied by the Turks and later served the rebellious *kuruz* soldiers as an army encampment.

In 1531 the **Protestant College** was established here in defiance of the Habsburg attempts to re-establish Catholicism in the country. Sándor Petöfi and Mór Jókai were both pupils at this college. Those on the trace of F. A. Maulbertsch's works in Hungary will find plenty in Pápa. He painted the ceiling frescoes (scenes from the life of the martyr Stephen and of the Ascension of Mary) in the single-aisled Baroque church on Szabadság tér. The chapel of the Esterházy Castle was built in the 18th century on the foundation walls of the old castle opposite the church. It also contains a fresco by Maulbertsch.

Left: To each his own fuel – it could be the famous Blue Franconian wine.

Celldömölk

The journey along the road from Pápa to Sümeg via Celldömölk and Jánosháza takes you through a varied landscape of undulating wooded countryside, through fields and vineyards. **Celldömölk** lies on the left bank of the Marcal river and at the foot of a 21 m high basalt peak, the Ság mountain. Reading the poet Dániel Berzsenyi (1776-1836), who writes with passion of his homeland the "Ság mountain lost in mist", you might assume he is writing about the seat of the gods or about a brother of Mount Everest. This is not the case because the summit of the mountain is easily accessible in a comfortable walk. If you have not already had your fill of Hungary's preserved and restored Baroque architecture, drop in on the center of the little town, where you will find a church that once hosted pilgrimages and the chapel of Calvary.

About 40 km south of Celldömölk on Highway 84 beyond Jánosháza lies **Sümeg**. Its 13th century castle, partly reconstructed, partly still in ruins, dominates the entire area. It is built on a steep hill with vineyards sprawled at its feet, and provides a wonderful panoramic view of the surrounding countryside. In autumn the sky is broad and clear, the air, brought by the wind from Balaton, seems pervaded with the taste of wine and may whet your appetite for a Riesling. A tour of Sümeg is best begun at **Szabadság tér**. Walk first down Deák Ferenc utca towards the square of the same name. Beautiful Baroque houses line the way, as well as parts of the old town wall. In the single-aisled Baroque church on Deák tér, the Parish Church of Christ's Ascension, you will find some of F. A. Maulbertsch's finest works. He painted the entire interior of the church with scenes from the Old and New Testaments. He portrayed himself twice. The shepherd in the *Adoration*, offering cheese (side altar, right) was the artist's own features, as

The Rába, which springs in the Alps of Styria, changes its easterly course here and flows to the north, now wide enough to carry ships. You can take a dip in the fresh, icy cold river at the beach local. Körmend, a town with 11.000 inhabitants, was created after the borders were secured in the 11th century. The present-day castle on Szabadság tér retains within its walls the old fortified castle with its four corner towers. It has been rebuilt several times, and today exhibits grandiloquent Baroque features with a few Classical elements. For example, the gable with the coat-of-arms of the Bathyány family is carried by six Ionic colums, which are supported in turn by a long balcony with a balustrade, resting on six Doric columns. The park is a nature conservation area and has a lake on which you can take boat trips. There are many old trees in the park, and magnolias too, said to be the finest in Hungary.

On the Way to Szombathely

The next sizeable town, Szombathely, lies around 30 km to the north on Highway 86, which frequently crosses the railway track running alongside it. You soon get used to the hysterical screams of the locomotives at the railway crossings whether there is a gate or not. The route via Sárvár, through the lowlands of the Rába, is twice as long but worth the ride. If you can, find time for a paddle-boat trip to Sárvár and on to Györ. You will be traveling downstream and so it is not at all tiring. You can stretch your legs for a while in **Zsennye**. The castle built between the 16th and 18th centuries is thought to stand on the ruins of a castle of the Order of the Knights Templar. Near the well-kept Arboretum is the "Thousand Year Oak", which has a trunk circumference of 10 m. The great tower and the portal of the parish church in **Rum** are among the few remaining relics of Gothic art in Hungary.

was the young, round-faced man wearing a typical yellowy-orange jerkin of the time, kneeling before the patron bishop Biró (on the wall of the organ loft).

The splendid stuccoed **Bishop's Palace** on Szent István tér was built by Biró, archbishop of Veszprém. The balcony of the palace is supported by two Atlases and has a railing of pierced stone. The bishop's coat-of-arms is above the balcony and shows that he was the first owner of the house. Today it serves as a boarding school.

You may not wish to travel further south but take a drive along the Austrian border from Körmend to Köszeg instead. A small road lead straight across the Kemenes crest, an area of gentle, wooded hills, to route 8 near the town of Vasvár. **Körmend**, standing on the left bank of the river Rába , is now only 15 km away.

Above: Shopping is one of western Hungary's major activities. Right: The town of Sümeg viewed from the (almost) impregnable fortress wall.

Sárvár (*sár* = mud, *vár* = castle) can be described as a Hussar-town, castle-town and spa-town. It takes its name from the **castle**, which already stood there at the time of the land-taking. In the 12th century Sárvár was a royal residence and part of the western belt of fortresses. Over the centuries the castle has had many owners with the net and fortunate result that each new owner extended the castle and strengthened it in a new way whilst retaining its traditional defensive function. Its present pentagonal shape it acquired during the tenure of the Nádasdy dynasty. The first member of this illustrious family to live here, the humanist scholar Tamás Násady, turned the castle into both a military fortress as well as a stronghold of Hungarian intellectual life and the Reformation. The first Hungarian translation of the New Testament by János Szylveszter was printed in 1541 in the castle's own printshop. (The first complete translation was printed in 1590 by Gáspár Károlyi. It is as important for the development of the Hungar-ian language as Luther's translation was for the German language.) The line of Nádasdy descendents mirrors the changing relations between Hungary and Austria. There was the "Conqueror of the Turks", "Black Beg", then there was the "Conspirator against the House of Habsburg", who was executed, and then the "Loyalist to the House of Habsburg", who was honored by Maria Theresa with the Grand Cross.

In the 18th and 19th centuries the castle once again changed owners several times. The last private owner was the royal house of Bavaria. Ludwig III died here in 1921. Today, once again close ties exist between the small town of Sárvár and Bavaria, but the reason for this fraternizing is hops and malt and Kaltenberg beer. The "castle brewery" produces 800 liters of Bavarian beer a day. Fresh from the barrel it is a great tonic before setting off to see the museum rooms of the castle and the festival hall with its beautiful ceiling paintings that make one forget the tasteless electric lamps that illuminate the

59

place. While drinking your beer, don't forget that the maximum blood alcohol limit for drivers is 0.0 milliliters.

Szombathely is accessible on routes 88 and 86. The name means Saturday Place (*locus fori sabbati*) indicating that in medieval times markets were legally held here on Saturdays. This area has been inhabited since the Stone Age. The Romans built onto the old Celtic settlement and called their town *Savaria*. It was elevated by Emperor Claudius to the higher status of a *colonia*.

The archaeological finds from this time are ranked third in Hungary behind *Aquincum* and *Gorsium* in terms of quantity and quality. Attending the Summer Festival in the ruins of the **Temple of Isis** and listening to Sarastro calling in his resonant bass upon Isis and Osiris to always act with wisdom one might think that this scene from Mozart's *Magic*

Above: Catholic processions are still part of a long tradition in western Hungary. Right: A fountain in Szombathely.

Flute was composed especially for this stage. The temple complexes of the Egyptian cult of Isis which spread to the Roman provinces were destroyed in an earthquake in 455. It was not until 1955, 1500 years later, that the ruins were rediscovered on present-day Rákóczi utca. With the exception of the temple façade and its reliefs, the complex has not yet been fully restored. The town center of Szombathely, known as Steinamanger under Frankish rule in the 8th century, is a protected area today. The most Classical but also Baroque buildings with their rows of pictures give the town center its special character.

The huge **Bishop's Palace**, built in the typical eighteenth-century style, dominates Berzsenyi tér. Pillars divide its richly stuccoed façade, the balcony with its stone balustrade is supported by four columns. The group of statues on the attic symbolizes the cardinal virtues: prudence, justice, fortitude and temperance. One of the town's seven museums, the first archeological museum in Hungary, is housed in the great hall of the Bishop's Palace. A pompous stairway decorated with scenes from the crusades takes you to the first floor. Here you will find murals and scenes by F. A. Maulbertsch.

The **museum village** northwest of town on Lake Gondola transports the visitor back to the good old days of peasant life. There is quite a number of similar museums around the country, set up with the aim of preserving some of the old traditions. But such things can only continue to exist together to exist together with people. Lake Gondola offers a variety of activities on its 12 hectares. Part of it is devoted to swimming and boating, part of it to fishing.

The town's three large churches, the Franciscan church (Derkovits Gyula utca), the Church of St. Martin and the cathedral (Templom tér) are in Baroque style. Gothic parts of the Franciscan church survived both the assault of the Turks and the great fire that ravaged the town in the 18th century. The formerly Gothic Church of St. Martin is said to have been built on the foundations of the house in which St. Martin was born. The cathedral, which has dominated the square since the end of the 18th century, was hit by several bombs during the Second World War. Among other things, the frescoes and ceiling decorations by Maulbertsch – late works by the artist – were irrevocably destroyed.

The Church of Ják

14 km south of Szombathely on a verdant hill stands the church of **Ják**, one of the Benedictine abbey churches dedicated to St. George. It was consecrated in 1223, and is a jewel of Romanesque architecture. Once again religion has chosen the most beautiful setting. Márton of Ják, known as the Great One (Marthius dictus Magnus), lord of these lands, founded this imposing, two-towered church. He built the church on the highest

and most central point of his land. Márton of Ják could look out over his lands from here to make sure that all his farmers had turned up for church. For the law here was: Those who neglected to attend church on Sundays were punished with the whip. The church area itself is devided up by octagonal bundles of pillar. The western façade makes an especially strong impression, with its two towers flanking a double portal. Its unity makes it one of the most beautiful parts of the church. Life-sized representations of Christ and ten of his apostles have been placed in the niches of the gable. The other two apostles stand to the right and left of the tower façade. Only Christ's head and those of the two apostles on either side of him are original. The others were added during the Baroque era. The portal's own decoration consists of a rich mixture of abstract ornamentation and mythological animals. Ják's overall design is more complex than that of St. James, the so-called "Scottish" church in Regensburg, which is regarded as the

61

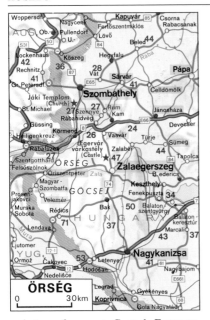

ÖRSÉG

0   30km

archetype for most Central European Norman art. The door was Márton of Ják's visiting card, so to speak. It shows his wealth carved in stone. Walking around the church it soon becomes obvious that no expense was spared when it came to employing stonemasons. Of significance inside the church are the few remaining murals and the architectural planning. The **Chapel of St. James**, built at the same time as the church, stands separately opposite the main façade. It was used for weddings, baptisms and blessings which were forbidden in the churches of the order.

22 km to the north of Szombathely is **Köszeg**, a picturesque little border town with a population of 13.000 at the foot of the Hungarien Alps tucked in a green landscape. It makes an ideal starting point for walks, to the highest elevation, the **Irottkö** (833 m) for example. A walk through the town center is a perpetual

Right: Carrying home the harvest the old-fashioned way.

confrontation with history. Finds going back to the Bronze Age show that this area of Hungary was settled at a very early time too. In chronological order Illyrians, Celts, Romans and Avars settled here before the arrival of the Magyars in the 10th century. The emblem of Köszeg is **Jurisics Castle**. Its construction was begun in the mid-13th century. Very soon a town had sprung up around it, protected by its walls and bastions. Karl Robert granted it the status of a "royal free town" in 1328.

Over the centuries Köszeg belonged sometimes to Hungary, sometimes to Austria, in which case it was called Güns. In 1532 the fortress commander Miklós Jurisics defended it against Suleiman II and his 20.000-strong army with only a small band of loyal soldiers. After 19 assaults Süleyman finally gave up. The **Heroes' Gate** at the end of Város utca was constructed in 1932. It not only keeps the memory of this victory alive, but also commemorates those who fell in the First World War. At the beginning of the 17th century the Haiducks of the Transylvanian Prince István Bocskai arrived at the gates of the town to free the people from the Habsburg yoke. At the beginning of the 18th century it was Prince Rákóczi's *kuruz* soldiers who fought the Emperor's men here, and set the town on fire before sounding the retreat.

During the following years primarily German merchants, vintners and artisans settled here and in the surrounding area in the wake of Habsburg repopulation policies. A veritable construction frenzy began, for which parts of the town wall and the watch towers were sacrificed. The new buildings were in the Austrian Baroque style, nouveau riche and stately. Industrialization, just beginning in Austria, stole the livelihoods of the Köszeg craftsmen. But the town refused to modernize. Like Sleeping Beauty it fell into a deep sleep and preserved its harmonious,

historical beauty. **Jurisics tér**, with its statue of Mary – in the Middle Ages a pillory stood here – is the town's most beautiful square. The Baroque houses (nos. 2-4, 6 and 7) still seem to be dreaming of times gone by, protected by the two churches, the Gothic Church of St. James and the Baroque Church of St. Emeric.

Mysterious Örség

Between routes 7 and 8 and bordered to the east by Highway 74 lies a true paradise for walkers and cyclists. It is here that you will find the hills, woods and meadowlands of two small regions known as Örség and Göcsej. They have many surprises and have caused many a Hungarian poet's heart to beat faster. Just before his death, Dezsö Kosztolányi (1885-1936) wrote: "Here, where the land seems gently conjured by the foothills of the Jura mountains, the air is softer than elsewhere." And indeed it is softer, for southern winds moderate the currents blowing in from the Alps. The

Örség has protected the western border since the time of the Árpáds. Watchhouses stood on the hills, from which the scattered villages could be seen. Houses for the increasingly large families of the guards sprung up over time and formed hamlets. The local woods supplied the timber for construction. Until well into this century, the low, whitewashed and thatched cottages were built according to traditional designs. Beams were roughly joined together at the corners of the house without use of nails, and the gaps between them filled with clay. This was in plentiful supply, for below a 10-15 cm layer of humus lies a hard layer of clay, impenetrable to water. Meadows and pastureland for cattle grow well on this earth, but grains cannot be farmed.

However, it does provide the material for an extensive pottery industry. The old tradition of Hában ceramics is still preserved primarily in **Magyarszombatfa**, a village on the Yugoslavian border with 300 inhabitants. You can buy some of these products in the **Fazekasház** (pot-

63

ter's house), now a museum. The town of **Velemér** lies only 3 km to the southeast. The beautiful 13th century single-aisled village church alone makes a visit worthwhile. If you are interested in the murals which date from 1380, you can ask for a key to the church at the school house.

12 km north of Magyarszombatfa is the town of **Őriszentpéter**, which has 1200 inhabitants. The 13th century village church is one of the most beautiful Romanesque buildings in the country. The richly ornamented portal is similar to the main door of the church in Ják. Őriszentpéter is the ideal place to stay. Inns and a camp-site offer reasonably priced accomodation and provide a good base for hikes and day trips; to the ancient community of this area, for example, **Szalafő**, only 6 km to the north. The hamlet consists of eight groups of houses, of which the nicest is the "Pityerszer", in which you will find a museum.

Above: Harvesting potatoes by hand, a hard but socially fulfilling job.

Along the Yugoslavian border, particularly in the triangle where Yugoslavia, Austria and Hungary meet, you will still find a lot of Slovenes. They are members of a Slavic race which expanded as far as Szentgotthárd on Hungarian territory. Slovene customs and language have survived thanks to the nationality policies layed out in the Hungarian constitution. The little town of **Szentgotthárd** is well worth a visit. It is situated on the right bank of the Raab, where it is joined by Hungary's shortest river, the Lapincs. In summer this river is hardly more than a narrow stream, but when the snows thaw it becomes a raging torrent. The museum named after the ethnographer Pavel Agoston has exhibitions devoted to the various local ethnic groups, including the Slovenes of course.

Szentgotthárd grew from a Cistercian abbey built by Béla II. (1173-1196), but only a few ruins of the original building remain today. The present church was built in the mid-18th century in the Viennese Baroque style. The painting in the first arched bay of the nave is by Stephan Dorffmeister. It depicts the battle of Szentgotthárd which took place on August 1, 1664. It was then that the Imperial General Count Raimund Montecuccoli, who made three demands for his military campaigns – money, money and more money – defeated the Turks with his army of mercenaries. The prolonged Turkish rule and Hungary's seven year War of Independence against the House of Habsburg (1704-1711) did not make this poor district any richer. From the end of the 19th century the financial situation was eased somewhat by a gently flourishing industry, producing mainly tobacco and silk. But it was only when the first Hungarian oil was discovered here in 1937, that wealth was brought to the area.

Turkish Relics

The administrative center of these oil fields is in the district capital of **Nagykanizsa** (where routes 7 and 74 intersect), which has around 56.000 inhabitants. The **fortress** here was the second largest in Hungary. It was razed to the ground in 1702, having been badly damaged in 1690 in a three-day battle with the Turks. Its stones were also used to build new houses, and many were used in the construction of the two-aisled Baroque **Franciscan Church**. The 15th century Gothic Madonna, carved from wood, stands on the altar to the right of the entrance and offers the observer a calm point of focus amidst the Baroque and Rococo complexities. The red marble baptismal font was made from the hand basin of the last Turkish commander of the fortress, Mustapha Pasha. György Thury was the commander of the fortress from 1568-1571. The life- sized bronze statue of this legendary hero, to the east of the ruins, is by Miklós Borsos, one of Hungary's most important contemporary sculptors. The **György Thury Museum** (1, Szabadság tér) houses a very good

ethnographical and local historical collection. The information on the woods, its flora, fauna and forestry is particularly interesting.

Route 74 takes you through undulating hills and some beautiful scenery. **Zalaegerszeg** on the Zala was first referred to in documents from the 13th century. A fortress and swamplands protected the town from falling into foreign hands. However it was burned down on several occasions. Ferenc Deák was born here in 1803. He was the speaker of the Parliament who called for passive resistance against the Habsburg overlords and demanded the return of Hungary's constitutional rights. The parish church, the town hall and the district house are Baroque. In an Art Nouveau house (9, Bathyányi utca) you will find the **Göcsej Museum**. Together with an ethnographical collection it also has a fine art exhibition including works by various painters and sculptor Zsigmond Kisfaludi-Strobl (1889-1975), creator of the Liberation Monument in Budapest. The oldest open-air museum is the **Göcseji Falumúzeum** in the north of the town on a dead branch of the Zala. Here you can see houses and workshops from villages in the area, grouped around a more than two hundred years old water-mill.

The **Castle of Egervár** stands in a beautiful valley about 10 km to the north. It was built in the mid-16th century in Renaissance style on the ruins of two castles from the 13th and 15th centuries. At the beginning of the 18th century the Széchenyi family renovated the castle in Baroque style. Today, completely restored, it serves as a hotel. In the summer months concerts are held in the courtyard. The acoustics are remarkable and the concerts are attended by many people. Egervár's Gothic parish church, built by Franciscans in the 15th century, was also renovated in Baroque style in the 18th century. The interior is predominantly Rococo.

THE SMALL PLAIN

General Information: The towns on the western border of Hungary tend to host consumer tourists from Austria. Add to this the summer crowds on their way to the Balaton and you have overload on the border crossings especially in summer of course. As with all touristically well-trodden areas, the roads are lined with signs saying "pension" or "Zimmer frei", indicating rooms for rent. These lead often to nice, sometimes inexpensive lodgings in private homes. For overall information in Budapest, contact TOURINFORM, Petöfi u., Budapest V, Tel: 117- 9800. In the following the region has been divided into its main cities.

SOPRON
Accomodation
MODERATE: **Lövér, Várisi út 4. Tel: (99) 11-061; Palatinus, Új u. 23, Tel: (99) 12-395.** Sopron, **Fövénverem u. 4, Tel: (99) 14-254.** *BUDGET*: **Lokomotiv**, Szabadság körút 1, Tel: (99) 14-180; **Pannónia**, Lenin körút 75, Tel: (99) 12-180; **Panoráma üdülöszálló**, Panoráma u. 38, Tel: (99) 12-745. *BED AND BREAKFAST*, **Átrium vendégház** (guest house), Köszegi u. 3, Tel (99) 13-799; **Patkó panzió**, Somfalvi ú, Kossuth-major, Tel: (99) 14-648. *CAMPING* (only during the tourist season): **Lövér**, Pócsi-domb, Tel: (99) 11-715; Ozón kemping, Sopronbánfalva, Malom köz 10, Tel: (99) 16-248.

Tourist Offices
Ciklámen Tourist, Ógabona tér 8, Tel: (99) 12-040; **Express** (for students and youths), Mátyás király u. 7, Tel: (99)12-024; **IBUSZ**, Lenin körút 41, Tel: (99) 13-281

Restaurants
The three moderate hotels of Sopron mentioned above have moderately priced, good food. Other good restaurants are: **Fenyves étterem**, Várisi út 4; **Gambrinusz étterem**, Új u. 2; **Bisztró**, Lenin körút 79; **Szélmalom Vendéglö**, Fráknoi út; **Alpesi Vendéglö**, Hársfa sor 42. **Caesar's borozó**, Hátsókapu u. 2, specializes in wine, as the name indicates.

Sightseeing
Sopron is famous for its substantially extant old town which is being extensively restored after several decades of neglect. Museums: **Mining Museum**, Templom u. 2, opening hours: 10 a.m. - 2 p.m. (Wed. closed) from April 1 to October 31, open until 5 p.m.; the rest of the year. **Franz Liszt museum**, Május 1. tér 1, opening hours: Tues.-Sun. 10 a.m. - 6 p.m., April 1 - Oct. 31, 10 a.m. to 5 p.m. the rest of the year. The old **Synagogue** has the same hours. Sopron's **Catholic Church Art Collection**, Orsolya Tér 2, April 1 -

October 31, Tues. - Sun. 9 a.m. - 5 p.m., until 4 p.m. the rest of the year. **Baker's museum**, Bécsi u. 5, opening hours: Tues., Thur., Sat.: 1 p.m. - 5 p.m., Wed., Fri., Sun.: 9 a.m. - 1 p.m. Other museums: **Modern lapidarium**, Fö tér 1; the **Old Apothecary**, Fö tér 2; **Fabricius House**, Fö tér 6. East of town lie two important palaces: In Nagycenk stands the **Széchenyi palace** (including a hotel) and in Fertöd is the famous **Esterházy palace**.

GYÖR
Accomodation
MODERATE: **Klastrom szálló**, Furst Sándor u. 1, Tel: (96) 17-368; **Rába szálló**, Árpád u. 34, Tel: (96) 15-533. *BUDGET*: **Kiskútligeti fogadó**, Kiskútliget kemping (96) 18-986. In **Mosonmagyaróvár: Fekete Sas szálló**, Lenin út 93, Tel (98) 842; **Minerva szálló**: Engels Frigyes u. 2, Tel: (98) 15-602. *CAMPING*: Kiskútligeti kemping, Györ, Tel: (98) 18-986. **Magyar Autóclub kemping**, Gabona rakpart 6, **Mosonmagyaróvár**, Tel: (98) 15-863.

Restaurants
The road here is lined with restaurants of varying quality. An "experience" is the airplane place just west of Györ on the fork to Csorna. Otherwise: **Rába étterem**, Árpád u. 34; **Park étterem**, Tanácsköztársaság útja 19; a cheap alternative is the self-service **Mária étterem**, Aradi vértanúk útja 12.

In **Mosonmagyaróvár**, **Széchenyi étterem**, Városház u. 2; **Várpince étterem**, Vár u. 2.

Tourist Offices
GYÖR: Ciklámen Tourist, Aradi vértanuk útja 22, Tel (96) 11-557; **Express** (for students and youths), Bajcsy-Zsilinszky u. 41, Tel: (96) 18-853. **IBUSZ**, Tanácsköztársaág útja 29-31, Tel: (96) 14-224. **MOSONMAGYARÓVÁR: Ciklámen Tourist**, Lenin u. 88, Tel: (98) 11-078; **IBUSZ**, Lenin u. 132, (98) 15-135.

Sightseeing
GYÖR: Xantus museum (Széchenyi tér 5), for local history and ethnography (closed Mondays). **Széchenyi Museum** (Apothecary), Széchenyi tér 9 (closed Saturday). **Kovács-Margit Exhibition**, Rózsa Ferenc u. 1 (closed Mondays), **Roman and modern lapidarium**, köztársaság tér 5, (closed Mondays). Numerous beautiful Baroque houses. Thermal waters at Marx tér 1. Lébénymiklós' Romanesque church ca. 20 km west of Györ.

MOSONMAGYARÓVÁR: An old fortress, a thermal bath, the Hanság local museum (Lenin út 139). The town is often overlooked by tourists racing from the border to Budapest.

SZOMBATHELY AND KÖSZEG
Accomodation
SZOMBATHELY: *LUXURY*: **Claudius szálló**, Bartók Béla körút 39, Tel (94) 13-760. *MODERATE*: **Isis szálló**, Rákóczi Ferenc u. 1, Tel: (94) 14-990; **Savaria szálló**, Mártírok tere 4, Tel: (94) 11-440. *BUDGET*: **Tourist szálló**, Jókai Park, Tel: (94) 14-168. *CAMPING*: Kondics u. 4, Tel: (94) 14-766.

KÖSZEG: *BUDGET*: **Írottkö szálló**, Köztársaság tér 4, Tel: 333); **Park szálló**, Felszabadulás Park, Tel: 322. **Strucc szálló**, Várkör 124, Tel: 281. *CAMPING*: Alsó körút 79/b, Tel: 89.

Restaurants
SZOMBATHELY: **Gyöngyös étterem**, Savaria u. 8; **Korzó étterem**, Mártírok tere 5; **Kispityer halászcsárda** (fish specialties), Rumi u. 18. KÖSZEG: **Szarvas étterem**, Kossuth Lajos u. 6; **Kulacs étterem**, Béke u. 12; **Hegyaljy étterem**, Rohonci u. 40.

Tourist Offices
SZOMBATHELY: **Savaria Tourist**, Mártírok tere 1, Tel: (94) 12-348; **IBUSZ**, Savaria u 3-5, Tel (94) 14-141.
KÖSZEG: **Savaria Tourist**, Várkör 57, Tel: 195; **IBUSZ**, Köztársaság tér 4, Tel: 336.

Sightseeing
Szombathely has maintained a very pretty inner city, noted for its shopping. Its main feature is an open-air village museum (**Skanzen**) made up of peasant houses gathered from the region. Other museums: **Iseum Garden of Ruins**, Rákóczi u. 1 (closed Mondays). **Museum of the Revolution**, Alkotmány u. 2 (closed Mondays). **Savaria Museum**, Kisfaludy u. 9 (closed Mondays). **Linen Museum**, Traktoros u. 1 (closed Sat.-Sun.) Köszeg's Jurisics tér is the town's main focus. Nearby **Íróttkö** mountain offers hikes. **Bük**, 20 km to the east of Köszeg, is a spa.

ÖRSÉG
Accomodation
SZENTGOTTHÁRD: *BUDGET*: **Turistaszálló**, Népköztársaság u. 8, Tel: 381. ÖRISZENTPÉTER: *BUDGET* and *CAMPING*: **Örségi fogadó**, Városszer 57, Tel: 155. KÖRMEND: *MODERATE*: **Rába szálló**, Bercsény u. 24, Tel: 89.

Restaurants
SZENTGOTTHÁRD: **Hármashatár étterem**, Széchenyi u. 1; **Makk Hetes vendéglö**, Árpád u.; **Zöldfa halászcsárda**, Széchenyi u. 18. ÖRISZENTPÉTER: **Örségi kisvendéglö**. KÖRMEND: **Rába étterem**, Rákóczi u. 2; **Centrál étterem**, Vida J. u. 6; **Halászcsárda**, Bajcsy-Zsilinszky u. 18.

Tourist Offices
SZENTGOTTHÁRD: **Savaria Tourist**, Kossuth Lajos u. 3, Tel: 28. ÖRISZENTPÉTER: **Savaria Tourist**, Városszer 23, Tel: 153. **KÖRMEND: Savaria Tourist**, Rákóczi út 11.

Sightseeing
The Örség is a remote area with sleepy landscapes and villages. Besides archelogical finds, the local museum of Szentgotthárd (Hunyadi u. 9) is devoted to the Slovene minority. **Pittyerszer**, near Öriszentpéter consists of old typical houses of the region.

ZALAEGERSZEG / NAGYKANIZSA
Accomodation
ZALAEGERSZEG: *MODERATE*: **Arany Bárány szálló**, Széchenyi tér 1-3, Tel: (92) 14-100; **Balaton szálló**, Balatoni u. 2. *BUDGET*: **Göcsej fogadó**, Kaszaházi u. 2, (92) 11-580. NAGYKKANIZSA: *MODERATE*: **Centrál szálló**, Szabadság tér 23, Tel: (93) 11-000. *BUDGET*: **Pannónia szálló**, Vörös Hadsereg u. 4, Tel: (93) 12-188.

Kemping fogadó (bed-and-breakfast and camping), Tel: (93) 19-119. There are quite a number of camping sites in the immediate area of both towns. Around Zalakaros one also finds two inexpensive hotels (quite jammed in the summer), the **Napfény** and the **Termál**.

Restaurants
ZALAEGERSZEG: In the hotel Arany Bárány, **Göcsej étterem**, Dózsa liget 1; **Halász-vadász** (spezializing in fish and game), Kaszaházi u. 2; **Nefelejcs étterem**, Dísz tér. NAGYKANIZSA: The **Centrál** hotel has a restaurant. Otherwise: **Ady étterem**, Ady u., and **Kanizsa étterem** on Szabadság tér.

Tourist Offices
ZALAEGERSZEG: **Zalatour**, Kovács Károly tér 1, Tel: (92) 11-443; **IBUSZ**: Dísz tér 4, Tel: (92) 11-458; **Cooptourist**, Kossuth Lajos u. 36, Tel: (92) 11-331. NAGYKANIZSA: **Zalatour**, Lenin u. 13, Tel (93) 11-185; **IBUSZ**, Szabadság tér 21, Tel: (93) 11-296.

Sightseeing
Zalaegerszeg is known for its **village museum**. Nearby is a museum documenting the diminutive Hungarian oil industry. Falumúzeum u. 5 on 2 respectively, the village museum is closed as of October 31. **Kisfaludy Stróbl collection**, Batthyány u. 2, includes the Göcsej museum documenting Zalaegerszeg's history. To the southwest of town lies the Little Balaton lake and the spa **Zalakaros**. Nagykanizsa's claim to fame rests in the **György Thury museum**, boasting a display of logging.

LAKE BALATON

NORTHERN SHORE
VESZPRÉM
TIHANY
SOUTHERN SHORE

Lake Balaton and its immediate sur-roundings mean cash for Hungary: More than a third of the country's income from tourism comes from the Balaton. It lies only one hour's drive from the country's metropolis and is easily reached on the M 7 highway. No wonder it has become the most important local holiday resort for the people of Budapest.

This largest of all lakes in central Europe represents a major source of hard currency for the highly indebted nation. And the government is quite aware of its economic importance: 500 million dol-lars are said to have been invested in the development of the infrastructure around the lake since 1987. And a large propor-tion of this money is being used for plans which will directly benefit tourism.

In addition to five new harbors for yachts and sailboats, the long overdue cleaning up of the beaches is being accel-erated. The vital improvement in the qu-ality of the water constitutes a further project in this Five Year Plan. At many places supply facilities leave much to be desired; supermarkets and shopping cent-ers should change this situation. A further component in this comprehensive de-

Preceding pages: A magic moment on Lake Balaton near the town of Balatonkenese. Left: Joyful pennants on a Balaton ferry.

velopment program will be the electrifi-cation of the railway line on the southern shore; at present trains, especially the goods trains around the lake, are a terrible nuisance to all those seeking rest and re-laxation.

Not All Roses

Increasingly since the 1970s efforts have been made to preserve the region's natural resources. Several conservation areas and nature reserves have been iden-tified in areas of important botanical, zoological, scenic or historical interest. Most of them are on the northern shore of the lake. By the beginning of the '90s around three dozen nature reserves ex-isted already and the inclusion of other endangered zones is envisaged. The aim is to protect flora and fauna, especially since air pollution and acid rain has now begun to affect the Lake Balaton area.

A few environmental bureaucrats with a knowledge of history point to various forestry laws which were progressive at the time they were enacted, but active en-vironmental conservationists such as István Illés are very worried: "The costs of restitution will be a thousand times higher, and the penalties will not (have to be) paid by those who caused the dam-age, or those whose careless actions

71

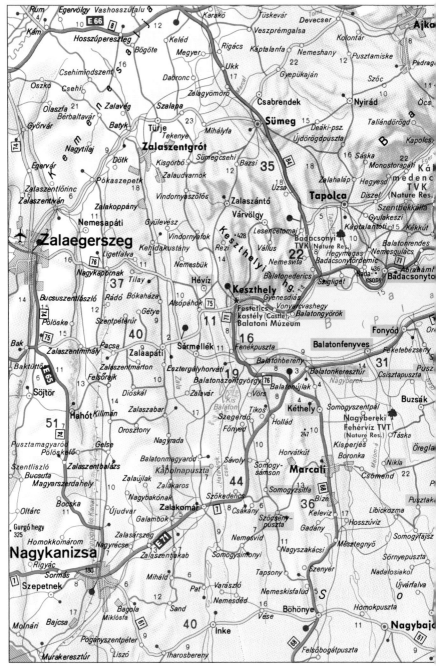

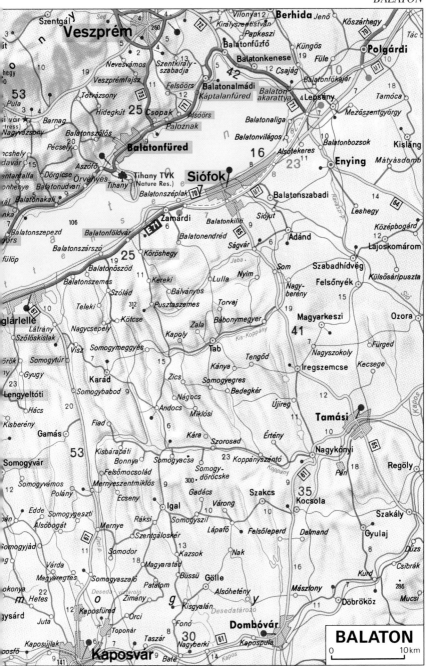

BALATON

0   10km

caused the situation to arise in the first place". He adds in no uncertain terms: "I am referring to the pollution of the rivers and lakes, into which sewage from distant towns was dumped. A community can save millions if it decides not to build its own waste-water plant. On the other hand, those people who happen to live on the estuaries of the polluted rivers will have to come up with billions in order to repair the damage."

And while money plays an important role indeed, it nevertheless takes second place to good will, rationality and expertise. Author Illès has no illusions about future prospects in terms of environment.

"In the past few years the first steps have been taken to rectify matters, but those who are fighting for the environment, which affects us all, and those who set a good example, will in the future have a long, hard job trying to convince

Above: Forbidden pleasures – the sign says "swimming forbidden". Right: Waiting for the elusive fogas.

other groups in society that they are right."

But let us turn to more pleasant things – the natural phenomena around Lake Balaton. The lake is thought to have been formed during the period between the last two ice ages – between 19 and 17.000 years ago. In comparison to the quantity of water in other lakes the Balaton, with its 1.9 billion cubic meters, to put it simply, is shallow. Geologists are interested in the clearly defined features of the area: They talk of the nine "faces" of Lake Balaton, including the peaks of extinct volcanoes.

Journey's Beginning

Our round-trip starts in **Balatonakarattya**, the nearest town to Budapest. Until 1990 the holiday resorts to the south were only open to army officers, party members and important state officials. Former castles, mansions, estates and parks filled with ancient trees are the great attractions here. Our anti-clockwise

round-trip begins on the northern shore of the lake, where there are more sights than on the scenically (more) monotonous southern shore. In clear weather you can see across almost all of the more than 78 km length of the "Hungarian Sea" from the **Magas Part** above **Balatonkenese**. In the town center there are two churches under preservation orders, and a nobleman's farmhouse, dating from 1830 and now serving as a csárda. The estate owner's pseudo-Baroque house must be the only two storied farm around Lake Balaton. The lower section once housed the "business" rooms. The upper area is lined with round pillars and used to house three rooms for living and the kitchen.

A few minutes' drive from the Balaton, **Veszprém**, with a population of 63.000, is the seat of the district of the same name and the center of the north of the lake. Veszprém has become more attractive since the building of a pedestrian zone. The double-arched bridge, which is 150 m long and 46 m high, crossing the river

Séd, is one of the main sights in this episcopal town that lies sprawled on several hills between the Bakony mountains and the Balaton. Several sacred buildings should also be mentioned: the Bishop's Palace and the Chapel of Gizella, the oldest parts of which date back to the 13th century, St. Michael's Cathedral with its splendid crypt, the Chapel of St. George, the Franciscan Church and the Church of St. Stephen, the Provost's Palace and the church and convent founded by a Greek order of nuns in the 12th century. Secular buildings, such as the Old Town Hall, are a bit of a rarity in town.

Herend's Porcelain

13 km from Veszprém is **Herend**, famous for its porcelain factory which celebrated its 150th anniversary in 1989. An exhibition in the museum details the history of the company. Let us return to the Lake though: In the spa town of **Balatonalmádi** there is an avenue of black

poplars, which has been placed under a preservation order, and the very popular **Old Park** (Öregpark) which was established in 1890.

If you are interested in geology or mineralogy pay a visit to the exhibition in **Almádi** (the locals always leave out the word Balaton from the name of the town) above Káptalanfüred railway station. Here you will find information on the shining, purplish red Permian sandstone (The Permian era was 240-200 million years B.C.), an ideal building material, as can be seen from the Baroque church of **Felsöörs** which was built using this sandstone at the end of the 12th century, during the rule of the Árpáds. Its tower is decorated with unique carvings, the so-called Knots of Hercules, ancient ornamental motifs designed to ward off demons. The building used as the Provost's residence is also of architectural interest. It now houses an interesting exhibition of local history.

A walk from Felsöörs through **Malom-völgy**, the Valley of the Mills, is recommended to those with an interest in botany. **Alsóörs** is famous for the trees in its arboretum, planted in the 1950s. The oldest mansion in Hungary, dating from the 15th century, can also be found in this spa town.

The slopes of **Paloznak** alone would make a detour from another holiday resort worthwhile. The Protestant church has a belfry which has been placed under a preservation order and for being a fine specimen of traditional folkloric church architecture. When the Roman-Catholic church was being restored a few years ago a Gothic gate came to light. The Romanesque windows suggest that an older church must have stood here before the 14th century.

Balatonfüred stands against the backdrop of Mount Tamás and Mount Péter,

with Mount György to the west. It is somewhat sheltered from the north winds by the chain of hills in front of it. The "fresh" air which blows into the spa from the four valleys not only refreshes the air but cleanse it too – if it were not for the thousands of cars! One of Balatonfüred's attractions is an old cemetery with charming weathered gravestones and the **Small Forest** or Kiserdö which is spread over an area of 10 hectares. In 1784 the district administration ordered the inhabitants of all the neighboring villages to help water the shady lime trees and the elms planted around the Füred well in times of drought. The fame of the spa soon spread. Indian Nobel Prize winner Rabindranath Tagore was a frequent visitor. In gratitude to the town he planted a tree in the grove which has since been named after him. Decades later came a memorial plaque with his verses inscribed in Hungarian:

When I am no longer on this earth,
O tree,
Let your new leaves whisper in spring,
Above the heads of those
who come here;
The poet loved while he lived.

Some of the most popular walks from Balatonfüred take you through **Koloska Valley**. Conservationists believe that the **Kéki Valley** (*kéki* = blue) could also be prepared for hikers. A visit to the relatively small cave with thermal waters already suggests the impressive limestone formations of the Bakony. Near the road on the edge of the town of **Veszprém-fajsz** is a photogenic calvary and a wonderful view over the lake and from the plateau of the hill across to the Bakony Hills.

The 14 m deep mineral water well near the beach pool of **Csopak** is a secular meeting place for the plain old thirsty and for those taking water for medicinal purposes. One well, whose medicinal waters used to be sold under the brand name of *Saint Joseph*, was plugged a few years

Right: Artistic stonemasonry over the entrance of the Tihany abbey.

ago on orders from Badacsony's Office in Cellars. The bottling plant was demolished and a park built on the site. The substitute was not bad either: Csopak is still famous for its wine, sought-after throughout the country. Within town limits you will also find the **Kökoporsó-domb,** whose name translates roughly as "stone coffin hill". This is where a Roman sarcophagus was discovered.

The most beautiful and the largest castle of the Balaton Highlands is unfortunately closed to tourists. It stands near Csopak in **Nosztori**. Bishop Ranolder had the single-storey building erected in 1861. It now serves as the district's Institute for Plant Protection. At about the same time as the castle was built, a medieval church was demolished in **Nemes-Pecsély**. Some of it was used in the construction of a riding school in 1862 alone for the vaulted stable ceiling supported by sandstone pillars. Near by you will find three other old buildings which house traditional collections from abandoned farmhouses and local wine cellars.

The Jewel of Tihany

The **Tihany Peninsula** is one of the most beautiful regions around Balaton, and conservationists have been quick to realize what has to be done here. As early as 1952 it became the first conservation area in the country. Scientists point out that its woods, hills, ponds and springs are evidence of a unique – and not so ancient – coming together of geological forces. The Óvár hill appears to have been inhabited as far back as the Bronze Age. Later the area was settled by Celts. Some Avar graves have also been discovered in **Diós**. The Benedictine monks – incidentally the oldest order of monks in the West – came here in 1055. Most tourists mecca to the Abbey Church built between 1719 and 1754. In the summer season organ, chamber and choir concerts are held here. András I, one of Hungary's first Árpád kings, is buried in the crypt. The site of the grave has not been changed since 1060. It is made of white limestone and bears a Greek-Orthodox

cross. There is a fine view over the lake from the hill where the abbey stands.

Belsö-tó (the Inner Lake) is one of the special geological features of the Tihany Peninsula. It lies approximately 25 m above the water level and does not seem to be connected to Lake Balaton. For a long time scientists assumed that it had been formed by the effects of the winds in the sediment of the "Pannonian Sea". But following drilling tests, the Geological Institute ascertained that the inner and the outer lake were both formed from volcanic craters during the Tertiary period. Today the outer lake is overgrown with thick reeds and is home to greylag geese. Mallards, gadwalls and ferruginous ducks have also returned to this nesting ground after a long absence. The reeds are still harvested by hand in the traditional manner. Reed ducks are particularly popular in the winter months when the lake is frozen.

Above: A lonely chapel watches over the higlands north of the Balaton.

In the local villages you will come across many thatched houses, for whenever a new roof is put on a farmhouse it is thatched. Man, of course, is nature's greatest enemy, for with every broken reed several square meters of reeds "drown". This is because below the surface of the water the plants are individually joined together by a fine network of air-filled roots. These long roots need to breathe and the vital oxygen is fed to the roots down the reeds. Two types of plants are strictly protected on the peninsula: the yellow lily and the star hyacinth, which turns violet when it flowers in autumn. But despite the hundreds of thousands of tourists who invade Tihany and "occupy" it during the summer season, or invade from the south by ferry, biologists have still been able to identify almost a thousand different species of insect and 800 species of butterfly living more or less happily on the peninsula.

Continuing the round-trip in westerly direction, the next stop is **Örvenyés** where there are both natural and historical monuments to see. The last of the watermills still in use dates back to the year 1748. But half a century ago grain was still being ground in dozens of mills. Not far away is a 250 year old stone bridge which crosses the river Pecsély. In **Balatonudvari** in the local cemetery you will find more than a dozen early 19th century heart-shaped gravestones, which are unique in Hungary. The inscriptions are badly weathered and can only be deciphered with great difficulty.

Balaton's High Lands

A few minutes drive away from Lake Balaton near **Nagyvázsony** is the Kinizsi family's castle, first mentioned in the 15th century. The dynasty's leader then was one Pál Kinizsi, a man of legendary strength, who served as a general under Mátyàs Corvinus. For centuries, until 1945, the castle was then owned by the Zichy dynasty. Today the ruins serve as a backdrop for an open-air theater and are sometimes used in the making of historical films. Only ruins remain too of the Romanesque church in **Boldogasszony-Dörgicse**.

In **Óbudavár**, the smallest town on the north shore, on the road to Nagyvázsony, stands a vaulted stone building which was used until only a few years ago as a wash house by the woman of the village. It was built on top of a spring which flowed through the back wall and covered the floor with up to 30 cm of water. The wash house has been under a preservation order since 1979.

The nearby village of **Szentantalfa** also deserves attention, with its pretty farmhouses and three churches. In the church of **Zánka**, only a few kilometers away, the chancel is supported on two pretty pillars with capitals. It was only when the regional agricultural cooperative's bulldozers had already recklessly destroyed most of a former Roman villa not far from the village of **Kékkút** (blue

well), famous for its mineral water, that the National Office for Environmental and Nature Protection declared the Káli Basin a conservation area. The **Káli Basin** is an ancient site on which traces of life from as far back as the Neolithic Age have been found. "All geological, botanical, zoological and historical treasures in the area are protected through the sensible management of tourism."

Seas of Stone

The most famous attractions in the area are the so-called Seas of Stone which were formed by the after-effects of volcanic activity, when sand layers from the Pannonian Sea were cemented by pebbles. According to the experts, the Seas of Stone near **Szentbékkálla** has the most beautiful and unusual formations. It is the best preserved sea of this kind and has remained largely unscathed by stone quarrying. In the town of Szentbékkálla itself there is an impressive and splendid Baroque church built by Bishop Eszterházy in the last decade of the 18th century. The frescoes show scenes from the life of Saint Benedict.

Beautiful basalt formations of volcanic origin, the so-called Stone Sacks, have taken shape on the slopes of Fekete (Black) Mountain, described as the most beautiful region in the Káli Basin, above **Kapolcs** near **Királykö** (Royal Rock) and near the **Ördögattja** (Devil's Dam). A walk among the ponds and the springs offers some of the most splendid panoramas of the area. This walk is recommended to tourists (with robust shoes!). Climbing the narrow summit of the 347 m high **Tóti peak**, however, is only suitable for expert climbers. From here you can also enjoy a wonderful panorama.

The best view of the whole basin, the woods and peaks of the Bakony Hills, the meadows and the distant vineyards is found at **Kövágoörs**. Badacsony Hill and its immediate surroundings from **Bala-**

tonederics to **Ahámhegy** were declared the second conservation area in the Balaton region about fifteen years after the Tihany peninsula.

The conservation order was declared following the closure of the **Badacsonytomaj Quarry**, where the systematic destruction of the environment had been going on for decades. **Badacsony Hill**, which dominates the northern shore of the lake, is regarded by lovers of the Balaton area as one of the most beautiful areas on the lake. Tens of thousands of fruit trees and hundreds of thousands of vines give the landscape its special character in spring and autumn.

Wine Without Roses

An eighteenth-century, architecturally playful winery is a popular tourist destination in **Badacsony**. It was the former residence of Róza Szegedy. A literature

Above: Young love on the Balaton promenade. Right: Getting ready for the big catch.

80

museum has been established here in honor of her husband, the poet Sándor Kisfaludy. It is hardly necessary to mention that this wine town also has an excellent wine museum.

Included in the conservation area are the basalt hills, the many vineyards on the hills, the castle ruins of **Várhegy** and the village of **Szigliget**. The Classical **Eszterházy Castle** is set in a park with 500 trees. The castle has been the home of the "Literary Foundation of the Hungarian Writers' Union", a conservative conformist Communist organization since 1945.

The town of **Öregfalu** – Old Village in English – above Szigliget has retained the atmosphere of centuries past. Almost 70 mostly thatched farmhouses remain standing to form one of the most beautiful villages on Lake Balaton and indeed in the whole country. They too are protected by the National Office of Protected Buildings.

In **Újfalu** you will find the most beautiful coats-of-arms in the Balaton region.

It was chiseled in stone in 1683 and graces a Rococo winery which dates back to 1780-82. It depicts a chubby- cheeked Bacchus straddling a wine vat. Under him are statues of the goddesses Ceres and Diana, symbols of agriculture and shepherds respectively. In the central wall niche Saint George fights his eternal battle with the dragon.

Szent György Hegy (Saint George's Mountain) is behind Badacsony Mountain. The slopes of this hill grow superior wines to those of its big brother, where the famous *Gray Monk* (*Szürkebarát*) thrives. Nevertheless Saint George is simply unable to compete with the popularity of Badacsony, even though the shape of its rounded summit is as unmistakable as that of the Badacsony Mountain. One special attraction here, however, are the tower-like basalt formations that have come to be known as the "Organ of Badacsony".

The double cavern of **Tapolca** has been protected since 1942. It consists of the Spital Grotto and the Lake Grotto, but has been closed to the public since a cave-in. The grottos also dried up naturally. The 340 m cave could be driven through and was for a long time one of the largest springs of karstic waters in the country. The grottos were particularly suitable for the treatment of respiratory illnesses. Success rates of 60 to 70 percent were the rule in the treatment of asthma and bronchitis.

Problems of a completely different kind have arisen in the **Keszthely Hills**, where environmentalists and conservationists say that the mining of natural resources has completely destroyed the scenery.

Even today only the bravest Hungarien politician will call for the closure of mines for the sake of ecology, despite the recognized economic significance of raw materials for the country. Traces of ocher, a pigment containing iron ore were discovered on the east side of the **Biked Mountain**. This is an important export which earns the country its essential hard currency.

BALATON'S SOUTHERN SHORE

At Keszthely on the west bank you are already on your way to the southern shore. The districts of Zala and Somogy both begin here. The two parks in **Keszthely** are veritable urban oases. The town's most important sight is the **Festetics Castle**, which has been painstakingly restored over many years. The building has a wonderful library, beautiful furnishings, and is one of the most popular places not only in Transdanubia but in the whole country. Some of the rooms are open to the public, others are used as offices. In the high season concerts are held, sometimes by candle light, with a 19th century ambience. The castle's English garden also deserves a look. Entry is free, as it is to the **Helikon Park**, a conservation area that spreads over 15 hectares down to Lake Balaton. The former Franciscan church in town has been redesigned several times. The birthplace of Carl Goldmark (composer of *The Queen of Saba*) has also been beautifully restored. The two kilometer long row of chestnut trees beginning at the **Balaton Museum** is under protection order.

Hardly anyone will miss the chance to visit the Romanesque church in the cemetery of **Egregy**, not far from Hévíz. This too is under a preservation order, as are several wonderful old farmhouses and mansions in **Balatongyörök**.

Hévíz

The spa town of **Hévíz**, with its radioactive and sulfurous thermal waters, has been one of Lake Balaton's main sources of vital hard currency for years. It is particularly popular with Western visitors. The thermal lake, which stretches for 4.4 hectares, is the largest in Europe and the second largest in the world.

Left: The thermal lake of Hévíz, a natural wonder with curative effects.

It was not only environmentalists who realized that **Kisbalaton** (Little Balaton) was in danger of imminent death. This lake is 40 square kilometers in size, of which 16 square kilometers are open waters, and is similar in formation to Lake Balaton. Its waters were deep, once upon a time, but extensive drainage and water regulation has resulted in the Kisbalaton becoming a swampy morass. A further result was the gradual silting up of the mouth of the Zala at Lake Balaton.

The creation of a drainage system for this river also had a devastating effect, for it has prevented the natural depositing of fertile silt. Industrial expansion, which resulted in the dumping of pollutants into the Zala, almost killed the Kisbalaton a few years ago. Various so-called "technical successes" and natural catastrophes (droughts, for example) only served to accelerate the destruction over the years. A complex system of locks is now in place to clean the waters flowing into the lake. This effectively improved the quality of water in Lake Balaton over the last few years although it is still not as clean as it might be. The Five Year Plan to improve the infrastructure of the Balaton also is providing a large amount of money for this project.

The Office of Environmental Protection acted resolutely. The regeneration of the Kisbalaton is one of their most prestigious projects, and is carried out so conscientiously that during the egg-laying season, and when the young birds have hatched, even the guards are prohibited driving their boats to the nesting grounds. Kisbalaton is not only a wonderful ornithological site, but plants are protected here too. The look-out tower offers a good view across the lake.

A day trip to **Kápolnapuszta** is recommended. Black buffaloes were once bred for their milk (high fat content). But it became necessary to rescue the breed from extinction. The consumption of buffalo meat is now banned and mechanization

has largely meant that these erstwhile beasts of burden have become redundant. In 1956 all that remained was a herd of 50 buffaloes, living on a reservation that was also open for tourists.

The Southern Shore Begins

The most beautiful thing about the southern shore of Lake Balaton, the lake's conoisseurs say in jest, is the enchanting view of the volcanic mountains of the northern shore it affords. But all jokes aside, the southern shore almost overwhelms its visitors with its countless architectural, and, more rarely, geological or scenic sights. It has a wide and extremely flat beach which is ideal for children. The lake waters are very shallow here; you often have to wade for hundreds of meters into the lake before it becomes deeper.

Above: The Festetics castle in Keszthely.
Right: The best view of the lake's southern shore is from the train.

Most tourists drive past **Balaton-keresztúr**, even though it has one of the prettiest churches in the area. It was built between 1753 and 1758, and has some luxuriant Rococo frescoes. Somewhat more spartan in concept is the closed-off nudist camp of **Balatonberény**, one of the few in the country. In **Somogyzsitfa**, specifically in the section of Szöcseny-puszta, you will find a beautiful castle which now houses a school of forestry. The arboretum has many exotic tree species. Not far is an 800 m alley of horse-chestnut trees, not as long as, but often favorably compared with the one of Készthely.

There is another castle in **Kéthely**, which functions as an old people's home today. Curious tourists are usually permitted to look round the building if they ask at the reception. There is also a church with beautiful wood carvings.

The area of **Nagyberek** can be dangerous. In former times it provided excellent refuge place for those who knew the area well. It is not advisable to leave the

marked paths of these swamplands, for you are in great danger of sinking into some parts of the moor. The most interesting part of Nagyberek is Fehérvízi öslap – "the primal swamp of Fehérvíz". It has now been declared a conservation area. The region is well- known for its bird life: The white egret is found here, along with little egrets, night herons, purple herons and spoonbills. Moorhens have also made their home here and in winter you can spot the odd osprey.

During the summer season a narrow-gauge train takes passengers from Balatonfenyves to the simple medicinal spa at **Csisztapuszta**. The train ride is an ideal way to get a good impression of the area. An ultramodern riding hall was built near a wonderful hunting lodge by the Balatonnagyberek estate in **Balatonfenyves**. The horses are bred in the neighboring Pusztaberény Stud Farm. **Fonyód** is usually ignored by tourists, despite the fact that it has a restored former dairy farm, which has now been turned into a full-fledged tourist center. It is for the most

part merely seen as the docking place for the ferry to and from Tihany. But from the hill where the castle stands it offers a splendid view of the northern shore.

The lack of scenic attraction on the southern shore is compensated for by its charming architecture. Every second village has either a castle or some former mansion to see. The former castle of Count Zichy in **Lengyeltóti** was turned into a hospital after the last war. In **Öreglak** you will find the castle that once belonged to the Jankovich family, surrounded by a 32 hectare park with a rich selection of tree species, but has unfortunately been neglected. Another castle belonging to the Jankovich family, this one in Romantic style, is in **Szöllösgyörök**. A medical institute was set up in the middle of its well-maintained 45 hectare park. The complex can only be viewed with special permission. The former Széchenyi castle in **Somogyvár** is also used as a medical institute. The **Breza Forest** extends nearby, a nature reservation with countless botanical

treasures. The town itself was the administrative seat of the Somogy district for almost 700 years – the largest district in the country. Since 1972 work has been in progress restoring the basilika and the foundation walls of a monastery on the Kupavár castle hill, which offers a splendid view over Lake Balaton.

The family mansion of the poet Dániel Berzsenyi, a historical monument, stands in **Nikla**. The former mansion of the Bogyai family is set in a large park in **Pusztakovácsi**. Five kilometers from Boglárlelle, in **Szöllöskislak**, a small castle offers wine tasting in a folkloric setting – for hard currency.

Boglárlelle, at the foot of three small hills of volcanic origin (between 128 m and 165 m high) is an artists' colony. On the cemetery hill (Temetödomb) stand two chapels simply called the blue and the red and famous throughout Hungary.

Above: Summertime crowds enjoying a particularly healthy form of fast food. Right: Bull's eye!

Local sculptors display their works in these chapels, and during the summer season they both provide floor space for art exhibitions. Sometimes an open-air theatrical performance takes place up in front of the Red Chapel. The house in which the painter Lajos Kunffy once lived, and the park surrounding it, is in **Somogytúr**.

Zala, a few minutes' drive away also merits a visit worthwhile. This is where the painter and graphic artist Count Mihály Zichy, whose claim to fame rests with his collection of pornographic works, was born in the old mansion. The building is under preservation order and has been turned into a museum. It gives a wonderful impression of the life of the Hungarian nobility around the turn of the century. But it also provides insight into the creative work of the painter.

The End of the Journey

Let us return now to the lake. The great attractions in **Balatonföldvár** are the pro-

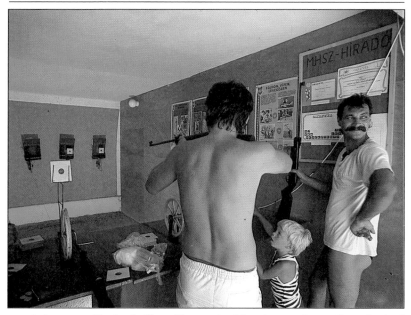

tected plane trees. The local office of forest management had an unusual look-out tower built there, which is also accessible by car. Besides its very well developed – overwhelming one might even say – the town of **Köröshegy** also boasts several architectural jewels, namely two beautifully restored farmhouses, a former Széchenyi Castle and a Gothic church, dating back to the 15th century. About 8 kilometers away near **Kereki** are the ruins of Fejérkö Castle, built in the 15th century as well as a simple Classical church dating to 1830.

The popular resort of **Siófok** is the southern shore's metropolis. The enormous amount of construction undertaken over the last few decades has meant that the town has taken on almost disturbingly large proportions. The town is directly connected to Budapest by means of the motorway M 7, which easily accounts for the touristic boom. Apart from a few villas from around 1900, it has little in the way of historical sights to offer the visitor. A double avenue of plane trees on

the lake shore and a well- maintained park from the turn of the century are both enjoyed during the summer months by thousands of holiday makers.

Imre (Emeric) Kálmán has given millions of people countless pleasant and sometimes sentimental hours of pleasure. He composed about twenty operettas, including the highly successful *Circus Princess*, *Countess Mariza*, and the *Csárdás Princess*. The famous composer was born in Siófok in 1882. Being a Jew, he was forced into exile in 1940, but had the good fortune of dying a successful man in Paris in 1953. Holiday makers in Siófok usually prefer to make their acquaintance with Hungary's most popular pop singers who give an almost obligatory annual open-air concert there in the summer season. Hungarian pop music is regarded as particularly progressive throughout Eastern Europe. Its inability to achieve much success outside the country is due in part to the Hungarian language, which is so different to other languages on the European continent.

LAKE BALATON
Access
Lake Balaton is easily accessible by train, bus and car. Regular routes have been established from Budapest by bus and train and for motorists, the easiest way is to take the M7 until Lepcsény where it joins Route 71 which travels all along the northern shore. Or proceed on the M7 to Siófok. Route 70 from Budapest through Érd, Martonvásár and Székesfehérvár is more picturesque. Coming from Vienna, the simplest way is to cross the border at Hegyeshalom, proceed to Györ, where signs show the way.

Ferries and cruises
There are regularly scheduled ferries touring or crossing the Balaton, especially during the season. A shuttle runs the Tihanyrév (pier)-Szántódrév route every 40 minutes in Summer, from 6:20 a.m. to midnight, and in Winter from 6:30 a.m. to 7:30 p.m. The tourist offices should be able to give information on special tours, dancing cruises and the like. Otherwise, for everything concerning shipping or sailing, contact **MAHART**, in Badacsony, Tel: (87) 31-240; in Balatonföldvár, Tel: (84) 40-304; in Balatonfüred, Tel: (86) 42-230; in Fonyód, Tel: (84) 60-012; in Siófok, Tel: (84) 10-050; in Tihany, Tel: (86) 48-485.

Warning: Remember that the summer months around the Balaton mean crowds. The touristic infrastructure is fairly well established. After the season, ca. September 15 - May 15, there is no garantee that the places listed below will be open.

THE NORTHERN SHORE
Accomodation
VESZPRÉM: *BUDGET*: **Veszprém szálló**, Budapest u. 6, Tel: (80) 24-876.
VÁRPALOTA: **Palota szálló**, Szabadság tér 5, Tel: (80) 50-753.
BALATONALMÁDI: *MODERATE*: **Auróra szálló**, Bajcsy-Zsilinszky út 14, Tel: (86) 38-810; **Villa Pax Corporis**, Bajcsy-Zsilinszky út 8, Tel: (86) 36-808.
BUDGET: **Tulipán szálló**, Marx tér 1, Tel: (86) 38-317. *CAMPING*: **Kristóf Kemping**, Tel: (86) 38-802.
BALATONFÜRED: *MODERATE*: **Margaréta**, Széchenyi u. 29, Tel: (86) 43-824; **Annabella**, Beloiannisz u. 25, Tel: (86) 42-222; **Hotel Marina**, Széchenyi u. 26, Tel: (86) 43-466.
TIHANY: *LUXURY*: **Club Tihany**, Rév u. 11, (86) 48-088.

Restaurants
The most famous food on the Balaton is *fogas*, a kind of pike-perch whose exploitation in the lake has rarified the supply and pushed up the price.
Veszprém: Veszprém szálló at the hotel by the same name; Magyaros étterem, Kossuth Lajos u. 6; Dózsa étterem, Dózsa György tér 1. **Balatonfüred**: Try at the hotels listed above; Balaton étterem, Kisfaludy u. 5; Magyar Tenger vendéglö, Kossuth Lajos u. 11; Halászkert, Szechényi tér 1; Tölgyfa csárda, Csárda u.. **Tihany**: Sport étterem, Fürdötelep; Fogas Vendéglö, Kossuth l. u. 1; Kecseköröm csárda, Kossuth L. u. 13.

Tourist Offices
VESZPRÉM: **Balaton Tourist**, Münich Ferenc tér 3, Tel: (80) 13-750; **IBUSZ**, Kossuth L. u. 6, Tel: (80) 12-425; **Express** (for youths and students). **BALATONFÜRED**: **Balatontourist**, Blaha L. u. 5, Tel: (86) 42-822; **IBUSZ**, Petöfi u. 4/a, Tel: (86) 42-438; **Cooptourist**, Huray u. Tel: (86) 43-271. **TIHANY**: **Balatontourist** (in summers only), Kossuth u. 20, Tel: (86) 48-519.

Sightseeing
Veszprém attracts quite a few visitors, with its Baroque houses and churches. Above all **Herend**, a little to the west is famous for its ceramics. Balatonalmádi is a touristic center as is Balatonfüred, though the latter still reflects some of its flashiness of earlier days. Its spa specializes in heart and circulatory dieseases. Tihany's abbey can be seen from a great distance, but its natural beauty can only be seen on the spot.

Museums
VESZPRÉM: The **Castle Museum** in the castle is open Tues.- Sun. 10 a.m. - 6 p.m.; **Bakony Museum** (regional) Lenin liget 5. **Museum of Transdanubian Construction**, Házgyár u. 1, open Mon. - Sun. **BALATONFÜRED**: **Jókai Memorial Museum**, (closed Mondays) **TIHANY**: **Tihany Museum**, Pisky sétány I; A **potter's house**, Visszhang 10; Open-air **Ethnographical Museum**, Batthyàny u. 36 (closed from October 31 - May 1).

FROM TIHANY TO KESZTHELY
General: Camping sites, bed-and-breakfasts, hotels, restaurants and beaches are by and large well indicated on the narrow stretch of land between Tihany and the Badacsony hill. This region includes at least two inland centers with some touristic infrastructure, Nagyvázsony and Tapolca.

Accomodation
KESZTHELY: *MODERATE:* **Helikon szálló**, Balaton-part 5, Tel: 12-951; **Phoenix szálló**, Balaton part, Tel: 12-630. *BUDGET* and *CAMPING*: **Amazon szálló**, Szabadság u. 11, Tel: 12-248; **Castrum camping**, Móra Ferenc u. 48, Tel: 12-120; **Zalatour camping**, Balaton-part.

NAGYVÁZSONY: *BUDGET*: **Hotel Kastély**, Kossuth u. 12, Tel: (80) 31-029; **Fogadó**, Sörház u. 2, Tel: (80) 31-015.
TAPOLCA: *BUDGET*: **Hotel Gabrielle**, Batsányi tér 7, Tel: (87) 12-642.

Restaurants

KESZTHELY: **Béke étterem**, Kossuth Lajos u. 50; **Juventus étterem**, Mártírok u. 1; **Georgikon étterem**, Fö tér; **Halászcsárda** (fish specialities), Balaton-part. NAGYVÁZSONY: **Vár csárda**, temetö u. 7; **Restaurant Vázsonykö**, Kinizsi u. 84. TAPOLCA: **Bauxit étterem**, Ady Endre u. 22; **Balaton étterem**, Deák Ferenc u. 2; **Tavasbarlang vendéglö**, Arany János u. 16.

Tourist Offices

KESZTHELY: **Zalatour**, Fö tér 1, Tel: 12-560; **IBUSZ**, Széchenyi u. 1-3, Tel: 12-951; **Express** (for youths and students), Kossuth Lajos u. 22, Tel: 12-032. NAGYVÁZSONY: **Balatontourist**, at the fortress, Tel: (80) 31-015. TAPOLCA: **Balatontourist**, Deák F. u. 7, Tel: (87) 11-179.

Sightseeing

The inland landscape here consisting of volcanic formations, is memorable. Keszthely's **Festetics castle** is a Baroque pearl with very beautiful interiors. The museum is open from April 1 to June 30 from 10 a.m. - 6 p.m. exc. Mondays, and until 7 p.m. between July 1 - August 31. **Balaton Museum**, Múzeum u. 2 (exc. Mondays). Keszthely is overall a pleasant town to visit. As the name of the first restaurant suggests, Tapolca's reputation lies in its aluminium ore, a museum has been dedicated to that metal (Batsányi tér 2). A special site is the **cave lake** at Kisfaludy u. 3, which opens at 8 a.m. and closes at 5.30 p.m. in Summer and at 4.30 p.m. otherwise (closed Sundays). The **Kinizsi fortress of Nagyvázsony** is worth a visit. Local activities include horseback riding.

HÉVIZ

This famous spa with a thermal lake lies a few kilometers west of Keszthely and is a must even in Winter.

Accomodation

LUXURY: **Hotel Aqua**, Kossuth L. u. 13-15, Tel: 11-090; *MODERATE:* **Hotel Thermal**, Kossuth L. u. 9-11, Tel: 11-190; *BUDGET:* **Hotel Napsugár**, Tavirózsa u. 3-5, Tel: 13-208. **Pension Piroska**, Kossuth lajos u. 10, Tel: 12-698.

Restaurants

Debrecen étterem, Rákóczi u. 1; **Rózsakert étterem**, Rákóczi u. 19; **Cimbalom csárda**, Petöfi u. 6; **Vadaskert csárda**, Vadaskert.

Tourist Offices

Zalatour, Rákóczi u. 8, Tel: 11-048.

BALATON SOUTH SHORE

General: Much of Balaton's tourist industry seems to have settled on the southern shore, especially on the stretch from Boglárlelle to Siófok. Route 71 is lined with restaurants and supermarkets, souvenir shops, bars and rooms for rent. Prices in season are high compared with other less touristic areas of Hungary. If renting a room, inspect it carefully before saying "yes", otherwise you might find yourself sleeping on an ancient sofa in a hastily remodelled garage.

Accomodation

BOGLÁRLELLE: *BUDGET* and *CAMPING*: **Platán panzió** (bed-and-breakfast), Hunyadi u. 56, Tel: (84) 50-203; **Sellö camping** site, near the ferry embarcation.
BALATONSZEMES: **Lido panzió**, Ady Endre u. 53, Tel: (84) 45-112; Szemes has five camping sites including one, the **Hullám** (Tel: (84) 45-116), for students only. Telephone numbers: (84) 45-112, 45-114, 45-115, 45-177.
BALATONSZÁRSZÓ: **Vasmacska panzió**, József Attila u. 17; **Tura camping**, Tel: 40-254.
BALATONFÖLDVÁR: *MODERATE:* **Hotel Neptun**, Tel: (84) 40-388; **Hotel Fesztivál**, Rákóczi u. 40, Tel: (84) 40-377. *BUDGET* and *CAMPING:* **Hotel Juventus**, József Attila u. 9, Tel: (84) 40- 379; **Magyar Tenger camping** site, Tel: (84) 40-240.
SIÓFOK: *MODERATE:* **Európa**, Petöfi sétány 5, Tel: (84) 13-411; **Hungária**, Petöfi sétány 13, Tel: (84) 10- 677; **Hotel Lido**, Petöfi sétány 11, Tel: (84) 10-633. *BUDGET:* **Hotel Vénusz**, Kinizsi u. 12, Tel: (84) 10-660; **Hotel Napfény**, Mártírok u. 8, Tel: (84) 11-408; **Motel**, Kinizsi u. 6, Tel: (84) 10-644; **Touring Hotel**, Foki-hegy, Tel: (84) 10-684; **Panzió Oázis**, Szigligeti u. 56, Tel: (84) 12-012. Camping sites along the beach.

Restaurants

There are innumerable places all along route 71 and off it that offer anything from fast food to solid fare at reasonable rates.

Tourist Offices

BALATONFÖLDÁR: **Siotour**, Hösök útja 9-11, Tel (84) 40-099. SIÓFOK: **Siotour**, Szabadság tér 6, Tel: (84) 10- 900. Branches of Siotour the southern coast are indicated by road signs.

Museums

BALATONSZÁRSZÓ: Memorial museum to the poet **József Attila**, József A. u. 7 (closed Mondays), opening hours: 10 a.m. - 6 p.m. (until 2 p.m. from November 1 - March 31). **BALATONSZEMES**: **Postal Museum**, Bajcsy-Zsilinszky u. 46, open: May 1 - Sept. 30, 10 a.m. - 6 p.m. SIÓFOK: **Museum for Water Economy**, Sió u. 2, open April 1 - Oct. 15, 9 a.m. - 6 p.m..

AROUND PÉCS

PÉCS
SZIGETVÁR
SIKLÓS

Warm breezes from the Mediterranean basin still reach Baranya district in Hungary's southwestern belly. From the slopes of the Mecsek hills the view sometimes stretches for miles over the crouching Villány elevations, into the plains of northern Croatia. A vast array of interesting fauna and flora have gathered here; the Romans brought wine, the Turks found propicious weather to plant fruit trees, and on warm summer days the casual traveler with a nose for the south will recognize the unmistakable aroma fig trees. The regional capital is **Pécs**, a bustling city of 175.000 people, with two universities, a fine theater, libraries, a very restored inner city, good restaurants, recreational spots and a healthy climate.

Once a large Celtic settlement nestled at the foot of the Mecsek it must have reminded the Romans on their trek through Europe of their home city. They called it *Sopianae* and made it the capital of southern Pannonia. Huns, Goths of all sorts, Avars and the Franks followed leaving varying degrees of traces, now for the most part exhibited in the **Janus Pannonius Museum**. When the Hungarians arrived in 899, the city was already

Preceding pages: The Swabian church in Palkonya still bears Ottoman traits. Left: The Great Cathedral of Pécs.

called *Quinqua Ecclesiae*, five churches. King István I elevated it to a bishopric in 1009 and soon it became a busy cultural and trade center. In 1367 Europe's fourth – short-lived – university opened its doors in Pécs.

The Turks had little trouble overcoming Pécs' week defensive wall which extended around nearly 175 acres, and their 143-year occupation left an indelible mark on the city and its surroundings. The minaret of Pasha Hassan Jakovali's mosque on Petöfi Square, the Catholic church turned Mosque and turned Catholic church again on Széchenyi Square are, next to the four- towered cathedral, the town's hallmarks. A fairly busy mercantile life continued in spite of wars. It stalled temporarily at the end of the 17th century under the impact of the voracious Austrian army and the plague.

Coal mining in the 19th century and the birth of other local industries, notably Vilmos Zsolnay's pottery and later porcellain factory, once again put Pécs on the trade map. Notwithstanding political changes that swept Hungary during the 20th century, the city has suffered no major setback since then. Pécs was spared bombings and sieges during World War Two, though other side- effects of fascism such as the deportation of the Jewish community took their social

93

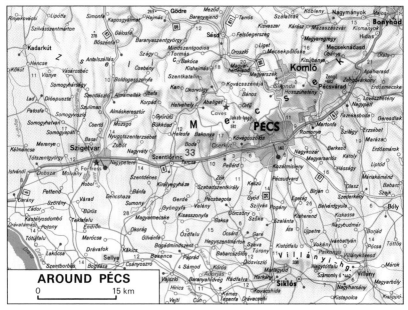

AROUND PÉCS

0   15 km

toll. The synagogue built in the 1860s by the Budapest architects Gerster and Frey, still stands on Kossuth square.

Walking Around

Kossuth square is as good a place as any to begin a visit of the city. On the corner of Bem u. is a self-service restaurant with a pleasant local flavor serving breakfast and other meals for a pittance and where smokers are firmly prohibited from darkening the already dingy atmosphere. The little street leading west through a newly built shopping center emerges at the **central post office** whose tympanon of sparkling pyrogranite bears Hungary's royal insignia and postal symbols. The large avenue here, Rákóczi út, forms a part of the innercity periphery. A few hundred feet to the west where it joins the Szabadság u. is a statue of Zsolnay watching earnestly over his em-

Right: The fountain with the bulls in Pécs, a gift from the Zsolnay factory.

ployees. The small **ethnographic museum** nested in at number 19 offers a collection of national (German, Hungarian, Serbian) costumes from the surrounding area, household items from cooking jars to spinning wheels, and upstairs a flight of rooms from peasant houses.

Further along Rákóczi út stand the remains of the **mosque of Pasha Jakovali Hassan**, built in the early 16th century, once upon a time the centerpoint of a busy religious community that included a pilgrim's house and a dervish school. After the Turks left the mosque served as a Catholic church, but in 1955 it was restored to its original form. A small museum recalling some military, private and religious aspects of Turkish life was opened in the entrance hall, thanks in part to financial help from the Turkish government. The Islamic students at the university sometimes use this mosque for their services. The **Hotel Minaret** diagonally opposite was once a Franciscan monastery. Its church stands on the ruins of a mosque, which once stood on the ruins of a church. **Sallai u.**, a pleasant pedestrian shopping street, connects Rákóczi út. to the center of town. Its portals, shop signs and intricate stucco work inherited from the prosperous 18th and 19th centuries are perhaps more interesting than the shops themselves. On **Jókai square** at the end of the street stands a fountain covered in eosin glazing, a product of the Zsolnay factory to honor its 100th anniversary. The "elephant block", a cluster of shops between Jókai and Széchenyi squares with a pleasant courtyard (an elephant marks the spot) was named after a store offering among other things wares from the colonies run by György Pucher.

Széchenyi square, the epicenter of Pécs life, is one of the more architecturally eclectic spots in Hungary, provided of course one takes the foundations of the buildings into account. Much of what had been left by the Turks or was reconstructed during the 18th century succumbed to the prosperity of the 19th century. House number 2, for example, had been familiarly referred to as the "rat castle" owing to its delapidated condition, until a gentleman named Lórant built the **Lórant Palace** in its stead in 1883. Today, fully restored, it recalls the work of the great secession architect Ödön Lechner. The neighboring house was built at first by the Jesuits in the early 18th century partly using Turkish grave stones. Across the street stands the **Hotel Nádor**, erected in 1846, redesigned and totally rebuilt in 1902 and painstakingly renovated in 1989-90. At one time Pécs's literary, political and social crème de la crème gathered in the coffeehouse on the ground floor.

The most striking construction on Széchenyi Square, however, is the former **mosque of Pasha Kasi Gassim**, the largest in Hungary. It was built on and from the remains of the St. Bartholomew Catholic church. Jesuit priests catholicized it after the expulsion of the Turks,

installing a choir and tearing down most of the adjacent buildings including the minaret which was replaced with a tower. The Austrian governor of the city, count Vecchi, did his share by pilfering the lead that covered the dome and robbing the graves under the floor. Like the mosque of Jakovali, that of Kasi Gassim was also restored around the mid-20th century. The characteristic ogee windows reappeared, the dome was replaced and several Turkish inscriptions from the Koran laid bare. After this restoration, Pécs decided to erect the statue of János Hunyadi in honor of his famous victory over the Turks at Belgrade in 1456. Its eye-catching, assymetrical location on the square is neither an accident nor uncontroversial.

Another interesting item on Széchenyi square is the pyrogranite **fountain** with four bull heads designed by Andor Pilch in honor of Zsolnay that stands at the southern tip of the square in front of the church and cloister of the Sisters of Mercy (now belonging to the surgical fa-

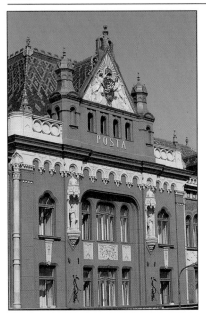

sively used as an apartment house, a hospital, a theatre and a school.

The last important sight not to miss in Pécs is the **cathedral**. Firstly, its four majestic towers can be seen from miles away. Secondly it has been a part of Pécs history since the 11th century in spite of the obvious fact that nothing about it suggests such august age: The interior is a mixture of Baroque and Gothic, the frescos by Bertalan Székely and Károly Lotz are somewhat more modern. The exterior dates to the end of the 19th century and was intended to look like the original cathedral. The Turks of course found the whole construction ideal for use as a mosque.

Already in the days of St. István, the bishop lived on the western side of the square, albeit the building itself has changed over the centuries. The same applies to the parish archives that have traditionally been stored in buildings on the eastern flank of the square. **St. István square**, adjacent to cathedral square, is one of the favorite meeting place for the city youth. Farther to the west stands a section of the old city wall equipped with a solitary barbican. Recent local digging brought several interesting "tidbits" to light: a 4th century cemetery chapel, mosaics, bits of carved stone and even frescos, which have been carried off to the archeological section of the Janus Pannonius Museum.

culty of the school of medicine). One can leave Széchenyi square by the Lajos Kossuth street in the east, a pleasant pedestrian zone with a number of interesting buidings. The most striking is the beautifully restored **Pannonia Hotel** in Secession style by Andor Pilch. Further down the street is the national theater dating back to the end of the 19th century and the church a few hundred feet further, for all its apparent greyness has a typically Pécsy history, having once been a mosque, then a Greek Orthodox church before going over to the Order of Saint Paul. During the War of Independence the Turkish building was destroyed and rebuilt in more conventional style with a cloister. After the order was disbanded by Emperor Joseph II toward the end of the 18th century, the building was succes-

Museum Row

And while on the subject of museums: In Pécs a series of important museums have been clustered in or near the **Káptalan u**. behind the parish archives. On Janus Pannonius u. is one exhibiting the works of Tivadar Csontváry (1853-1919), a leading painter of his time. In Káptalan u. 6, where the canon once resided, is a small the museum devoted to Ferenc Martyn, a multi- talented gentleman, painter, graffic artist, sculptor and

Above: Pyrogranite artistry on the main post office in Pécs. Right: Selling Jesus or two-bit novels. Far right: The mosque with minaret of Hassan Jakovali.

porcellain designer. House number 5 has paintings by another 20th century artist Endre Nemes who expressed his alienation at the times he lived through in a sometimes oppressive surrealism. Victor Vasarely has his own museum. A native Pécser who lived for decades in Paris, he experimented with geometric shape and optic games, achieving international recognition in the sixties. Finally, Káptalan utca 2, where numerous medieval and renaissance elements were uncovered, one finds an exhibition of the works of Zsolnay and his family: huge vases painstakingly decorated with a hodge-podge of Turkish, Chinese, Japanese and folkloristic motives, a beautiful blue, white and gold table setting as well as a borderline kitsch bowl bearing little piggies.

Outside its inner city, Pécs has other culturally interesting sights: the medieval churches in Pécs-Málom and Cserkut, south and west of the city respectively and the little grave chapel (*türbe*) of the Turkish holy man Idris Baba (west). Visits to some of these dispersed locations can be easily coupled with hikes along the winding roads on the city's vine- and tree covered slopes.

The paths are well marked and provided with agreeable resting spots generally with spectacular views over the city and surrounding countryside. The finest observation post, a veritable crows nest, is the television tower.

Rest and Recreation

Beyond the crests, tucked away in the valleys of the Mecsek on a very, very winding road is **Orfü**, a pretty little village at the gates of a pleasant recreational area. A string of four artificial lakes here offer swimmers, rowers and even anglers ample opportunity to let it all hang out. The hunting exhibit and water-mill museum are both worth a visit, but it is Mother Nature who created tne most beautiful spots in the area. The caves of the Bánosi mountain and in particular in the Bodó mountain in neighboring **Abaliget** are among the finest in Europe.

97

The latter is also being used by doctors to help cure bronchial diseases. Another interesting spot is **Magyarhertelend**, to the northeast of Orfü as the crow flies: The lake, or rather large pond, outside the village is thermal. Further eastward on the way to **Komló**, a little village that overgrew its boundaries owing to coal mining, is another recreational center, **Sikonda**, with a small thermal lake. From Abaliget it is possible to loop westwards through the Mecsek, through sleepy little villages such as **Hetvehely**, where the Baroque church still displays its Gothic origins. The baptismal font in the church of Szent-Lörinc on route 6 belonged once upon a time to a Turkish bath.

In spite of its size **Szigetvár**, a small town 33 km west of Pécs, is known to every Hungarian for its role in resisting the Turks. Built on a swamp (as the name island-fortress suggests), it was among the few fortresses to be properly modernized by the local strong man Bálint Török after the Mohács defeat. It held out three sieges, in 1541, 1554 and 1556. According to Hungarian historians, in 1566, Miklós Zrínyi, Ban of Croatiá, held Szigetvár at odds of 20 to 1 for a total of 33 days. In spite of a promise of safe-conduit, he refused to surrender and, dressed in his finest clothing, led the remaining soldiers of his garrison into a crazy, fatal sortie. Poets sang this heroic feat down the centuries. His resistance prevented the Turks from proceeding further to Vienna. Moreover their greatest Sultan Suleiman II died a few days prior to Zrínyi's sortie. His heart and innards were buried in a small chapel (*türbe*) a few miles outside the town where his tent had stood. After 1566 the fortress was rebuilt with a mosque in the middle. The foot of the minaret can still be seen on the western wall. The rest of the building is devoted to Zrínyi-related ephemera.

A little museum on the street leading to the fortress gives a general history of Szigetvár, but it is Turkey that hangs like

Above: The warm climate of southern Hungary makes for warming wines.

a conscience over the town. The **mosque** on today's Zrínyi square became a Catholic church with paintings by Dorff-meister on the inside harmonizing with typically Ottoman ogee windows. The Franciscans took over the mosque of Hadji Hussein on Zárda u. On Bástya u. stands the old **caravanserai**. Behind the fortress is Cumilla's fountain whose waters, it is said, have magic powers. And every Saturday a bell in the Catholic church donated by emperor Joseph II tolls for the courageous soldiers of 1566.

To the west of Szigetvár comes **Dobzsa** where the 1853 *talpás ház* – a house built on beams – of one István Benked has been turned into a museum exhibiting items of everyday Hungarian peasant life. **Ibafa**, 13 miles northeast of Szigetvár is known throughout Hungary from a tongue twister celebrating its priest's wooden pipe (*az Ibafai papnak fapipaja van*). Whether its pipe museum came first is a matter of intense speculation amongst amateur philologists.

The Ormánság

Among the costumes and furnishings exhibited in the ethnographic museum in Pécs are some from the *Ormánság*, a word deriving from the Turkish word for forest. This region with its own cultural and social habits lies to the south of route 6. There are no signposts indicating where it begins or ends. The capital, if any, is **Vajszló**, a village of barely 2000 souls that acquired rights in 1354. Since the peasants in the Ormanság were not allowed to acquire land, they tried to keep their birth rate down to one child per family, hence the low population.

Sellye, about 12 km west, devoted its small museum to the region. Less publicized, yet fascinating as they are generally considered only typical of eastern Hungary, are the painted coffered ceilings in several regional churches. The work, dating often to the early 16th cen-

tury was performed by local carpenters, who also did the painting. The motives derive mostly from nature; one coffer in the church in **Drávaivány** portrays a mermaid in naive style. Other churches with well restored painted coffered ceilings and choirs are east of Vajszló in **Kórós**, **Adorjás** and **Kovacshida**, all on the way to **Siklós**, a busy, bustling community about 11.000 strong known generally for its wine and marble which has been extensively used in Hungary. The fortress overlooking the entire region might not be the oldest, but it is one of the most complete in Hungary. It belonged for a while to the Garais, a powerful dynasty from which sprang two royal palatines. Later it was granted to the Perényi dynasty. In spite of its apparent impregnability, the Turks captured it in three days. In the 18th century the Batthyány family, whose coat-of-arms carved in stone still adorns the southwestern portal, occupied the fort and partially rebuilt it according to the Baroque *Zeitgeist*. Today the mighty old pile of stones attracts thousands. One wing serves as a hotel, it has a restaurant, the dungeon and torture chamber with its walls impregnated with screams are open to the public. One flight of rooms is furnished in 18th and 19th century fashion.

Also worthy of note in Siklós are the Franciscan church on the eastern access to the castle and the 18th century Greek Orthodox church to the east of town. To the northwest lies the little village **Mariagyüd**. Pilgrims still flock to its church in quest of healing, for here, according to local sources, several miracles took place. In 1737 for example, the prayer to the Virgin Mary for succor against the plague was immediately answered. To the south of Mariagyüd one can also heal one's agues in the thermal and mineral waters of the town of **Harkány**.

Locals describe this southern fringe of the Villány " mountains " as having been

"ploughed by the devil". It is climatically the hottest spot in Hungary and the landscape brings once again the Mediterranean region to mind, with barren, rocky slopes interspersed with vast vineyards.

Hungary's Napa Valley

On the road to **Villány**, in **Nagyharsány**, the pretty Gothic church with its fragments of frescos and single column holding up the sacristy, had to be shared by several sects during the Turkish occupation. Since 1968 a former quarry near the village has become the meetingplace for sculptors who can use the fresh air, the free space, the warm weather, perhaps, too, the good local wine to fire up their imagination. The open air museum, with its eclectic collection of modern sculptures standing around like abandonned children is an oddity in Europe's cultural scene.

Above: The "land ploughed by the devil" still attracts human workers.

Villány is the Napa Valley of Hungary. The local museum gives the best overview with exhibits of countless bottles and labels, prizes written in French, the *lingua vinica*, presses, spraying contraptions of all shapes and sizes, harvesting paraphenalia, and a cellar where the mold growing from the green wood barrels will soon have taken everything over. In town and in the surrounding communities cellars are often dug straight into the hillsides. The owners (mostly of German descent) have built simple white houses at the entrances. Only the pungent smell of fermenting wine in fall suggests the nature of the activities in these houses that line the Villány hills. A museum in **Villánykövesd** documents the history and traditions of the local German community. On the way back to Pécs one should glance at the church in **Palkonya**, an ex- mosque redone in Baroque style.

We are about to leave Baranya county. Route 6 slithers eastward along the Mecsek to **Pécsvárad**, an ancient fortified spot at the foot of mount Zengö, the Mecsek's highest peak (682 m). It then continues to Bonyhád, into the next chapter, passing by **Zengövarkony**, where the old peasant house of the Dékany family has been turned into a museum. In the following village, **Mecseknádasd**, stands a similar museum devoted to the German peasants who settled here in the 18th century. In nearby **Óbánya**, shortly before reaching the village itself, lie the ruins of a 10th century castle (Réka vár) where, so the historians say, St. Margaret of Scotland, an Árpád princess, was born.

An alternative to reach the next chapter in this book, however, is to follow the road that leads through Hosszuhetény, Magyaregregy and Szászvár, each of which has been graced with the ruins of a fortress. If intending to head further east, it is also wise to feast ones eyes on the hilly, forest-covered landscapes. After a few weeks in the puszta, they suddenly take on the aspect of a rare delicacy.

PÉCS

Access: From Budapest either by car over Route 6 (ca. 200 km), or by train from the Déli pályaudvar (southern) train station.

Accomodation

MODERATE: **Hotel Pannonia**, Rákóczi u. 3, Tel: (72) 13-322; **Hotel Hunyor**, Jurisics Miklós u. 16, Tel (72) 15- 677; **Hotel Nádor**, Széchenyi tér 15, Tel (72) 10-779. **Hotel Fönix**, Hunyadi u. 2, Tel: (72) 11-680. *BUDGET:* **Hotel Dömörkapu**, Gyükés dülö 1, Tel: (72) 15-987; **Hotel Fenyves**, Szölö u. 64, Tel: (72) 15-996; **Hotel Camping**, on the Mandulás camping site, Tel: (72) 15-981; **Minaret panzió**, Sallai u. 35., Tel: (72) 13-322. *CAMPING:* **Mandulás camping**, Tel: (72) 15-981) **Dozsó** camping site, Felsövámház u. 72, Tel: (72) 13-648.

Restaurants

Hotels **Hunyor**, **Pannonia**, **Nádor** and **Fönix** all offer a wide range of fares at reasonable rates. A pizzeria in the Fönix might provide a much needed change of fare. The **Vadásztanya**, Ürögi u., specializes in venison and exotica such as kangaroo...**Borostyán étterem**, Kossuth Lajos u. 64; **Misina étterem**, Misina-tetö; **Szölöskert**, Jurisics M. u.; **Tettye étterem**, Tettye tér 4. The **Konzum étterem** on Kossuth Lajos tér, a self-service, is interesting for its local color.

Tourist Offices

Mecsek Tourist: Széchenyi tér 1, Tel: (72) 14-866; **IBUSZ**, Széchenyi tér 8, Tel: (72) 12-148; **Pannon Tourist**, Déryné u. 1, Tel: (72) 11-326.

Sightseeing

Pécs is a pretty town with many historical sights, a relative wealth of Turkish relics, a street devoted to museums (Káptalan u.) and a number of well-restored buildings from the 19th century. Museums include: On Káptalan u.: No. 2: **Zsolnay Museum**; No. 3: **Mecsek Mining Museum**; and the **Vasarely Museum**; No. 4: **Modern Hungarian painting**; No. 5: **Nemes Endre Museum**. All closed on Mondays. **Archeological Museum**: Széchenyi tér 12. **Mosque of Hassan Jakovali and Museum**: Rákóczi u. 2 (closed Wednesdays). **Museum of the City**, Felsömalom u. 9. **Synagogue**, Kossuth tér, open afternoons only from May 1 to October 31. The **Cathedral** is open from 9 a.m. to 6 p.m. every day except on Sundays and on religious holidays when it opens its doors in the afternoons only for visitors.The surrounding countryside has a great deal to offer as well. To the north lies the recreational area of **Orfü**, with lakes and an interesting set of caves. For **Accomodation**, inquire at the camping site, Dollár u. 1., Tel: (72) 78-070. **Restaurants**: **Bisztró**, Dollár u. 14; **Klub Pécsi-tó**, Ady E. u. 1;

Vaskakas, Mecsekrákosi u. 29. The lakes at Orfü are well equipped for vacationers, with tennis courts, fitness centers, canoing, sailing and surfing. Visit also the nearby caves. **Remember**: The outdoor season ends around October 15 and comes alive again around April 15.

SZIGETVÁR

Accomodation

BUDGET: **Hotel Oroszlán**, Zrínyi tér 2, Tel: 284; Tourist lodgings have also been arranged in the castle. The Oroszlán, gives information. **Tourist office**: At the Hotel Oroszlán. **Restaurants**: **Kert étterem**, Rákóczi u. 26; at the Hotel **Oroszlán**; in the fortress itself.

Museums

The **Zrínyi-Miklós Museum** on the castle grounds stays open from 8 a.m. to 6 p.m. during the peak season (April 1 to September 30).

SIKLÓS

General: This old fortress town lies in a hot dry plain known for its tasty wines and thermal waters (in Villány and Harkány respectively). The fortress has several museums and hosts a chamber music series.

Access: From Pécs take either Route 58 straight south to Siklós and Harkány, or take Route 57 off of which leads a road to Villány. There are regular busses to Siklós from Pécs.

Accomodation

Hotel Tenkes in the fortress, Tel: 12-270; the local **tourist office** is also located in the hotel. **Hotel Központi**, Kossuth tér 5, Tel: 54.

Restaurants

In the **fortress** and the **Hotel Központi**; **Vasúti étterem**, Vasút u. 9; **Sport étterem**, Felszabadulás u. 74; **Tenkes étterem**, Széchenyi u. 12.

HARKÁNY

Accomodation

MODERATE and *CAMPING:* **Hotel Baranya**, Bajcsy-Zsilinszky u. 1, Tel: (72) 80-160; **Hotel Dráva**, Bajcsy-Zsilinszky u. 3, Tel: (72) 80-434; **Hotel Napsugár**, Bajcsy-Zsilinszky u. 5, Tel: (72) 80-300; **Camping site**, Bajcsy-Zsilinszky u. 4, Tel: (72) 80-117.

Restaurants

In the hotels mentioned above; **Nimród étterem**, Bajcsy-Zsilinszky u.11.

Sightseeing

The Siklós **castle** has several exhibits including a torture chamber and modern ceramics and paintings (closed Mondays). Near Villány is a **Wine Museum** (closed Mondays). The open-air sculpture museum **Nagyharsány** is accessible to all.

ALONG THE BLUE DANUBE

MOHÁCS
BAJA
KALOCSA
RÁCKEVE

Highway 6 from Pécs to Budapest runs through **Bonyhád**, a small provincial town which serves as the capital of the area known as "Swabian Turkey" for the Swabians who settled here after the Turks left. Even today the locals around this region speak German dialects. The countless traditional farmhouses in the surrounding villages are also interesting, and many of the villagers still wear traditional costumes too. But inevitably you come upon the Danube, that long, quiet stretch dividing eastern and western Europe. Unfortunately no passenger ships have shuttled between Budapest and Yugoslavia for years. Perhaps the Danube Steam Ship Company feels it is not necessary to show their passengers this partly flat, partly dry and sleepy landscape after they have seen the nicer parts to the north of the capital.

But let's climb aboard anyway, with the famous Danish storyteller, poet, dramatist and travel writer H. C. Andersen and let ourselves be transported to the ship in our imaginations:

"Our journey began in gently rolling, fertile green hills. Along the way we passed two overloaded ships with more than 100 passengers aboard. We were

Left: One of the few bridges crossing the Danube, here at Dunaföldvár.

told that these people, who were singing at the tops of their voices, had been on a pilgrimage. ... While we were discussing this, a storm suddenly came down between the mountains like an avalanche. The Danube became a torrent in the cloudburst, and our ship suddenly picked up speed. To the left between the green foliage of the plants a series of little villages suddenly appeared. Like floating colonies, the Danube seemed to carry them on its back. Each house also had a watermill, its wheels turning constantly. The millers' lads pressed pell-mell at open windows to catch a glimpse of our ship and its passengers. All this spawned a prankish kind of cheerfulness that stayed with us until Pest.

We still had three days in front of us before our journey's end, and we still had to travel through Mohács, Baja, Tolna, Paks, Földvár and Ercsi. In every town more passengers boarded our ship. In the afternoon we arrived in Mohács, where we stayed until early the following day."

MOHÁCS

The name of this town will always be associated with the battle which was fought near by on 29th August 1526. A 25.000 strong Hungarian army was defeated by a Turkish army far superior in

numbers, and the king, Ludwig II of Habsburg, died (allegedly) drowned in a river with his back to the action. On this bloody day not only countless soldiers perished, but Hungary's independence was lost too. After considerable work the battlefield was rediscovered. In 1975 mass graves were found, in which 280 Hungarian soldiers had been laid to rest. Nearby the archaeologists' spades uncovered further graves. The 450th anniversary of the battle was celebrated on 29th August 1976. On this occasion a memorial park with symbolic graves was opened at **Sátorhely** (7 km southwest of the town).

Mohács, where our journey begins, is a typical example of the towns along the Danube. Its main street, the **Szabadság utca** (Street of Freedom) begins where you disembark from the ship. The Turks are never far away, though their modern appearance is inoffensive: The **city hall**

Above: The wooden masks of the Busó are supposed to drive winter away.

has clearly oriental lines, coffee- houses filled with chattering Hungarians are christianed "Török Kavéház" (Turkish coffee-house). And house number 2 on Szabadság utca, built on Roman foundations, was once upon a time used as a bathhouse for the occupying Turkish army.

Not far away, in Kálvin Street, there is a nice single-aisled Baroque **Protestant church** from the 18th century. The **Catholic church**, built in 1776 and also in pure Baroque, is one of the oldest buildings in the town. Its main altar in particular, a work by the famed Stephan Dorffmeister, is worth seeing. The **Greek-Orthodox church** in Tolbuhin Street with two towers gracing its façade, was built in the same period and style. Close by, at 2 Kisfaludy Street, you will find a simple Baroque building. Formerly a Greek trading house, it has Byzantine reproductions of the saints in the niches in the upper part of the façade. After countless sights Szabadság Street ends at a colorful town center park.

A short walk leads to **Hösök tér** (Heroes' Square), where the erstwhile episcopal church proudly stands, commissioned in 1739 by the bishop of Pécs, Zsigmond Berényi. It was built in Baroque style and contains a number of interesting statues. Close by is the **Bishop's Palace**, built all in all between 1714 and 1799. Today it is a school. In 3, Szerb Street, in the **Dorottya Kanizsay Museum**, an exhibition commemorates the Battle of Mohács. In a more pleasant vein, pottery plays an important role in Mohács' arts and crafts and today there are still a few master potters who produce the unglazed black Mohács pottery, a Turkish import in fact.

Many traditions associated with masks and disguises survive in Hungarian villages today. By far the most decorative Shrovetide procession in Hungary is most probably the carnival parade of a southern Slavic ethnic group in Mohács, the so-called "Busójárás" (Busó parade). In their language the word means changing clothes, transformation or rebirth. The *busók* (masked men) wear huge wooden face masks, and each movement they make is ritually prescribed. Originally only adult men were entitled to carry the *busó* mask, and younger lads were given other ones.

"We left Mohács. Our ship was filled with more than 300 passengers and more were to join us on the way to Pest. Trunks, sacks and cases were piled up as high as the ship's wheel. You had to search everywhere above and below deck, just to find a place to stand."

BAJA

You can still travel to **Baja** in this way if you choose one of the ferries which are shuttling between the banks of the Danube all day until evening. Otherwise you will have to travel to **Bátaszék** and then join highway 55, which cuts through the swampy **Gemenc Nature Reserve**.

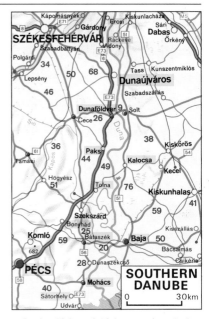

In the 18th and 19th centuries, during the Golden Age of Danube cruises, Baja was one of the most important trade centers of the lowland plain. After the Second World War thanks to the economic chimeras of the new Communist regime, the emphasis was shifted to industry. The center of the town is the generous **Peace Square** (Béke tér) lined with tourist offices, bars and restaurants. It is a favorite meeting place in summer. Béke tér is situated on the bank of the Danube tributary, the Kamarás, called simply the Sugovica by the locals.

Some of the buildings here have particularly interesting architectural traits, such as the **István Türr Museum**, an ex-bank built in Classical style in 1847. It contains a very informative exhibition on local history (with the emphasis on the Danube and water distribution) and also a picture gallery including 20th century Hungarian works. The Baroque churches in the town are also worth visiting as is the **synagogue** which now serves as the local library.

Above: Kalocsa's folkloric museum boasts some beautiful samplers of floral designs.

Petöfi Island is to Baja what Margaret Island is to Budapest – a place of relaxation and culture. It plays host to the Baja Summer Days, the Folkloric Festival along the Danube, and to numerous sporting events.

Before the waters were regulated in the last century, **Szekszárd** stood on the banks of the Danube. This is why the town center was built on hills at a safe distance from possible floods. 38, Széchenyi Street you will find the **Augusz House**, built in 1820 in neat Classical style, used to be a casino. Its cultural and historical significance lies in the fact that Franz Liszt, who often gave concerts in the town, used to stay here on his visits and also composed many works here. The old center of Szekszárd was **Béla Square**. A small community already existed here in Roman times. An abbey and a castle were added during the Middle Ages. Later, much later, one of Hungary's

most famous buildings in Classical style was erected on Béla u., the district governmental building designed by one Mihály Pollack and executed between 1828 and 1832. The Hungarian King Ludwig II and his noblemen stopped at this location in 1526 on their way to Mohács a few days before the tragic battle. An archive with numerous medieval documents and letters by Franz Liszt has been established in the building and the erstwhile dungeons. There is a large wine cellar next to it. But beware of the *Szeksárd Vörös* (red wine) which is extremely tempting.

THE BISHOPRIC OF KALOCSA

Kalocsa is probably the oldest and most interesting town on the southern Danube from a political point of view. It developed in a marshy area to the east of the Danube. István I founded an archbishopric here in the 11th century. This had a positive influence on the subsequent development of the town. In the

Middle Ages the bishops of Kalocsa often rose through the ranks to become important politicians, diplomats and military leaders. During Turkish times the population fell drastically – a result of the soldiers stationed in the castle thus bringing the war home. Kalocsa was never able to re-establish its prominent position, even later when the Turks were ousted in the 17th and 18th centuries, and when new people settled here. But the name Kalocsa has become important once again for two things in particular. Today it is famous for the paprika it produces, and for its folk art. Most of the blouses and tablecloths are embroidered with what are known as "Kalocsa floral motifs". In the second half of the 19th century Kalocsa embroiderers used only white, blue, black and red yarns but since the 1920s multi-colored patterns have dominated. The women who designed the patterns were called "writers" and they became famous throughout the region and indeed the country.

Folk Painting

Another equally important art is traditional wall painting (*pingálás*). Kalocsa is one of the few regions in Hungary where the women painted the interior walls of the houses themselves and painted flowers on the exterior façade facing the street. Plant designs are the most common ones in this colorful mural art, although now and then they will ship in pictures of birds. All this can be seen in the **Museum of Folk Art** at 1-3, Mihály Street, a little house with a thatched roof and in the **Museum** at 25, István Street. The beautiful Baroque **archbishop's residence**, built between 1776 and 1799 using remains from the castle, is at Szabadság tér.

Most of the east wing of this building is taken up by the library which contains 120.000 volumes. This valuable collection includes 57 codices and 508 first editions. The oldest codex dates from 1040. Among the most famous books in the library is a Bible signed by Martin Luther himself. The library's festival hall was completed in 1780. F. A. Maulbertsch did the painting. Among the guests here was Franz Liszt, who gave several concerts here. Behind the building stands a romantic, architecturally eclectic **cloister**, built in the second half of the 19th century. The archbishop also kept his horses here, in stables with four towers, built in the 18th century, and his grain in a silo from the same period. Also on Szabadság tér is a Baroque **cathedral** designed by Andreas Mayerhoffer, with two towers, beautiful stucco-work and a chancel.

Since the mid-1970s the name **Paks** has become synonymous with one thing: a nuclear power station. When it was built, its 11.000 inhabitants felt, that it promised many things. Today, after Chernobyl, they feel a little different about it. The mid-19th century was Pak's Golden Age, a period during which numerous patrician houses sprung up in the center of the town. Among them is **Szeniczey Manor** built between 1850 and 1874 in Classical style. In the 19th century the great Hungarian politician Ferenc Deák often stayed here. The **Fischercsárda** is an ideal place to enjoy a meal and watch the Danube sliding past.

Dunaföldvár has always been an important crossroads joining the west and east of the country. It was first mentioned in a document dating from the year 1009. In the 12th century King Béla II founded a **Benedictine Abbey** here. The tower built in the 15th and 16th century to improve its defenses, still stands today. But today it is a museum of local history and prison museum. Other monuments worth seeing are the **Roman Catholic church**, built between 1723 and 1729, the **Greek Orthodox church**, built in the second half of the 18th century in Baroque style and, not to forget, the late-Baroque **Franciscan church**.

had the "good fortune of enjoying the harmonious juxtaposition of the enormous industrial complex and the residential area". It is no wonder that the town was honored with the name Sztálinváros (Stalintown) – but of course only for as long as this name was fashionable. However, not everything disappeared beneath the huge concrete blocks. In the small heart of the "old town" there is still a **Greek-Orthodox church**, built in Baroque style in 1696.

RÁCKEVE

The 5 km long island of **Csepel** begins a little to the north of Dunaújváros. Its northern tip forms the industrial area of Budapest. It is to this island that the citizens of Budapest come on day-trips and to get away from it all. The largest place on the island, and the most popular with the tourists, is **Ráckeve**. It was originally founded by people who had left their Serbian hometown of Keve, fleeing from the Turks. Its most famous building is a Baroque **castle**, designed by Johann Lukas Hildebrand and built in 1702. Unfortunately its rooms were used as a warehouse for many years. Amongst the most interesting parts of the castle is the **Greek-Orthodox church** with its fan vaults. It was built in 1487 in the late-Gothic style. The interior walls were covered with Byzantine paintings. The two Gothic chapels were added in the 16th century. At the same time the ground floor of the separate bell tower was built. In 1758 it was finished in the architectural style of the day.

The Baroque **Catholic church**, built between 1791 and 1799 also has its merits. A short walk through the town is recommended if only to admire the splendid architecture of the local buildings. In Kossuth Street, for example, there is a vaulted cellar and a painted arch belonging to a merchant's house dating from the 15th century. An inn has nested inside it.

Most Historians of 20th century love **Dunaújváros**. It was in its time "the first Socialist town in our homeland", as the propaganda proudly proclaimed. And the propaganda was not wrong, for this gigantic project represents the physical realization of Stalinist dogma. A few decades ago there was only a small village standing here. Today it has grown into an industrial town with a population of 65.000. Building work began on the foundry in 1950, and already by 7 November, 1951, the anniversary of the Russian Revolution, iron smelting began. The great speed with which this was all achieved was of course only possible with a great deal of hard work and dedication. Unfortunately planners forgot to calculate the cost of dragging in all the ore and coal, so the plant's steel instead of being competitive is too expensive.

At the end of the third year the young town already had 20.000 inhabitants who

Above: The Serbian-Orthodox faith prevails in the beautiful church of Ráckeve.

ALONG THE DANUBE

General: Cruise ships seldom make any major stops between Budapest and the southern border at Mohács, therefore the traveler wanting to inspect some of the sites along the Danube will either have to go by car, bicycle (a pleasant alternative as the landscape remains flat most of the way, or by bus from town to town. Travel information here has been provided for the major towns along the river, beginning with Mohács.

Crossings: There are bridge crossings only in the following places: Baja, Dunaföldvár, and to the island of Csepel in Ráckeve. Other crossings are with ferries for a small fee and generally a little longer than business hours.

MOHÁCS
Accomodation

BUDGET:. **Hotel Csele**, Kisfaludy tér 6, Tel: 10-825; **Hotel Korona**, Jókai u. 2, Tel: 10-541. Other accomodation at Sátorhely, **Sátorhely fogadó** (bed and breakfast) Tel: 10-322; to the north in Somberek, Tel: 10-855; the nearest camping is 15 km upstream in Dunaszekcsö.

Restaurants

Cselecsárda, Szölöhegy; in the **Korona Hotel**; **Halászcsárda** (fish specialities), and **Révkapucsárda**, both on Kisfaludy tér; **Wernesgrüner sörözö**, Dózsa György u. 1.

Tourist Offices

Mecsek Tourist, Tolbuhin u. 2, Tel: 10-961. **Special note**: Besides its historical importance, Mohács is also known for its carnival procession, the *busójárás*, when people don frightful wooden masks to chase winter away.

BAJA
Accomodation

MODERATE: **Hotel Sugovica**, Petöfi-sziget (island), Tel: (79) 12-988; The island also has a camping site, Tel: (79) 11-174. *BUDGET*: **Hotel Duna**, Béke tér 6, Tel: (79) 11-765.

Restaurants

Sugó étterem in the Hotel Sugovica; nearby on Petöfi island is the **Védió étterem**; **Duna étterem**, Béke tér 6; **Csitanyica vengdéglö**, Szabadság 84.

Tourist Offices

Pusztatourist, Béke tér 8, el (79) 11-153; **IBUSZ**, Béke tér 7, Tel: (79) 11-161; **Express** (for youths and students), Béke tér 6.

SZEKSZÁRD
Accomodation

SZEKSZÁRD: *MODERATE*: **Hotel Gemenc**, Mészáros L. u. 4, Tel: (74) 11-722. *BUDGET*:

Hotel Tourist, Kálvária u. 1, Tel: (74) 12-228. **FADD-DOMBORI** (north of Tolna): *BUDGET*: **Hotel Hullám**, with camping site and restaurant.

Restaurants

In the **Hotel Gemenc**; **Kispipa étterem**, Széchenyi u. 1; **Halászcsárda** (fish specialities), Zrínyi u. 60; **Krokodil**, Oseri J. u. 114.

Tourist Offices

Tolna tourist, Széchenyi u. 38, Tel: (74) 12-144; **IBUSZ**, Széchenyi u. 19, Tel: (74) 11-947.

KALOCSA

has a reputation for itself and for paprika. No wonder then, that a museum has been devoted to the red gold (the only hotel in town bears this name). The library of the archbishopric on Szabadság tér is also worth seeing, however.

Accomodation:

Piros Arany Hotel, I.István Király útja. 37.

Restaurants

In the **Piros Arany**; **Kalocsai csárda**, I. István Király útja 87; **Diófa vendéglö**, Petöfi S. u. 67; **Mátyás vendéglö**, Petöfi S. u. 2.

Tourist Offices

Pusztatourist, I. István Király útja 35, Tel: 799.

DUNAFÖLDVÁR AND DUNAÚJVÁROS
Accomodation

MODERATE: **Hotel Aranycsillag**, Vasmü u. 3, Tel: (25) 18-045. *BUDGET*: **Hotel Szélkakas panzió** (bed and- breakfast), Lokomotiv u. 1/a, Tel: (25) 17-989. *CAMPING*: Tel: (25) 17-627.

Restaurants

Aranyhordó, Erdösor 31; Halászcsárda Dunagyöngye, Sziget u. 2; **Kis Csillag**, Vasmü u. 39.

Tourist offices

DUNAFÖLDAR: **Tolna tourist** has an office at the fortress. **DUNAÚJVÁROS**: **Korányi Sándor** u. 1, Tel: (25) 16- 607; **IBUSZ**: Vasmü u. 10/a, Tel: (25) 16-487.

RÁCKEVE
Accomodation

MODERATE: **Hotel Keve**, Elnök tér 12, Tel: (26) 85-147; The **house-boat** in the Malom-öböl (gulf) on Tinodi u., Tel: (26) 79-162. Further accomodation in bed-and-breakfasts in Dömsöd to the south and Peróg to the north. The **Apaj Hotel** in Kiskunlacháza (Bankháza-Hajóstanya) Tel: (26) 85-303 is a good address to know.

Restaurants

Duna étterem, Kossuth u. 18; **Fekete Holló étterem**, Kossuth u. 1; **Savoyai-kastély étterem**, Kossuth u. 95.

Tourist Offices

Dunatours, Kossuth u. 12, Tel (26) 85-372.

BUDAPEST
Paris of the East

BUDAPEST
DANUBE BEND
WEST OF BUDAPEST

BUDAPEST

Hungary's capital has been called the "Paris of the East" and the "Pearl of the Danube" since 1873, when the towns of Buda, Pest and Óbuda were united. Those who doubted the truth of these comparisons learned their lesson at the latest in Paris in 1988 when the UNESCO declared Budapest's Danube panorama and the Castle District as "especially valuable heritage with universal significance for mankind" to be listed between the Acropolis in Athens and the Great Wall of China.

The Castle District

The Castle District spreads on a 60 m high, 1500 m long and 500 m wide stone plateau which runs parallel to the Danube. The full majesty of the castle itself is best appreciated from the Pest bank of the river. "It is like looking at a beautiful painting", Miklós Oláh (1493-1568) wrote in his book *Hungaria*. Settling the rocky elevation and systematic organization of its defensive system,

Preceding pages: Buda and Pest glow in the setting sun. Left: The neo-Gothic façade of the Parliament on the Pest bank of the Danube.

began in earnest under Béla IV (1235-70) after the Mongols had destroyed Pest on the left bank of the Danube. The majority of the population, that came to live on the hill, was German. But French, Italians, Walloons and Jews also found their way here. Each group had its own streets. The invasion of the Turks in 1541, however, brought an end to the continued development of this castle town which now had 20.000 inhabitants.

The fire which was lit in 1686 to celebrate the ousting of the Turks destroyed whatever had survived the Ottoman occupation. The castle and its town were rebuilt mainly in Austrian Baroque style, but suffered great damage again during the course of the 1848-49 Revolution. In the winter of 1944-45 they were once again reduced to rubble in the hail of bombs and grenades. During the subsequent restoration work, however, the architects took both historical sources and urban planning issues into account. Surviving medieval parts, such as windows, oriels, niches and portals were not bricked up, but were incorporated into the new houses. Bridges thus spent the past and conjured up at least visions of this ancient part of town. Modern buildings arose only where the war had annihilated all traces of the past. The **Hilton Hotel** is a fine example of a successful

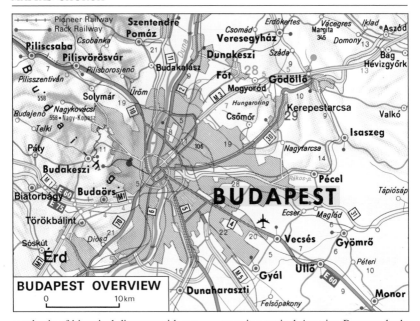

BUDAPEST OVERVIEW
0   10km

synthesis of historical distance with spatial unity. A late-Baroque façade, the tower of the medieval church of St. Nicholas, its north wall with three Romanesque windows, the medieval cloister and a Renaissance well were all successfully combined with the very modern hotel architecture. The Church of Our Lady or **Mátyás Church** also forms a self-contained unit with the Statue of St. Stephen and the Fishermen's Bastion. As everything on the hill, the Church of Our Lady, originally a German church, has had a checkered past. It was first mentioned in a document from 1247, where it is referred to as the "fortress church". In 1255 it was renovated for the first time. But it was not until the 14th and 15th century that it was extended to its present size. The Turks turned it into a mosque – its interior was whitewashed and its statues and altars were removed. When the Turks had been ousted the Jesuits

Right: The roofs of Mátyás Church in the Castle District.

gave it a typical Austrian Baroque look, and turned it into a church again. In 1723 it was destroyed by a fire. Its current interior, an additional chapel, the murals and a colorful tiled roof all date from 1873-96. Frigyes Schulek, one of the innovative Hungarian architects of the end of the 19th century, created the church we see today out of the basic Gothic construction. Subdued light falls through the large stained glass windows made from drawings by Bertalan Székely and Károly Lotz. The light accentuates the beauty of the ceiling and the pillars, which are decorated with geometrical figures and stylized floral ornaments. The interior is rich in sacral elements – a Black Madonna on a late-Gothic altar (Loretto chapel), a neo-Gothic main altar, a neo-Romantic baptismal font. But it also has many parts which bear witness to Hungarian history. Frescoes by Lotz in the Chapel of St. László (north side chapel) show events from the life of the saint and King László (1077-95). Scenes from the life of Imre, the son of Stephen I, who died at an early

age, are found on the neo-Gothic side-altar of the Chapel of St. Imre painted by the artist Zichy. "Tolerant kings rule, intolerant kings tyrannize" were St. István's words to his son. In the Chapel of the Trinity the sarcophagi of King Béla III (1172- 96) and his wife Anne de Châtillon lie side by side. The many flags document the Hungarian people's almost irrepressible desire for independence.

The neo-Romantic and glowing-white **Fishermen's Bastion** built on the old look-out post is also one of Schulek's works. It takes its name from the fishermen who plied their trade in the shadow of the castle, and whose duty it was to defend this part of town. From the observation terrace you will find a fairy-tale view of the opposite bank, and from the highest tower you can see far into the Buda mountains. The **equestrian statue of István I** in front of the south side of the church was created by Alajos Stróbl. Events from the life of this great king are portrayed on the four white marble reliefs on the plinth. The **statue of the Trinity** in front of the western portal was erected by the local people to show their gratitude for having survived from the great plague epidemics of 1709 and 1710.

Time is one of the prerequisites to get to know the castle district better, for there is so much to see and enjoy here. About a day suffices to get an overall impression of the place, either on foot or more comfortably in a horse-drawn carriage directly into the **castle palace**. There is nothing left of the original castle built by Béla IV. Excavations reveal systematic construction beginning in the 14th century and climaxing during the great rule of Mátyás Corvinus (1458-1490). Nothing of this assumed splendor remains, for after the Turks withdrew even the ruins which could have been restored were torn down. In 1714 a smaller building was begun on the foundations of the old castle, which received several neo-Baroque extensions before around 1900. In 1945 the castle palace was devastated by fire. Renovation and rebuilding lasted well into the 1980s. Today the interior

Gül Baba türbéje (Tomb)

Margit-sziget

Országház (Parliament Building)

MOSZKVA TÉR

BATTHYÁNY TÉR

KOSSUTH TÉR

Hadtörténeti Múzeum (War History Mus.)

Bécsi kapu (Vienna Gate)

Szt.Anna templom (Church)

Hilton H.

Mátyás-templom (Church)

Vendéglátó ip. Múzeum (Mus.of Gastronomy and Trade)

Capucin Church

Tudományos Akadémia (Acad.of Sciences)

Magyar Állami Ope (State Opera)

Szentháromság-szobor (Statue of the Holy Trinity)

Halászbástya (Fishermen's Bastion)

Tourist Information Gresham palota (Palace)

Déli pályaudvar (Railway Station)

Panoptikum (Panopticum)

Buda Penta H.

Fehérvári kapu (Gate)

Budavári sikló (Funicular)

József Attila

Atrium Hyatt H.

Forum H.

Magyar Munkásmozgalmi Múzeum (Mus.of the Hung. Labour Movement)

Budavári palota (Royal Palace)

Nemzeti Galéria (Nat.Gallery)

Vigadó

H. Duna Intercontinental

Taverna H.

Széchenyi Könyvtár (Library)

Budapesti Történeti Múzeum (Hist.Mus.)

Semmelweis Orvostörténeti Múzeum (Mus.of Medical History)

Belvárosi plébániatemplom (City Parish Church)

Novotel

Szt.Gellért-szobor (Monument)

GELLÉRT-

Citadella

HEGY

Felszabadulási emlékmű (Liberation Monument)

Underground with Station

116

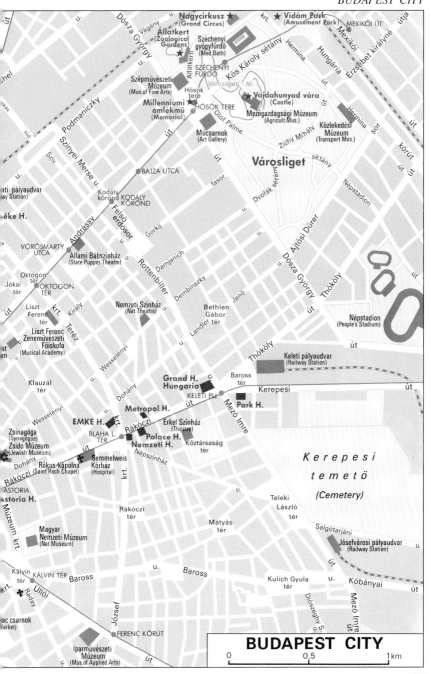

Nagycirkusz ★
(Grand Circus)

★ Vidám Park
(Amusement Park)

MEXIKÓI ÚT

Állatkert
(Zoological
Gardens)

Széchenyi
gyógyfürdő
(Med.Bath)

Kós Károly sétány

Hermina

Hungária

Erzsébet királyné útja

Dósza György

Vágány

u.

SZÉCHENYI
FÜRDÓ

Városligeti - tó

Szépművészeti
Múzeum
(Mus.of Fine Arts)

Hősök
tere

★ Vajdahunyad vára
(Castle)

Hermina

Podmaniczky

Szinyei Merse

Szív

hid

u.

Millenniumi
emlékmü
(Memorial)

HŐSÖK TERE

Olof Palme

Mezőgazdasági Múzeum
(Agricult.Mus.)

Zichy Mihály

Hermina
sor

körút

út

Múcsarnok
(Art Gallery)

Városliget

sétány

Közlekedési
Múzeum
(Transport Mus.)

ti pályaudvar
(ay Station)

BAJZA UTCA

fasor

Dvořák sétány

Ajtósi Dürer

Népstadion

út

út

éke H.

Kodály
körönd

KODÁLY
KÖRÖND

Andrássy

Felsö
erdösor

Gorkij

u.

Dósza György

Thököly

út

VÖRÖSMARTY
UTCA

Állami Bábszinház
(State Puppet Theatre)

Rottenbiller

Damjanich

Dembinszky

Oktogon
tér

Jókai
tér

OKTOGON
TÉR

Liszt
Ferenc
tér

krt.

Király

Teréz

Nemzeti Szinház
(Nat.Theatre)

Jenö

Bethlen
Gábor

Népstadion
(People's Stadium)

Liszt Ferenc
Zeneművészeti
Föiskola
(Musical Academy)

st
m

Wesselényi

Landler tér

Thököly

út

Keleti pályaudvar
(Railway Station)

Klauzál
tér

Dohány

Grand H.
Hungaria

Baross
tér

Kerepesi

út

Wesselényi

u.

KELETI PU.

Mező Imre

Park H.

EMKE H.

Metropol H.

Rákóczi

BLAHA L.
TÉR

Erkel Szinház
(Theatre)

Zsinagóga
(Synagogue)

Palace H.

Nemzeti H.

Köztársaság
tér

Zsidó Múzeum
(Jewish Museum)

Dohány

Rókus-kápolna
(Saint Roch Chapel)

Semmelweis
Kórház
(Hospital)

Népszinház

krt.

Kerepesi

temetö

(Cemetery)

ÁSTORIA

Rákóczi

ASTORIA H.

Múzeum

krt.

Rákóczi
tér

u.

Teleki
László
tér

Salgótarjáni

Magyar
Nemzeti Múzeum
(Nat.Museum)

Mátyás
tér

Jósefvárosi pályaudvar
(Railway Station)

Kálvin
tér

KÁLVIN TÉR

Baross

Baross

Kulich Gyula
tér

u.

Kőbányai

út

Üllöi

József

u.

Diószeghy S.

Mező Imre
út

ac csarnok
arket)

FERENC KÖRÜT

Iparművészeti
Múzeum
(Mus.of Applied Arts)

út

BUDAPEST CITY

0   0,5   1km

rooms are museums. Individual parts of the building are denoted by letters of the alphabet. Wing A houses the **Museum of the Hungarian Workers' Movement**. In Wings B, C, and D you will find the **Hungarian National Gallery** which has exhibitions on Hungarian art from the Middle Ages to the present day. Wing E houses the Castle museum with the remains of the medieval castle (reconstructed knights' hall, church and dungeon). The **Széchenyi National Library** has a permanent home in Wing F.

You can also get to the hill from Clark Adam tér. An old cobbled street leads in a southerly direction via the southern tower to the castle's terraced park graded the **Statue of Prince Eugene**. Two stepped streets to the north of Clark Adam tér lead to Dísz tér. It is more comfortable to go by the funicular which leaves every three minutes from the north side of the castle

Above: The Fishermen's Bastion. Right: The Széchenyi chain link bridge, the most majestic of Budapest.

complex where the **Turul bird** greets new arrivals. Two streets, Franklin utca and Kagyló utca, lead from the river to the citadel. Both can be reached from Batthyány tér, which is dominated by the Baroque **Church of St. Anne**. In the former noblemen's inn you will now find **Café Angelika**, a popular meeting place for both young and old. House no. 3 (18th century) was built in 1790. The house next door, once a guest house and inn for the nobility, which contains a Rococo theater, was built around 1770. Kaiser Franz-Joseph and Casanova both stayed here. The statue on the north side is of Ferenc Kölcsey (1790-1838), the composer of Hungary's national anthem.

Franklin utca ends at the steps to the Fishermen's Bastion, which lead past sculptures and monuments to the Church of Our Lady. Kagyló utca is a romantic climb. It begans at Mária tér, which boasts a pretty Marian statue (1720), and leads through the Európapark to Bécsi kapu tér (**Vienna Gate Square**), the northernmost square in the castle district. This can also be reached from Moszkva tér, either on foot or by taking the no. 16 bus. The gate built in 1936 to commemorate the ousting of the Turks 250 years earlier replaced the erstwhile medieval city gate. A plaque commemorates the soldiers of many nations who helped bring about this victory. The square retains its ancient character, with eighteenth-century houses (no. 5), Baroque buildings (no. 6) and Classical buildings (No. 7), the Protestant church and its little statue. But this intimacy is unfortunately spoiled by the monumental neo-Romanesque archive.

The main streets of the Castle District all meet at squares and are joined by alleys and small streets. (All house numbers start in the south). Táncsis Mihály utca (formerly Jewish Street) and Fortuna utca (formerly French Street) meet at **Hess András tér**, at the memorial to Pope Innocence XI, between the lux-

urious Hilton Hotel and the excellent Fortuna restaurant, which has Gothic alcoves inside. Some of the houses on **Táncsis Mihály utca**, which runs parallel to the old fortress wall, have been built on medieval foundations. Some are Baroque, others Classical. The houses on Fortuna utca bearing uneven numbers are mainly Baroque. At no. 4 you will find the **Hungarian Museum of Trade**. The extensions of both streets behind Szent Háromság tér meet Úri utca at the bronze statue of Field Marshal Hadik. This statue was erected in memory of the Revolution of 1848-49. The house at Tárnok utca 14 dates back to the 14th century. Modern architects were able to reconstruct the medieval geometric façade paintings. No. 18 was once the citadel apothecary, and dates back to the 18th century. Today it is a museum.

Úri utca is the districts's longest street, and the most feudal in character. Its old, dignified houses have Romanesque, Gothic and Baroque stylistic features. From no. 9 you can get to part of the complex cave system under the hill. The house also has a 6500 square meter exhibition documenting the history of Hungary from its beginning. A walk in the shade of the chestnut trees on the **Tóth Árpád sétány** (promenade), which runs along the western fortress wall, makes a pleasant break. The promenade gives a spectecular view of the Buda hills. At the beginning of the promenade is the **Café Korona**, frequented by the literati, and is guarded by a small Hussar carved in stone. At the other end is the **War History Museum** in the right hand corner of Kapisztran tér, which has a statue of the monk Capistranus (1386-1456), who encouraged the Hungarians to fight against the Turks.

There are many restaurants to relax in, but we would recommend that you compare their price lists before making your choice. If you could use a few calories, the **Ruszwurm Pâtisserie** at 7, Szentháromság utca has Biedermeier furnishings and excellent cake. Under the Tóth Árpád sétány is the **Vérmezö** (Field of

119

Blood), where Ignác Martinovics (1755-1795) was executed with his supporters for championing the French Revolution.

Along the Danube

The narrow strip of land between Castle Hill and the Danube is known as the "water town" or *víziváros* in Hungarian, and has lived from the river ever since it was first settled.

The Danube already served as a trade route by the Romans, Avars and Huns. And present-day Budapest was a central point on this route. The Magyars recognized its convenient position and its usefulness when they arrived in the 9th century. Anchor taxes were already being levied here as far back as the 11th century. In the 13th century the ferrymen formed an organization; in the 14th century Buda earned storage rights and soon

Above: The Gypsy violinist Lakatos Sándor in the Mátyás Pince restaurant. Right: Rest and recuperation in the Gellért Bath.

became rich. King Sigismund (1387-1437) had the Danube cordoned off by a chain, so that no ship could escape his taxing grasp. Only the navy of King Mátyás Corvinus (1458-1490) could outdo his in terms of size and equipment. Even in Turkish times traffic on the Danube was heavy. On a single day, for example, 19 war ships and 20 freighters cast off from Budapest on their way to Vienna. After the victory over the Turks, Maria Theresia sent some "young ladies of Vienna unfortunately found wanting" on barges down the Danube to the deserted regions of southern Hungary, where they were to marry Her Majesty's soldiers who had settled there. At the same time German settlers, mostly Swabians, were also invited to establish themselves in a new Hungarian home.

The first steamship, the *Carolina*, docked in Pest in 1818. But it was not until 1830 that a regular shipping line to Vienna and south to the Black Sea came into existence. Since the completion of the Suez Canal Budapest has been joined

to the world's oceans. This explains the free port on **Csepel Island**, to the south of the city where seafaring ships drop anchor. Csepel has become Hungary's most important industrial area.

Only hydrofoils, the commuter boats (a remnant from the post-war period when Budapest's bridges had been destroyed), sports boats and anglers can make use of the Danube when the waters are at their lowest level. Measures can be taken against very high water levels, but not against drought. This particular problem though has never affected the spas and swimming pools, since they are supplied by many springs providing some 70 million liters a day. These mostly thermal waters, between 24 C and 78 C are said to heal articular, gynecological circulatory disorders. In addition to the springs there are artesian wells (Margaret Island and City Park). People have been coming to Budapest to take the waters for 2000 years, and it has been advertising its baths in brochures since the end of the 17th century. In 1934 it was given the of-

ficial title "spa town". The Turkish occupation was a Golden Age for Budapest's balneal culture. The bath houses, mostly built in Buda by Pasha Mustapha Sokolu, are still in use today, though most have now been restored and extended. The **Király Baths** (84, Fö utca) is a compact complex of buildings with four green cupolas with a golden half-moon on the highest cupola. It is one of the very rare preserved remains from this time. The burial chamber of **Gül Baba** (Mecset utca, has also been preserved. He was the dervish who introduced the rose to Budapest and was henceforth known as "Father of the Roses". Beneath the southern tower of the castle (Szarvas tér) you can also see a number of gravestones decorated with turbans. Some prayer niches in the Innercity Paris Church have also been preserved, as well as a late-Gothic ogee arch in the **Capucin Church** (30-32, Fö utca) which was built using stones from a mosque. Many Muslim buildings and ornaments were lost during re-Christianization. But a number of things also remained: coffee, tobacco and paprika, for example; and the stylized flower patterns, tulips, roses and carnations found on many ceramics and handicrafts are a fusion of Renaissance and Turkish elements.

The Citadel

The old citadel crowning Gellért Hill offers the finest view of the entire city and the surrounding countryside. The nearby **Liberation Monument**, erected to celebrate the Nazi defeat at the hands of the Red Army, is visible from most parts of the city. The bird's eye perspective shows clearly how the peripheral boulevards run in semi-circular fashion from and to the Danube. The citadel is the only fortress actually constructed as part of a vast system planned by the House of Habsburg to "tame rebellious Hungary".

The end of the Hungarian War of Independence (1848-49) marked the beginning of the tyrannical rule of Emperor Franz Joseph I, who had transferred command of Buda and Pest to his artillery commander Baron Haynau. Haynau, known as the "hyena of Brescia" for his suppression of the revolution in that North Italian city, became the "hyena of Hungary" too. Executions, disposessions and imprisonments were the order of the day. Soldiers taken prisoner by the Austrians were forced to build the citadel. It was to be an awe-inspiring construction with casements, moats, a drawbridge, bastions and sixty canons aimed at Buda and Pest. The occupying troops, however, never had occasion to fire them, except on the birthday of His Majesty. Their only other task was to hoist a flag when ships came into sight. This construction, built by slaves, soon became a royal joke. In 1897 the citadel was handed over to the City Magistrate who

Right: Selling handicraft on the Váci ut., a profitable sideline.

had it symbolically demolished by destroying some of the lesser walls. Today it houses a hotel, a restaurant and a wine bar. But the best thing which the citadel has to offer is the view. From here you can trace the course of the Danube all the way from Margaret Island to Csepel Island. You can see five of the city's eight bridges, which are among the most beautiful in Europe. The first bridge between Buda and Pest, that could withstand ice drifts and at the same time allow ships to pass, was the Lánchíd (chain bridge). It was inaugurated in 1849. Margit híd was completed 25 years later, Szabadság híd in 1896, Erzsébet híd in 1903, and Petöfi híd in 1937. Margit híd in the north and Petöfi híd in the south link the harmoniously arched peripheral boulevard on the Pest side (built over a drained arm of the Danube) and its rather tortuous counterpart on the Buda side. In contrast to the others, neither of these bridges has a raised iron construction. They offer an unhindered view of the river and the city.

Margaret Island

Margit híd not only joins Buda and Pest, but it also joins the mainland and **Margitsziget** (Margaret Island) by a smaller pedestrian bridge leading off it. The writer Mór Jókai described this island as "the fairy garden of Budapest". It is 2500 m long, 500 m wide and was formed in prehistoric times from sand and stone deposits. The island is entirely devoted to recreation. It has medicinal springs, swimming pools and lawns surrounded by a variety of trees, walks and a rose garden. This nature park in the middle of the Danube also provides for cultural events: Opera and operetta fans can visit the open-air theater.

The Romans not only loved the warm springs. For them the island was an important link in the *limes*, their outer line of fortifications. In the 12th century it gained a certain degree of independence

when it was made a royal hunting ground and called the *Island of Hares*. Palaces, houses and cloisters were built. The ruins of the **Dominican cloister** on the eastern side, above all its ground plan, carved in a stone in the well-house, suggest what the convent complex looked like when it was originally commissioned by Béla IV (1235-70). His daughter Margaret lived here in poverty and isolation after he vowed her to a nunnery if the Tatars would leave. The **Artist's Promenade** leads to the **Chapel of St. Michael** which was restored to its original form using stones from the old southern wall, including the windows, and from the 15th century foundations of the sacristy. It bears the oldest (14th century) bell in Hungary which serves to ring in feast-days.

A number of imposing buildings stands along the Pest bank of the Danube, the most impressive being the neo-Gothic **Parliament**. Its architect Imre Steindl wanted to "modestly represent the national but individual spirit in Gothic attire". The designers of the modern hotels on the Pest bank of the river must have had similar thoughts of modestly representing the extravagance of the 20th century. They received a good deal of negative criticism from the inhabitants of the city and a complaint from the UNESCO commission. The Pest bank of the river should have been rebuilt in original 18th and 19th century style when the buildings destroyed in the Second World War and the 1956 Revolution were being restored.

More Bridges

The **Lánchíd**, south of Margit híd is guarded on both the Buda side and the Pest side by two stone lions. Hungarians regard the bridge as the eighth wonder of the world. A model of it can even be found in the Deutsche Museum in Munich. It was built on the initiative of the great Hungarian politician and reformer Count István Széchenyi (1791-1860). He commissioned the Englishman William Tierney Clark to design it, and his fellow countryman Adam Clark (no relation) to build it. The latter also built the extension to the Lánchíd, a 350 m long tunnel under Castle Hill linking the Danube to the so-called Christine City. On the Pest side the view of the bridge is cut off by the **Gresham Palace**, an enormous housing block with a Secession façade. Even the janitor no longer knows exactly who all the tenants, subtenants and temporary tenants are. The building takes its name from the Gresham Insurance Company and was known for the "Gresham Dinner Circle", a group of artists, art patrons and collectors who met in a café on the ground floor every week until their group was dissolved in 1944. A few paces north on Roosevelt tér the **Academy of Sciences** proudly occupies the corner overlooking the Danube. It is a neo-Renaissance building, constructed between 1862 and 1865. This too, as so many things in Hungary, was made possible by Count István Széchenyi, who donated 60.000 florins, the annual income from his estates, for the project. A commemorative statue to him stands in front of the academy.

The **Erzsébet híd**, Budapests longest and most graceful bridge, is the only bridge of those that were destroyed during World War Two, whose design underwent major changes on rebuilding. The former chain bridge was turned into a cable bridge without any of its former Art Nouveau ornamentation. The old pillars remained, the bothersome Pest approach to the bridge was also retained which blocks the view of the **Innercity Parish Church**.

This church is one of the most interesting monuments in the country. It was originally scheduled for destruction but earned a reprieve at the 11th hour, when its true value was recognized. It incorporates an array of stylistics elements from Roman to modern times. Stones

from the Roman military camp *Contra Aquincum* (3rd-4th century) were used to build the first early Romanesque church. The foundations of a tower from these ancient Roman fortifications and the leftovers of some walls were uncovered next to the church and turned into a playground for children. Some remains from the original church in which Bishop Gellért was buried are located in the south tower. A Romanesque church grew out of the first one in the 12th century. It was here that Elizabeth, later Saint Elizabeth, was betrothed to Ludwig IV of Thuringia when she was only four years old. Under Sigismund of Luxemburg (1387-1437) and Mátyás Corvinus (1458-1490) the church was extended by a Gothic and late-Gothic aisle. Having survived its transformation into a mosque during Turkish times (the *mihrab,* a prayer niche in the chancel wall, recalls this period) it was renovated in Austrian Baroque style in the wake of the general subordination to the House of Habsburg. After the Second World War the badly damaged church was not only renovated but was also freed from the eclectic elements which the architect Imre Steindl (1839-1902) had added to it. To hear Mozart's *Requiem*, for example, in this church is one of the unforgettable memories of Budapest.

In contrast to the Pest approach to Erzsébet híd, the Buda side is lively and elegant. The bridgehead is guarded by the **Statue of St. Gellért** which stands halfway up the steep escarpment. It was from here that heathens threw the Bishop from the rocks in 1046 – either tied to a cart or in a barrel – historians are still arguing about which method was actually used.

Szabadság híd, whose original name, Franz-Joseph, still stands on the bridgehead joins Fövám tér (the main customs square) with Gellért tér. The bridge rests on two pillars and has a delicate iron construction which looks like lace. The supporting construction is crowned by

Right: Milling crowds in the 19th century covered market on Fövám Square.

the mythical **Turul bird**, totem of the ancient Magyars. Opposite Fővám tér the "stomach of Budapest" yawns, a large **market hall** built at the end of the 19th century, a huge brick and steel construction typical of this period. Here you can buy absolutely anything to fill your stomach and tickle your palate: Tables bend under the colorful abundance of garden and farm produce; row upon row of sausages hang close together; meat, fowl and fish, fresh or smoked, are laid out for the customer. Countless varieties of pickled vegetables and canned fruits peer from the shelves. In the gallery you will find various folkloric items, manufactured goods and handicrafts.

The **Vigadó**, which was entirely resuscitated after World War Two, including round arches, pillars, friezes, reliefs and dancing figures, proves that this would have been the correct course to take when restoring the Pest bank of the river. Budapesters have nicknamed this former ballroom where concerts and other events take place, "a crystallized stone Csárdás". An attempt to rebuild the south tower of the small **Serbian-Orthodox church** was, however, unsuccessful, for it lists a little. The church has wooden carvings, frescoes and a wonderful iconostasis, and stood directly on the banks of the Danube when it was first built (1791-1801). But around 1870 the bank of the Danube was built up and widened which had the effect of narrowing the river bed. The river was also made deeper and was freed from the sandbanks. It was only in this way that the devastating floods could be avoided, which had visited the town annually. The Danube could flow more quickly and the ice floes, which until then had piled up on the sandbanks and dammed the river, could be carried off by the water.

The Innercity

Buda, on the right bank of the Danube, has the ambience of a provincial town, with its extensive residential areas stretching out towards the west. But **Pest**,

on the other side of the Danube, is very much a metropolis, at least within the confines of the peripheral boulevards. Life is faster here, and far more crowded too, on the pavements as well as on the roads. It is in Pest that you can buy almost anything your heart desires. Goods in the small shops are moderately to exorbitantly over- priced. In the department stores prices are lower, but the choice of wares is not always the best. The most popular shopping area is **Váci utca** and the little streets around it between Erzsébet híd and Vörösmarty tér. The area has brought forth a myriad of bars and restaurants of all shapes, sizes and styles, even American style of McDonald's. Kígyó utca leads to Felszabadulás tér, which is, however, no longer a square (*tér*), but simply a broadened street. Today there is a subway where the town gates once stood in the Middle Ages. The Baroque **Franciscan church** and the

beautiful **Naiad Fountain** are calm points of focus amidst the hectic bustle. In contrast, the little passage, the Párizsi udvar and the baroque Art Nouveau houses next to it, with their Moorish and Venetian features, are anything but calm. The "square" leads imperceptibly into Kossuth Lajos utca and then into Rákóczi út, which ends at the eastern train station. It crosses the small peripheral boulevard, which is called Tanács körút, to the left and Múzeum körút to the right where the **Hungarian National Museum** is situated in the middle of a park surrounded by wrought-iron railings. The museum is a Classical building dating from 1840. It not only provides an overview of Hungarian history from the land- taking (896) to the 1848-49 Revolution, but also houses Hungary's greatest treasures, the Holy Crown of St. István and the royal insignia. Múzeum körút joins Kálvin tér to the south. The simple church here has excellent acoustics and is the venue for extremely popular concerts. Üllöi út, the road which leads to the airport, begins on

Above: Shopping in Budapest's pedestrian zone. Right: Nightlife in the Béke Hotel.

this square. No. 33 is the **Museum of Applied Arts**, a Secessionist construction by Ödön Lechner.

In Tanács körút (left of Rákóczi út) on the corner of Dohány utca is the Romantic synagogue which incorporates Byzantine and Moorish features. The side wing houses the "Collection of Jewish History and Religion". Most of the houses on Rákóczi út date from the second half of the 19th century. The **Chapel of St. Roch** was built after the plague epidemic in 1711 and the St. Roch hospital was built in 1811, replacing the quarantine barracks. This was the markplace of Dr. Ignác Semmelweis, known as the "savior of mothers" for having discovered the cause of the deadly childbed fever (the house where he was born in 1-3 Apród utca on the Buda approach of Erzsébet híd houses the "Semmelweis Museum for the History of Medicine"). The building has a beautiful 18th century façade. In **Café Hauer** at 49, Rákóczi út, you can treat yourself to some excellent cake in a Biedermeier setting. It also makes an

ideal stop before a visit to the **Erkel Theater**, the city's second opera house just around the corner on Andrássy út.

The most splendid street in Pest has to be the two-and-a-half kilometer long **Andrássy út**, which runs from the city center to the City Park. Many of its houses are protected buildings. Most of them are decorated with neo-Renaissance and neo-Baroque sgraffiti, sculptures, reliefs and mosaics. The first third of the street leads into **Oktogon tér**, which takes its name from the corner houses which give it its octagonal shape. The second third of the street, whose row of trees gives it the feeling of a promenade, takes you to Kodály körönd. Villas with gardens grace the last third.

In house No. 3, which has a beautiful gateway and ceiling frescoes in the stairway, you will find the **Posta Múzeum** (Post Office Museum). But the showpiece is the **Opera House** (No. 22), built from plans by Miklós Ybl between 1875 and 1884, and restored at great expense one hundred years later. The interior

matches the splendid exterior. It has a wide stairway, a horseshoe-shaped auditorium on three levels and many ceiling frescoes and murals. In **Nagymezö utca**, which intersects with Andrássy út near the opera house, you will find several smaller theaters, the **Operetta House** (No. 7), the **Ernst Múzeum** (no. 8), and the **Moulin Rouge** night club (no. 15). Just before Oktogon tér, Pest's most splendid street opens into two squares. The northernmost is **Jókai tér**, named after the writer Mór Jókai (1825-1904). His statue on the square was made by Alajos Stróbl. The square opposite was named after the composer Franz Liszt. However, the statue on the square is not of Liszt but the Hungarian poet Endre Ady (1877-1919). **School of Music**, a loadstone of Budapest's music scene as well as the school at which budding musicians are educated, is located at the

Above: Portrait artists with boasts on Vörösmarty Square. Right: One of many pompous allegories on Heroes' Square.

far end of the square. The **State Puppet Theater** (Babszinház) has made its home in a neo-Renaissance building behind Oktogon tér, at No. 69, Andrássy út.

The rounded shape of the **Kodály körönd** is marked by the arched façades of the four houses. The square's, or rather rotunda's, name comes from the composer Zoltán Kodály (1882-1967), who lived in house No. 89 until his death.

The final third of Andrássy út is very wide, and forms the approach to Hösök tere or **Heroes' Square**, with its **Millennium Monument**. This monument symbolizes Hungary's thousand years of history. The statue of the Archangel Gabriel standing on a high column dominates the scene. It is surrounded by a group of bronze horsemen, depicting chieftain Árpád and the other six Magyar tribes. Fourteen statues of Hungarian kings, princes and statesmen stand in the double semi-circular colonnade to the rear of the square. Beneath each one is a relief showing an event from his life. Four allegorical statues representing work and prosperity, war (a rearing horse), peace (a horse at rest), and finally learning and fame, stand on each corner of the colonnade. The square is flanked by two neo-Classical buildings, the **Szépmüvészeti Múzeum** (Museum of Fine Arts) and the **Mücsarnok** (Art Gallery). The former is one of the most important in the world. The core of its exhibits is made up of old masters and a collection of graphics. The collection of Spanish masters from the 15th to the 19th centuries contains 80 exhibits and the Italian masters are represented by several hundred works. In the Dutch section you will find paintings from almost all the schools from Gothic to the Mannerist. German, British and French art is also well represented.

Behind Heroes' Square is the **City Park** with a pond, castle and walks. The park stretches over an area of a square kilometer and is dominated by **Vajdahunyad Castle**. This group of buildings

was built for the millennial celebrations of 1896. The architects incorporated all of the architectural styles found in Hungary in this group of buildings. Today the complex is home to the **Agricultural Museum**. In the courtyard is a monument to Anonymous, the author of the *Gesta Hungarorum*, the oldest surviving Hungarian chronicle (12th century).

The Állatkerti körút begins right behind the **Museum of Fine Arts**, with the **Gundel Restaurant** (No. 2). A few meters away a gate mounted on two stone elephants marks the entrance to the **Zoo**. Budapest's **Circus**, which has made its home next to the zoo, is famous for its delightful program. The next attraction after the zoo is the **Vidámpark**, which means amusement park in English. Another form of recreation is in the **Széchenyi Bath** (No. 11), which has an open air pool and an indoor spa section.

The planners of the Andrássy út wanted this splendid street kept free of traffic. But they did not want to dispense altogether with fast connections to other parts of the city. So they burrowed underground and built the first underground on the continent, modeled on the underground in London. It was completed in 1896, after 20 months of building, right on time for the millennial celebrations.

If time allows you should spend a day in the hills of Budapest. If your feet are tired you can take a more relaxing trip on the **rack railway** which leaves from the Hotel Budapest. It connects with the narrow gauge railway at **Széchenyi Mountain**. The narrow gauge railway ends at **Hüvösvölgy**. A hike or walk in this area is a wonderful experience. It is almost impossible to lose your way here: Most of the paths are clearly posted and hiking guides of the area are available. Try the path from Hüvösvölgy through beech woods to **Kis Hárshegy** and through a grove of oaks where you will also find a lookout tower. A chairlift leads further (Libegö) to the **Jánoshegy** from Zugligeti út from where you can either go for a walk or enjoy the bird's eye view of Budapest from the lookout tower.

BUDAPEST
General

Budapest became one city when Buda and Óbuda on the left (west) bank of the Danube were incorporated with Pest on the right bank into a single administrative unit in 1873. It has 22 districts (in Hungarian: *kerület*, abbr. ker each named and numbered. An address in Budapest includes at least a Roman number referring to this district, or a four-digit zip code, whose middle numbers refer to the district; for example 1095 Budapest is in the 9th district.

Access

All of Hungary's major roads lead to Budapest, and all distances in the country are measured to the zero-shaped milestone to the south of Clark Ádám tér at the Buda end of the Széchenyi lánchíd (chain-link bridge). From Vienna follow the M 1 highway, from the Balaton its the M 7, from the southwest and southeast respectively come Routes 6 and 5, Route 10 bypasses the Danube Bend south of the Pilis mountains, Routes 11 and 2 come from the north along the left and right banks of the Danube respectively; and finally from the east and northeast come Route 4 and the M 3.

Airplanes of foreign companies land at the Ferihegy 1 terminal, the Hungarian MALÉV line serves Ferihegy 2. You can take a cab or a much cheaper bus to the center of town.

Trains from the west arrive mainly at the eastern train station (keleti), those heading south and east use the southern and western stations respectively.

Busses arrive at the main bus station on Erzsébet tér.

Accomodation

LUXURY: **Atrium Hyatt**, 1051 Roosevelt tér 2, Tel: 138-3000; **Duna Intercontinental**, 1052 Apáczai Csere János u. 4, Tel: 117-5122; **Forum**, 1052 Apáczai Csere János u., Tel: 117-8088 (the first three are all on the Pest bank of the Danube); **Béke**, 1067 Erzsébet körút 97, Tel: 132-3300; **Buda-Penta**, 1013 Krisztina körút, 41-43, Tel: 156-6333; **Gellért**, 1111 Szent Gellért tér 1, Tel: 185-2200; **Hilton Budapest**, Hess András tér 1-3, Tel: 175- 1000; **Thermal**, on 1138 Margit Island, Tel: 132-1100. *MODERATE:* **Astoria**, 1053 Kossuth Lajos u. 19, Tel: 117- 3411; **Budapest**, 1026 Szilágyi Erzsébet fasor 47, Tel: 115-3230; **Emke**, 1072 Akácfa u. 1-3, Tel: 122-9230; **Erzsébet**, 1053 Károlyi Mihály u. 11-15, Tel: 138-21-11; **Grand Hotel Hungaria**, 1074 Rákóczi út 90, Tel: 122-9050; **Ifjúság**, 1024 Zivatar u. 1-3, Tel: 135-3331; **Metropol**, 1074 Rákóczi út 58, Tel: 142-1175; **Nemzeti**, 1088 József körút 4, Tel: 133-9160; **Rege**, 1021 Pálos út 2, Tel: 176-7311; **Taverna**, 1052 Váci u. 20, Tel: 138-4999; **Volga**, 1134 Dózsa György út 65, Tel: 129-0200.

BUDGET and *BED-AND-BREAKFAST:* **Hotel Citadella**, 1118 Gellérthegy Citadella sétány, Tel: 166-5794; **Express**, Beethoven u. 7-9, Tel: 175-2528; **Strand**, Pusztakúti út 3, Tel: 167-1999; **Sport** 1021 Szépjuhászné út 9; **Trió**, 1112 Ördögorom út 20/d, Tel: 865-742.

CAMPING: **Hárshegyi**, Hárshegyi út 5-7, Tel: 115-1482; **Római-fürdő**, 1031 Szentendrei út 189, Tel: 188-167.

Note: Firstly, around peak season, especially in Summer when the Formula 1 races are taking place near Budapest, the entire city tends to be booked out. Secondly, do not forget the bargain lodgings offered by the private room service: tourist offices can book you into a room in someone's house or apartment. The system works well.

Restaurants

Budapest is an eater's paradise: For luxurious and not cheap fare, try any of the luxury hotels, for example. Other restaurants in this category are **Alabárdos**, I., Országház u. 2; **Apostolok**, V., Kígyó u. 4-6; **Citadella**, XI., Gellérthegy; **Gundel**, XIV., Állatkerti u. 2; **Mátyás Pince**, V., Március 15 tér 7; **Százéves**, V., Pesti Barnabás u. 2. *MODERATE:* **Halásztanya**, XIII., Váci út **47**; **Kis kakukk**, XIII., Pozsonyi út 12; **Petneházy lovascsárda**, II., Ady-liget, Fekete u.; **Régi Sipos halászkert**, III., Lajos u. 46; **Trombitás**, XII., Moszkva tér. *BUDGET:* **Apród csárda**, VII., Szondi u. 6.; **Bohémtanya**, V., Paulay Ede u. 6; **Megálló**, VII., Tanács körút 23; **Rózsa vendéglö**, VII., Rozsa Ferenc u.; **Tüköry sörözö**, V., Rosenberg Házaspár u. 15.

Cafés

They have made Budapest famous, and legend has it some stayed open throughout the war and the revolution of 1956. Among the most famous are **Gerbeaud** on Vörösmarty tér, **Hungária**, VII., Teréz körút 9-11; **Lukács**, VI Andrássy út 70; **Müvész**, Andrássy út 29; **Korona**, I., Disz tér 16; **Ruszwurm**, I., Szentháromság u. 3..

Tourist Offices

The most important addresses in this rubric are: **IBUSZ**, V., Petöfi tér 3, Tel: which runs non-stop, and **TOURINFORM**, V., Petöfi S. u. 17-19, with a multi-lingual telephone service under 117-9800. Branches of Budapest tourist exist in each train station, and at the following addresses: V., Roosevelt tér 5, Tel: 117-3555; VII., Klauzál u. 1, Tel 122-8848 and Erzsébet körút 41, Tel: 142-6521; XI., Bartók Béla út 42, Tel: 166-6194.

Baths

One way of making a trip in the bustling city more agreeable is to go to one of the thermal baths: **Gellért**, XI. Kelenhegyi út 4-6 (it has an open-air wave pool in summer); **Király**, II., Fö u. 84 (Mo., Wed., and Fri. for men only, Tue., Thur. and Sat. for women); **Rác**: I. Hadnagy u. 8-10; **Rudas** (for men only!), XI. Döbrentei tér 9; **Széchenyi**, Állatkerti út 11.

Nightspots

Several of the luxury hotels run nightclubs with basic floor shows: The Béke Hotel has its **Orfeum**, the **Havanna Club** has nested in the Thermal Hotel on Margitsziget, Hotel Emke boasts the **Maxim varieté**, and finally **Horoszkóp** show is in the Buda Penta. The **Moulin Rouge** at VI., Nagymezö u. 17 and the **Lido**, in the Belvárosi café on Szabadsajtó út 5, Tel: 118-2374.

The major hotels also keep their bars running late at night. Otherwise, drop into the **Casanova** on I., Batthyány tér, the **Pipacs**, V. Aranykéz u. 5, the **Phönix**, VII. Rákóczi út 90 or **Kati jazzbár**, VIII. Szentkirály u. 8. The **Café Pierrot** on I. Fortuna u. is a pleasant way to end the evening. The more active should try the **Petöfi csarnok** (hall) in the park: it becomes a wild disco on Saturday nights, attended by virtually thousands of Budapesters. A little quieter is the **Gösser Disco Bár** on V. Szende Pál utca 1.

Night services

Many ma-and-pa stores have turned to non-stop service in order to cash in on the night hawks. Their wares, ranging from sausages to cigarettes are 10 percent more expensive at night. An increasing number of fast-foodmongers have also gone 24-hours. The post offices next to the western (nyugati) and eastern (keleti) train stations never close. Pharmacies will indicate where the nearest paharmacy on duty is on a list beginning with the words *A legközelebbi éjszakai ügyeletet...*

Emergencies

Police: 07, **Ambulance**: 04, **Fire**, 05. **Towing**: 169-1831 or 169-3714. **Lost and found**: V., Erzsébet tér 5, Tel: 117-4961.

Festivalls and holidays

The first major event to take place in Budapest is the Spring Festival, 10 days or more of music and art centered in Budapest, but spilling into the country. The celebration of St. István's death on August 20th snarls all traffic: it comes with a great fireworks' display. The Formula 1 races in neighboring Mogyoród also create havoc with the city's infrastructure.

Transport

Budapest's public transportation system is a cheap and efficient way of getting around. It has an underground, busses, trams and trolley cars, plus a suburban train system. Driving in Budapest can be nervewracking, especially if one is unfamiliar with its jumble of streets. Taxis are abundant in number, dangerously reckless on the streets but relatively inexpensive. Several cab companies are competing on the market: **Budataxi**: Tel: 120-0200; **Citytaxi**, Tel: 122-8855; **Fötaxi**, Tel: 122-2222; **Gábriel taxi**, 155-5000; **Rádió taxi**, Tel: 127-1271; **Volántaxi**: 166-6666

Excursions

Consult any of the tourist offices to find out about tours in Budapest. These may be expecially handy if you are not planning to spend too much time in the capital. Boat tours including dance cruises and the like are also possible, consult the **MAHART** on the Belgrád rakpart.

Museums

With very few exceptions, all museums in Budapest are open from 10 a.m. to 6 p.m. except on Mondays. The highest concentration of museums is up in the castle which is divided up into several rooms. Building A is the Museum of the Workers' Movement. The National Gallery, covering Hungarian Art from the 11th to the 20th centuries, including stone carvings and religious art, is located in buildings B, C and D. The Royal medieval castle and a collection of Gothic sculptures is located in Building E. On the Tóth Árpád sétány on the northern side of Castle Hill you will find the **War Museum**.

Another museum concentration is near the Millenium monument. When facing the angel, The **Museum of Fine Arts** is on the left; to the right is the exhibition hall for changing exhibitions. The city park (*városliget*) has several museums: The **Agricultural Museum** is in one of the buildings on the Vajdahunyad complex. The **Museum for Transport** is on the Városligeti körút 11.

Hungarian National Museum, Múzeum körút 14-16 covers the history of the Hungarians up to the 1848/49 revolution. The royal insignia and the crown are in an upstairs room. There is also amuseum displaying geological, mineral and animal life in Hungary. One of the most complete collections of Hungarian folklore can be found at the **Museum of Applied Arts** on Üllöi út 33-37. The building itself, designed by the great Secessionist architect Ödön Lechner, is worth inspection. Another folklore- related museum is the **Ethnographic museum** on Kossuth tér.

THE DANUBE BEND

A trip along the Danube from Budapest to Esztergom and back again, either by boat or by car along the panoramic road which runs between the Visegrád and the Pilis Range has a variety of attractions to offer the sightseer. There is the beautiful, rich, natural riverine landscape and the mountain world, with its beech and oak trees, wild boars and deer, who frequently cross the marked hiking and riding paths. The **Pilis Range** consists of individual mountains made of limestone and therefore transpierced in several parts by canes. The slopes are generally steep (though the summits are rounded) and the stamina required to conquer one of them should not be underestimated. Among the most difficult are the Pilisteto (757m) and the Oszoly (329m).

The area between Budapest and Esztergom was inhabited as far back as the Bronze Age. Later Illyrian and Celtic tribes settled here. The Romans later made the Danube here part of the limes, that fortified line dotted with fortifications at the outer edge of their empire. In the 5th century Attila's Huns occupied this area for a short time, and when the Magyars arrived in the 9th century they found Slavic tribes inhabiting the region. Prince Géza chose Esztergom as his permanent residence after he had secured central power. Hungary's first stone fortress, combining religious and defensive functions was erected here in the 11th century. The land around the Danube Bend then flourished until the Mongols destroyed everything they could lay their hands on in 1241. The area recouped its losses and even became prosperous again, when new settlers arrived. But then it fell into the hands of the Turks in 1541. Whatever survived this reign of terror suffered under the sub-

Left: A Serbian-Orthodox cross glitters on a roof of Szentendre.

sequent War of Independence led by Ferenc Rákóczi II (1703-11) against the Habsburgs. Once again a new wave of settlers arrived, mainly Germans, Serbs and Slovaks.

Szentendre

The two important towns on the right bank of the Danube are Szentendre and Esztergom. **Szentendre**, 20 km north of Budapest and built on hills has around 19.000 inhabitants today. It was referred to for the first time in a document from 1146. The town center is a compact complex of architectural gems. Almost every house is under preservation order. The Serbian, that is southeast European atmosphere, still pervades the town to this day, especially when walking through tortuous, hilly alleyways, through passageways and up and down flights of crooked stairs. The first settlers arrived in 1389, fleeing from the Turks who had beaten the Serbian-Bosnian troops in the Battle of Kosovo. After János Hunyadi was defeated at the same location in 1448, a fresh wave of Serbian settlers arrived in Szentendre. But the majority came in around 1690, led by the patriarch Arsenije Crnojevic. Szentendre became the episcopal seat of the Greek-Orthodox Church and thereby a religious and political center for Balkan immigrants.

Of the seven tall church towers in the town, four belong to **Greek-Orthodox churches**. They are Baroque in style, and their interiors, especially their iconostases, are veritable jewels of the genre. The most beautiful is the episcopal church on Alkotmány utca.

Szentendre prospered after the ousting of the Turks. But it was not able to compete with Budapest in the 19th century. Today it is a small, sleepy but atmospheric town – except in the busy holiday months – with many interesting museums and buildings. The central square, Fö tér, is dominated by the slim tower of the

DANUBE BEND

0   10km

Greek-Orthodox **Church of the Annunciation**, with a façade adorned by balconies. It was designed by plans by the prolific architect Andreas Mayerhoffer in 1752. The **Pestilence Cross** in the middle of Fö tér was sponsored in 1763 by Serbian merchants. The railings are particularly beautiful examples of Rococo wrought ironwork. In the neighboring 18th century building (6, Fö tér) you will find the **Károly Ferenczy Museum**, exhibiting pictures, sculptures and tapestries which belonged to the Ferenczys, a famous family of artists, and also a local history and ethnographical collection. A visit in the **György Vastagh House** (Vastagh György u.) to the permanent exhibition of the ceramic artist Margit Kovács, who died in 1977, is an absolute must.

A curved alley leads from Fö tér up to Templom tér, where you will find the Catholic **Parish Church of Saint John**

the Baptist, the oldest church in town. Those parts of the church which survived Turkish destruction were restored in the 18th century in Baroque style. Individual Romanesque elements from the 13th century, and Gothic parts from the 14th and 15th centuries testify to its true age. In the house at 1, Templom tér is an exhibition in memory of the painter Béla Czóbel (1880-1976), the "grand old man" of Hungarian painting in this century.

In the northwest of the town is a large, open-air ethnographical village museum. Material has been gathered from various areas of Hungary, from furnished farmhouses to churches. These exhibits provide a good impression of the peasant life of the last few centuries.

On the way to Esztergom along the Danube you should not miss the second largest Danube island, the **Szentendre sziget**. There are four communities on the island, and a golf course in the romantic northern section. Numerous hiking paths, swimming areas and good restaurants make it an ideal place to stay a while. The

Right: Architectural ornaments recall the wealthy past of Szentendre.

easiest way to reach it is via the bridge of **Tahitófalu**. But there are ferries from both banks of the Danube arms that will carry you across too. The Pokolcsárda (meaning hell's inn in Hungarian) next to the disembarkation point opposite Tahitófalu is not only an excellent place to eat, but also affords a fine view of **Vác**, the largest town on the left bank of the Danube, with a population of 36.000. It was first mentioned in a document from 1075, and suffered similar waves of destruction and restoration to those of the towns on the right bank of the Danube. Like them it was rebuilt in the Baroque style in the 18th century.

Visegrád

The most popular holiday resort between Budapest and Esztergom is **Visegrád**. Its name derives from Slavic words meaning "high fort", suggesting that Slavs once settled here on the remains of ancient Roman fortifications. In 1250, nine years after the Mongol storm, Béla IV began the construction of the lower and upper **castles**. In the following centuries the complex became increasingly splendiferous until it reached its climax under King Mátyás when it became a veritable Renaissance miracle. Miklós Oláh (1493-1568), a contemporary writer and Achbishop of Esztergom, mentions 350 rooms, flower-filled gardens, lime trees in a splendid courtyard, a marble fountain from which red and white wine flowed on feast days and courtiers enveloped in silk brocade. Oláh also describes a chapel with red marble walls, a white alabaster altar and an organ with pipes of pure silver. For a long time this description was considered an old wive's tale. But excavations which have been carried out since 1934 seem to attest to its truth. The Turks, a landslide and the orders of the House of Habsburg to demolish all castles and fortresses in Hungary, turned the riches back into rags. The settlers who came here in the 18th century used the stones to build their houses. From the landing dock a path

leads to 13th century **Solomon's Tower** where a museum has been devoted to King Mátyás. A steep leads up to the stronghold upper fortress, which provides a wonderful panorama of the area. But the most beautiful view is to be found on the lookout tower on **Nagyvillámhegy**. From here you can see beyond the Danube into the Börzsöny Range opposite, with its up to 900 m peaks (paths are marked). For those who do not want to swim in the Danube, there is always the Lepence Pool in the forest. The village of **Nagymaros**, which has a population of 5000 and a pretty Gothic 14th century church, can be reached by ferry. The village once stood in the middle of a picturesque and ecologically important riverine landscape which was destroyed by the construction site of a controversial dam, a joint project between Austria, Czechoslovakia and Hungary.

Above: Iconic detail in the Serbian Orthodox museum of Szentendre. Right: Quiet flows the Danube.

The pretty village of **Dömös** (7 km beyond Visegrád on the road to Esztergom) once won a prize as the most beautiful village on the Danube Bend. It is historically significant, but is known mainly for being the starting point for walks and hikes into the Pilis, Visegrád and Börzsöny mountains. According to legend, the ceiling of the throne room in the Árpád castle, which once stood here, fell on King Béla I. Only ruins are left of the provost building built in 1107. In 1743 its stones were used for the construction of the single-aisled Baroque church. The mountains here provide for wonderful hikes, especially in the Fall, when the leaves don bright colors. Particularly advisable are walks to the **Prédikálószék** or to the bizarre rock formations of the **Vadálló cliffs**.

Esztergom

The episcopal town of **Esztergom** (60 km from Budapest, 32.000 inhabitants) has had an interesting history. As early as

the Neolithic Age there were settlers here. Celts and Romans have left their traces, and Charles the Great built his eastern-most fortress on this site after his son Pip-pin defeated the Avars in 976. Prince Géza built the first stone castle in Hun-gary here in 973, and his son István was crowned here. It was he who made Esztergom a royal residence and an epis-copal town. Under Béla III (1172-96) the town florished for the first time, and 300 years later it experienced a second Gold-en Age under King Mátyás, who gave it its Renaissance traits and turned it into the spiritual and cultural stronghold of the country. With only a few interruptions the Turks ruled the country and the castle between 1543 and 1683. Hungary's great poet Bálint Balassa was killed in one of the blazing battles to win back the castle in 1594. The Italian composer Mon-teverdi also fought in a battle for Eszter-gom. Not until 1820 did the town have an archbishop again. In 1822 construction was begun on the basilica on the **Cathe-dral Hill**. On the August 31st, 1856,

Franz Liszt conducted his own *Gran Mass*, composed especially for the in-augural celebrations (Gran is the German name for Esztergom). The **basilica** is the largest church in Hungary, modeled on St Peter's in Rome. Its bombastic propor-tions have earned for the architectonic experience of the architects Paul Kühnel, János Packh and József Hild. Unfor-tunately these surroundings fail to en-courage Christian thoughts or religious feeling. The burial chapel of bishop Tamás Bakócz on the left hand side of the church nave is the exception. It is a Re-naissance gem, built in 1506-11. It sur-vived the destruction of the old cathedral and was rebuilt in the basilica, stone by stone. The copy of Tizian's *Ascension* above the main altar of the sanctuary begs the question why no Hungarian painter was found to decorate the basil-ica. To the right of the high altar is the en-trance to the treasure vault which really contains treasures here, including chal-ices and monstrances from the 12th cen-tury, the cross of King Mátyás Corvinus,

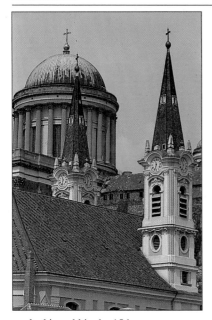

worked in gold in the 15th century, many valuable chasubles and a collection of naive sacred art.

Parts of the medieval **royal palace**, virtually unearthed and turned into a museum lie on a ledge near the basilika on the southern side of the hill. In the first room, alongside fragments of the medieval cathedral, is a model of the royal portal made from red marble, the "porta speciosa". A narrow passage leads from this room into the oldest preserved chamber in Hungary. A spiral staircase takes you to the "János Vitéz Room", the office of Archbishop János Vitéz (1408-1472), King Mátyás' mentor. The room is called "the room of the four cardinal virtues" because of the portrayal of the cardinal virtues on one of the walls. The "triumphal march of the planets" and a horoscope graces the intricate, vaulted ceiling. From here you come to the remains of the chapel built in the 12th century by Bur-

Above: The basilica of Esztergom, one of Hungary's earliest towns and bishoprics.

gundian masters with a wonderful rose window above the portal and fragments of the once flamboyant murals.

More Christian Traces

The **Viziváros** (water town) lies at the foot of the Cathedral Hill. Of all the Baroque buildings, the present-day **Parish Church** built by Jesuits is particularly impressive with its two towers flanking the façade. The town seems to be gathered around Széchenyi tér, once upon a timethe medieval market square. The Baroque houses, including the **Town Hall**, open up into green parks and exude great harmony. Museum connoisseurs will enjoy the **Museum of Christian Art** in the former Bishop's Palace (Zsigmond berény). It was founded in the 19th century. The core of its exhibits comes from the royal and episcopal treasuries, which were rescued from the Turks. This collection was increased through purchases and gifts. It includes the "Schnütgen Collection" from Cologne and the "Lemann Collection" from Vienna. This museum is very highly esteemed among European museums for its great wealth of paintings and art from all important eras of European religious art, its icons, chalices and sacred objects. A walk up **Szent Tamás hegy** (Hill of Saint Thomas) in the east of the town is rewarded by a charming view. The crucifixion scene standing here was erected in 1781, the chapel was built 40 years later. Kossuth Lajos utca leads to the wooded path that climbs up to the top of the 700 m **Dobogókö**. The watch-tower gives a wide view of the surrounding countryside. On a clear day one can even see the Tátra Mountains in Czechoslovakia. Another way of getting close to the stars though, is to visit the **Esztergom Observatory** (in the Sándor Petöfi House of Culture), which was erected on the site of Hungary's first observatory, built under King Mátyás.

ESZTERGOM
Accomodation
MODERATE: **Hotel Fürdö**, Bajcsy-Zsilinszky u. 14, Tel: 292; **Hotel Esztergom**, Primás-sziget, Nagy Duna sétány, Tel: 81-68. *BUDGET*: **Hotel Volán**, József Attila tér 2, Tel: 271. *CAMPING*: **Vadvirág**, Bánomi dülö.

Restaurants
Hotels **Volán** and **Fürdö** both have restaurants. **Kispipa étterem**, Kossuth Lajos u. 19; **Csülök csárda**; Batthyány Lajos u. 9; **Hurka csárda**, Babits Mihály út.

Tourist Offices
Komtourist, Széchenyi tér 13, Tel: 484; **IBUSZ**, Mártírok u. 1, Tel: 100.

Sightseeing
Esztergom is a museum town: **Museum of Christian Art** (Berényi Zs. u. 2), **Water Museum** (Kölcsey u. 2), **Bálint Balassa Museum** (Bajcsy-Zsilinszky út 63), **Fortress Museum** (Szent-István tér I), **Treasure Chamber of the Cathedral**.

Telecommunications
A word is necessary about it here: As of writing calls to Budapest have to go through an operator.

Note: Between the Árpád bridge in Budapest and the bordercrossing to Czechoslovakia in Esztergom, there are no bridges crossing the Danube, only ferries. Szentendre Island is connected to the left bank of the Danube by a bridge at Tahi.

DANUBE BEND
Accomodations
VISEGRÁD: *MODERATE:* **Hotel Silvanus**, Fekete-hegy, Tel: (26) 136-063. *BUDGET*: **Hotel ELTE**, Fö u. 117, Tel: (26) 28-165; **Hotel Vár**, Fö u. 9-11, Tel: (26) 28-264. *CAMPING:* Széchenyi u. 7, Tel: (26) 28-330; **Mogyoró-hegy**, Tel: (26) 28-217. The Danube Bend is a touristically frequented spot, meaning that a number of bed-and-breakfasts have mushroomed in the local towns on both sides of the river. Some are registered with the local tourist office, others have signs indicating "Zimmer frei", i.e., rooms for rent. You may want to stay in such quiet little villages as Nagymaros or Veröcemaros on the right bank.

Restaurants
In the hotels **Silvanus** and **Vár**; **Fekete Holló**, Rév u. 12; **Sirály étterem**, Rév u. 15; **Diófa Kisvendéglö**, Fö u. 48.
In **Nagymaros**, **Mátyás vendéglö**, Magyar u. 24; **Maros vendéglö**, Kossuth tér 2.

Tourist Offices
Dunatours, Fö u. 3/a, Tel:(26) 28-330.

Sightseeing
The **fortress** in Visegrád attracts a great deal of attention especially when it hosts the summer festival; and the **Pilis mountains** behind it are ideal for long hikes. The controversial dam of **Nagymaros** is also an attraction in its own right.

Museums
Mátyás király Museum, Fö u. 23, open from May to November (closed Mondays); the same applies to the **Salomon Tower**.

SZENTENDRE
Accomodations
MODERATE: **Hotel Danubius**, Ady E. u. 28, Tel: (26) 12-511. *BUDGET:* **Hotel Party**, Ady E. u. 5, Tel: (26) 12-491; **Hotel Sziget**, Pap-sziget, Tel: (26) 10-697. *CAMPING:* On the Pap-sziget, Tel: (26) 10-697. There are also several pleasant camping sites on the long Szentendrei Island that stretches all the way up to the Danube Bend itself. Inquire ath the tourist offices about bed-and-breakfast (*panzió* or *fogadó*) possibilities as well.

Restaurants
Aranysárkány, Vörös Hadsereg útja. 2; **Béke étterem**, Fö tér 19; **Muskátli**, Rakodczay u. 1; **Rab Rábi**, Péter-Pál u. 1/a; **Görög Kancsó**: Görög u. 1.; **Szigetgyöngye étterem**, Pap-sziget.

Tourist Offices
Dunatours, Vörös Hadsereg útja 1, Tel: (26) 11-311; **IBUSZ**, Vörös Hadsereg útja 15, Tel: (26) 10-515.

Sightseeing
Szentendre is one of the prettiest towns on the Danube. It is particularly famous for its Serbian-Orthodox churches, for its artists' colony and for its many art museums. A special treat is the **Café Nostalgia** after all is said and done. Numerous art galleries in Szentendre are open from Tues.-Sun. from 10 a.m. to 6 p.m. (April - Oct.31). **Barcsay Collection**, Dumtsa Jenö u.10; **Czöbel Museum**, Templom tér 1; **Ferenczy Museum**, Marx ter 6; House of Folk Art, Rákóczi u.1. the **Ethnographical Open Air Museum** on Szabad Farrás út is open from 9 a.m. to 5 p.m. every day, but only from April 1 to October 31.

VÁC
Accomodation
Tabán panzió, Korvin lépcsö 3; **Lovas panzió**, Váchartyán, Veres Pálné u. 3

Restaurants
Halászkert (fish specialties), Liszt Ferenc sétány 9; **Pokol csárda**, on Szentendrei Island; **Fehér Galamb**, Lenin u. 37.

Tourist Offices
Dunatours, Széchenyi u. 14, Tel: (27) 10-940.

WEST OF BUDAPEST

The district of Fejér west of Budapest has much to offer in the way of sightseeing and relaxation. 32 km from the center of town in the little village of **Martonvásár**, the Brunswick dynasty had a castle built in the middle of a 40 hectare park. The time of construction, 1773-1775, gave it initially a Baroque look, but a century later it was redone in neo-Gothic, according to English taste. The current attractions include the Beethoven Concerts held annually, as well as walks under tall trees along well-maintained paths. The concerts are held in homage to the great composer, who was a frequent guest of this castle between 1800 and 1806. This is where he met the three women who were to affect him until his death: Giulietta Guiccardi, and Therese and Josephine von Brunswick. He dedicated his *Moonlight Sonata* to Giulietta, the "beautiful devil". But his love for her was not requited. To his almost motherly soul friend, Therese von Brunswick, he dedicated one of his most beautiful sonatas, *op. 78 in F sharp major*. Therese, who founded the first Hungarian nursery school on the English model in 1828, was one of the most fascinating women of the 19th century. Her mortal remains rest in the crypt of the castle church.

Lake Velence

The **Velencei tó**, or Venetian Lake, begins only a few kilometers behind Martonvásár. From northeast to southwest it measures 26 square kilometers, it is 10 km long, about 2.5 km wide and 1 - 2 m deep. This shallowness means that it warms up quickly to 22- 26 °C in summer, and freezes solid in a real winter. No one knows where its name comes from. It

Left: A poetic instant in Hungary's oldest city Székesfehérvár.

hardly seems possible that people would have wanted to evoke the spirit of Italy's venerable town. It is more probable that the name derives from the metal weathervanes the local fishermen used to affix to their roofs. These, namely, were also called *Velence*.

Almost a third of the lake is covered in reeds which are harvested in winter and serve as nesting grounds for rare species of birds in spring and summer. According to one folk tale, three of the herons who migrate here every spring are in fact three sisters who escaped the Turks by turning themselves into these graceful birds. The lake is suitable for sailing, wind surfing and fishing (but only with a permit). **Pákozd** on the north shore can be reached by passenger boat from Velencefürdö, Gárdony and Agárd on the busy southern shore. This little village has an important history, for it was here that the Hungarians won a battle against the Habsburgs during the Revolution (1848-49). The obelisk commemorating the battle stands on a nearby hill right beside a small museum devoted to the great struggle. From here you can see far across the lake and into the **Velence Hills** in the north. These are the oldest elevations in Hungary formed from magma and granite. A walk through the wonderful woods to **Meleg Mountain**, the highest peak (351 m) near Nadap is charming and not at all tiring. The unique *ingókövek* or "oscillating stones" are colossal stones, fixed to the ground at one point only, that sway in the wind.

Székesfehérvár

About 10 km from the western end of Lake Velence and 69 km from Budapest is Hungary's oldest town, **Székesfehérvár**. It is surrounded by hills and looks across a wide plain. Before 1557, 38 kings were crowned here. Some of them were buried here too. Strictly speaking, Székesfehérvár's history begins with the

Roman town of *Gorsium*, a few kilometers to the southeast near the present-day village of **Tác**. Gorsium was a wealthy and important town at the intersection of seven trade routes, in an area which was already inhabited during the Copper, Bronze and Iron Ages. Excavations have been relatively easy, for Gorsium was only covered by a thin layer of earth and not by a new town. Indications of a prosperous past have come to light. Prince Árpád is supposed to have set up camp here after crossing the Danube. Prince Géza did not, however, he built his town on the old Roman town (an exception in the history of Hungarian town building). For strategic reasons he preferred the four small islands in the middle of the reed-covered swamplands of the time that marked the region's landscape at the time. Where the center of Székesfehérvár is located today he built Fehérvár, a for-

Above: The main square of Székesfehérvár with the "national apple" fountain by Béla Ohmann.

tified town defended by moats and trenches. He also built his castle and a chapel, his resting place after death. In the symbolism of ancient Hungarian, the word *fehér* (white) is the color suggesting the kind of honor due a person of the ruling caste. The oldest coherent written sentence in the Hungarian language found until now refers to this town. It reads "a feheruuara rea meneh hodu utu rea" and means "on the military road which leads to Fehérvár".

István I (997-1038) extended the town center using building materials found in Gorsium, and he made Székesfehérvár, which was first mentioned in documents from 1002 as *Alba Regia* and *Alba Civitas*, the center of his Christian state. His throne (*szék*) stood in the basilica which he had built. This was also where his crown and insignia and the State Treasury were kept.

In 1543, two years after the taking of Buda, the Turks arrived in Székesfehérvár. When they were ousted in 1688 the town had been reduced to ashes and was almost devoid of human life. Only the simple **Chapel of Saint Anna**, originally a modest cemetery church, survived as a witness to the town's glorious past. Koranic inscriptions and ornamental paintings on the walls show that it was used by the Turks as a prayer house. It stands in the present-day Arany János utca, surrounded by low, old town houses not far from the late-Baroque **cathedral** with its twin towers.

The old **basilica** also survived the Turkish wrath. Until the end of the 18th century masses were still held in its burial chapel. Bishop János Milassin had it demolished and used the stones to build himself a pretty **palace** in Zopf style. His coat-of-arms on the gable serves as an eternal reminder of the first owner. But although this building, with its Empire and Biedermeier furnishings and its valuable library, is among the gems of the town, it cannot compensate for his wanton destruction of the cathedral.

The Baroque Town

The new town which grew up in the 18th century bears all the typical hall marks of the Austrian Baroque. The damage it suffered during the Second World War was unfortunaly great. The loveliest square is **Szabadsag tér**. The sculpture at its center, the **Apple of the Nation** on the back of a lion, symbolizes the former importance of the old royal town. At the eastern end of the square is a **Garden of Ruins** with the remains of the royal basilica. The 106 m long stone wall here, however, is a remnant of the old castle. In the **Mausoleum of the Lapidarium** is a sarcophagus of Roman origin with Ventian-Byzantine stonemasonry. It was probably the last resting place of István I, but this cannot be said with any certainty because vandals, superficial archaeological work and floods caused by rising ground water have all made an irreparable mess of the kings buried here.

Some visitors to Hungary look almost exclusively for works by the great Austrian (born Swabian) painter Franz Anton Maulbertsch. They will find them in the Baroque **seminary church** in Petöfi utca. His frescoes covering Marian themes and his side altar paintings compete for magnificence with the Baroque seating and the glorious Rococo interior. The Baroque carvings in the **Cistercian church** built in 1745-51 are also worth seeing, especially the Rococo carvings in the sacristy.

The wonderful Rococo interior of the **Fekete Sas Gyógyszertár**, the "Black Eagle Apothecary" opposite the church, dates from the same period. Only a few paces from here in northerly direction is Gargarin tér and the **King István Museum**, which houses exhibits from all over the district from pre-historic times onward. The **István Csók Gallery** (1, Bartók utca) gives a good overview of Hungarian art in the 20th century. The architecture of the house at 12, Arany János utca, a single-storey dwelling built in 1781 in the style typical for the day, with a beautiful arcade in the courtyard, is far more impressive than the exhibition up on the first floor. It is devoted to the Ybl family whose most important issue was Miklós Ybl, an extremely prolific architect at the end of the 19th century responsible for, among others, the opera house in Budapest.

The Monks of Majk

If you drive from Székesfehérvár to the north via **Mór** and further along the foot-hills of the wooded Vértes hills, you will eventually come to the village of **Majk**. It is the site of one of Hungary's most interesting groups of Baroque buildings: the former "hermitage of the silent monks", the Camaldoli monks or Romualdines as they were also known. This order, which was a branch of the Benedictines, named itself after the settlement of Camaldoli in

the upper Arno Valley, which was established in 1018. Its sponsor was San Romualdo, Duke of Ravenna, Abbot of the Classe Monastery near Ravenna. He and his followers lived as hermits striving for a higher level of spiritual perfection. Although he had already come to Hungary in 1012 with 24 of his brothers to convert the local heathens, it was not until 1748 that the first Camaldoli monks actually settled in the country. They chose Majk, possibly because the Esterházy family was willing to donate some of its land to them. Aristocrats and church dignitaries supported them financially. Each of the 17 brothers of the order received an approxiamtely 100 square meter cell with a chapel and living quarters. The brothers dedicated their lives entirely to prayer and learning. They were only allowed to talk to each other twice a year. They had a huge vegetable garden in which their food was grown.

Above: Velence (Venice) Lake, a refreshing place only a stone's throw from Budapest.

What remains of this monastic community is a castle, the 17 cells and a lonely tower looking over a distant countryside, once part of a church that was destroyed at the end of the 18th century. Below ground is a historical puzzle that remains to be solved, a man-made system of caves eight stories deep. The passageways were discovered at the bottom of a well. Many objects such as coins, tools and ceramics were discovered here, some date as far as back to Roman times.

The industrial town of **Tatabánya** can be reached via **Környe** (where you come across the remains of the Roman settlement *Quirinium*). Tatabánya has ironworks, a cement factory, coal and aluminium works, and is on the motorway from Vienna to Budapest. About 10 km north of the exit is **Vértesszöllös**, where Hungarian archaeologists not only found the bones of prehistoric humans, who lived more than 5 million years ago, but have also found traces of primitive religious activity, tools and unique evidence of practical application of fire.

LAKE VELENCE

General: The lake, known as the "Balaton's grandchild" is another favorite vacation spot, especially for Budapesters looking for some quick relief from the city. Like the Balaton, its touristic infrastructure is fairly extensive, whereby the southern shore by far outweighs the northern shore. From about mid-September on many hotels and restaurants remain closed.

Access

Route 70 through Érd and Martonvásár or M 7 highway and take the Gárdony exit.

GÁRDONY AND AGÁRD
Accomodation

BUDGET: **Cápa Hotel**, Balatoni út, (in Velence), Tel: 498; **Hotel Agárd**, Akácfa u., Tel: 115; **Hotel Viking**, Gallér u. Tel: 577; **Touring Hotel**, on the beach, Tel: 118. *CAMPING:* **Nemeskócsag**, Akácfa u.; **Park**, Chernel I. u. 56-58. There are further accomodations in Gárdony, Kápolnyásnyék (inquire at the tourist offices) and of course in Székesfehérvár (see below).

Restaurants

At the **Touring Hotel**, **Nádas vendéglö**, Balatoni út; **Ponty étterem**, Szabadság u. 8, Gárdony; **Halászcsárda**, Balatoni út 2, Agárd; **Csutora kisvendéglö**, Balatoni út 133, Agárd. On the northern shore, east of Pákozd is a road leading to a pleasant little csárda on the lakeside.

Tourist Offices

Albatours has an office at the Nemeskócsag camping site, Akácfa u., Tel: 115. **Cooptourist** keeps an office Balatoni út 43, Tel: 48.

Sightseeing

Vacationeering on Lake Velence is the main sport: sun, surf, sail, tennis, bowling and so forth. Ship tours are available on the lake too. Try and visit the **nature reserve** between Dinnyés and Pákozd, famous for its ornithological life. Gárdony has museum in the **birth house of Géza Gárdony**, author of *The Stars of Eger*, a historical novel. In Pákozd is a museum and memorial to a major battle in 1848.

SZÉKESFEHÉRVÁR
Accomodation

MODERATE: **Hotel Alba Regia**, Rákóczi u. 1, Tel: (22) 13-484. *BUDGET*: **Hotel Velence**, Március 15. u. 10, Tel: (22) 11-262; **Törökudvar tourist lodgings**, Jókai u. 2, Tel: (22) 12-494.

Restaurants

In the hotels mentionned above; **Ösfehérvár étterem**, Szabadság tér 3; **Szabadság étterem**, Vörösmarty tér 1; **Árpád étterem**, József Attila u. 54; **Kiskulacs étterem**, Népköztársaság u. 56.

Tourist Offices

Albatours, Szabadság tér 6, Tel: (22) 21-235; **Cooptourist**, Rákóczi u. 3, Tel: (22) 14-391; **IBUSZ**, Ady E. u. 2, Tel: (22) 11-510.

Sightseeing

Ancient Roman remains ca. 25 km southwards in Tác. Medieval ruins on Fö tér, numerous museums: **Saint István Museum** (Gagarin tér 3), closed Mondays. **Fekete Sas Pharmacy Museum** (Március 15.u.), closed Mondays, **Construction Museum** (Arany János u. 10), closed Mondays, **Museum of the Aluminium Industry** (Zombori u. 12) closed Mondays and several galeries: **Art gallery** (Március 15. u. 6); **Csók István Gallery**, (Bartók Béla tér 1); **Schaár Erzsébet Collection**, (Jókai u. 11). The Franciscan Church on Fö tér.

TATABÁNYA AND TATA
Accomodation

TATABÁNYA: *MODERATE:* **Hotel Árpád**, Felszabadulás tér 1, Tel: (34) 10-299. *BUDGET:* **Rozmaring Inn**, Árpad u. 17, Tel (34) 10-824. *CAMPING:* **Nomád camping**, Tolnai u. 14, Tel: (34) 11-507.

TATA: *MODERATE:* **Hotel Diana**, Remeteségpuszta, Tel: (34) 80-388. *BUDGET:* **Hotel Kristály**, Ady E. u. 22, Tel: (34) 80-577; **Hotel Malom**, Szabadság tér 8, Tel: (34) 81-530; **Hotel Pálma**, Néppark, Tel: (34) 80-577. Inns and tourist lodgings are located at the **Öreg-tó camping**, Fáklya u. 1, Tel: (34) 80-496, and the **Fényesfürdö camping**, Fényes fasor, Tel: (34) 81-591.

Restaurants

TATABÁNYA: At the **Hotel Árpád**; **Hét Vezér étterem**, Kond vezér u..

TATA: At the **Hotel Diana** and **Hotel Kristály**; **Aranyponty étterem**, Vértesszölösi út; **Fényes étterem**, Görög hösök útja 2; **Halászcsárda**, Nagytó-part.

Tourist Offices

TATABÁNYA: **Komtourist**, Györi u. 12.

TATA: **Komtourist**, Ady E. u. 24, Tel: (34) 81-855; **Cooptourist**, Tóparti sétány 18, Tel: (34) 81-602.

Sightseeing

TATABÁNYA: The great millenial Turul bird up on the mountain and the Selim caves. Excursion to Zsámbék. **TATA**: The Öreg-tó (Old Lake), **German-Hungarian Museum**, Alkotmány u. 1 (closed on Mondays). The **Museum of Graeco-Roman sculpture** on Rákóczi u. (closed Mondays). The **Kuny-Domokos museum** in the old fortress (closed Mondays). A very worthwhile excursion is to the prehistoric excavation site of Vértesszöllös.

POLAND
• Brno
CZECHOSLOVAKIA
U.S.S.R.
Vienna •
• Bratislava   Miskolc •
AUSTRIA   The Mountains
    Around   Great Puszta
Györ •   Budapest
Little Plain   Budapest   Debrecen •
    HUNGARY
    Between
Balaton   Danube   Békés
    Southern   and Tisza   and
    Danube   Csongrad
Around   Szeged •
Pécs
• Zagreb   Pécs   ROMANIA
YUGOSLAVIA

BETWEEN DANUBE AND TISZA

JÁSZSÁG
JÁSZBERÉNY
CEGLÉD
KECSKEMÉT
KUNSÁG

Leaving Budapest in an easterly direction you soon come to the Pest Plain whose flatness and at times desolate feeling reminds one that it is indeed a just another section of the famous puszta. Most of the towns here still have their sights set very clearly on the capital. Their inhabitants make long journeys by car or by train on a daily basis, to work in the capital where wages are higher. But even the extra money that they can earn in the city has a long way to go, so most of the families try to earn extra income from raising small animals or growing vegetables.

This is the case in **Gödöllö**, a Baroque town surrounded by hills. It is one of the most popular destinations for art lovers. This is hardly surprising, for **Grassalkovich Castle**, whose vigorous history belies the sleepiness of the surrounding town, is well worth a visit. Once the place where royalty used to come to take a rest of from its busy social and political schedule, it is now an old peoples' home. In the meantime it played a significant role as the site of the war council during the 1848-49 revolution. The Red Army's General Chief of Staff had its headquar-

Preceding pages: Vacation homes east of Budapest. Left: Life in the country is often colorful thanks to the gypsies.

ters in the castle in 1919, and it also served Admiral Horthy well during the years 1920-1944. Despite extensive interior changes, at least it is still standing – in marked contrast to many other Hungarian castles which have fallen into disrepair for lack of money and interest. The Gödöllö castle, built between 1744 and 1747 in Baroque style, was commissioned by Count Grassalkovich. In 1867 it was renovated by the architect Miklós Ybl who added two cupolas. The Baroque **calvary** nearby and the **Statue of Mary** also deserve mention. A little further out off route 30 in the section of town called **Máriabesznyö** stands a Baroque church with several interesting features, notably an ebony statue of Mary and the crypt of the Grassalkovich family, decorated by the great Dorffmeister. On the whole, Gödöllö is a pleasant town to spend a little time in. Its high gables and peasant houses deserve a glance, and for a refreshing walk, there is always the arboretum on the road to **Isaszeg**.

On the northern border of the Great Hungarian Plain lies **Hatvan**, a local economic lodestone and an important crossroads between the western and eastern part of the country. The origin of the name is not clear, but some suggest that its distance to Budapest, 60 km, (60 is *hatvan* in Hungarian) played a role here.

149

Its history can be traced back as far as the Middle Ages. It was a small market town in the 13th to 15th centuries. In 1544 the townspeople themselves set their unprotected town on fire, rather than leave it to the Turks. In 1849 an important battle in the Hungarian Revolution took place nearby. Today Hatvan is a typical industrial town, with a new residential area called "New"-Hatvan built up in the way one might expect. And yet this town still has many cultural treasures, including a Baroque **castle** on the main square, which was built for the Grassalkovich family in 1754. Today it houses a small hospital and a park. Another important building on the square is the Baroque **Roman- Catholic church**.

Jászság

The area around the Zagyva river is called **Jászság** for historical and ethno-

Right: The Catholic church in Jászberény, a Baroque mark by András Mayerhoffer.

graphical reasons. But geographically it is little different to its surroundings. The history of the Jazygians can be traced far back in time. According to archaeologists a variety of peoples has always lived here. Traces have been found of settlements from the Stone Age to the Iron Age. The Jazygians arrived here under King Béla IV at the beginning of the 13th century. They migrated together with the Cumans from the area around the Caspian sea, and were granted royal privileges which applied until 1702 when Kaiser Leopold I sold the area to an order of German knights. Several decades later the Jazygians and the Cumans bought back their privileges. But the isolation and insulation of the Jazygians came to an end in 1876 when administrative reforms dissolved the Jász-Kun district and divided it up amongst several districts. This also signalled the end of the Jazygians' history.

Like the Cumans, the Jazygians earned their living mainly from cattle breeding. A wealthy farmer would own two or three farmsteads in addition to his own house in the town. This way of life presupposed the existence of an "extended family" to function. This meant that when a son married he did not leave the family home, but remained to work with his father on the lands they shared. Each farmstead specialized in a certain breed of cattle. This diversity was reflected in the popular Jazygian markets, attended by people from far and wide. The products of the Jazygian smithies, for example, and the furriers were particularly sought-after, for they were known for their high quality products.

Jászberény

To the south east of Hatvan lies **Jászberény**, a town of 31.000 inhabitants first mentioned in documents from 1357. It has always been the most densely populated town in the area. From 1565 it was awarded special privileges by the Sultan, and thus became an oasis in a region otherwise laid waste by the Turks. The inhabitants of other towns destroyed by the Turks fled to Jászberény, which contributed to its growth. By 1715 it was the sixth largest town in Hungary. But in the middle of the last century this growth stopped, and in the course of intense industrialization in other parts of the country it was overtaken by other cities.

The river Zagyva and its island is the main feature of the town. At the entrance to the island is **a statue of Déry**, one of Hungary's most popular actresses from the last century. Further along the path stands the **open-air theater**, built in 1959 with seating for 1400 people. Still further on you will see the Gothic **Franciscan church**, which dates back to 1472. This single-aisled building has its tower on the north side of the chancel, as is common in the churches of this particular mendicant order. The church was rebuilt in the second half of the 18th century in Baroque style. But its paintings are by masters from the 20th century. The church is next to a Baroque cloister built in 1730 whose dining room furnishings have been placed under the protection of a museum. In front of the church entrance stands a **statue of Mary** and in the garden are the stations of the cross, painted with traditional motifs, dating from 1776.

Kossuth Was Here

Jászberény's epicenter is **Lehel tér**, named after one of the Magyar chieftains. Its most important building is the Catholic parish church built during the 18th and 19th centuries. Its interior is also from the same period, yet many of its details still are Baroque, including the sculptures of the twelve apostles, the sacristy door and the candelabras. The parsonage church near by also has Baroque features. This contrasts with the **Rosalia Chapel**, built in 1839 in more

sober Classical style. But even this chapel has painted Baroque sculptures on either side of it. This group of monuments was enlarged in 1831 by the addition of a statue of the Trinity.

The square itself is usually buzzing with activity, people running around apparently indifferent to the significance of local monuments. If you look towards east you will spot a Classical building from 1827, whose courtyard reveals architectural traces of the earlier Baroque and Rococo periods. In the southern part of the square is the deepest **artesian well** in town, and opposite it the former **Pannonia Hotel**, built in 1837. Lajos Kossuth held a speech to the people here in 1849. The Classical **Town Hall** also has a great deal to offer art lovers, not only because it is a splendid building, but also because of the **Jász Museum** that has been housed in it since 1874. The most famous exhibit, the ivory "Horn of Lehel", is carefully kept separate from other exhibits. According to legend it belonged to the above-mentioned tribal

chieftain. It appears, however, to have been made in Byzantium in the 11th or 12th century. Lehel himself died in 955. The carvings show scenes from a Byzantine circus.

Most of the Plain between the Danube and the Tisza is included in the area known as **Kiskunság**. Like the Jazygians, the Cumans had fled from the Tatars at the beginning of the 13th century. They settled mainly in three towns: Cegléd, Nagykörös and Kecskemét. These flatlands melt into the Pest Plain, surrounded by the Gödöllö Hills to the north. It is bordered to the east by the Tisza and by the floodlands of the Danube in the west.

Cegléd is one of the typical towns of the Great Hungarian Plain. It also plays an important role as a crossroads between the various parts of the country. The first documents making any mention of the town date from 1290, but archeologists in

Above: One horsepower transportation, quiet and ecological. Right: Taking it easy out in the country.

their infinite wisdom suggest that it was a settlement even in prehistoric times. In 1444 it became a market town. During the Hungarian Peasants' War of 1514 the "Peasant King" György Dózsa held a famous speech here, after which 2000 men joined his army of disaffected peasants. Under the Turkish occupation it was the Sultan's town, and so escaped extermination. After the departure of the Turks, Cegléd retained its sense for independence. At the beginning of the Revolution of 1848, Lajos Kossuth began his recruitment drive here. This time again, many thousands of men were persuaded to fight following his impassioned speech. Kossuth's oak table, on which he stood to deliver the speech, stood on what is today **Freedom Square** (Szabadság tér). This place has been marked by a statue of Kossuth since 1902.

The town center consists of two adjoining squares: Kossuth Square and Freedom Square. On the first you will find a **Roman-Catholic church** built in 1825. It has a fire tower and a gallery

with an altar and two sculptures of an-gels. The eclectic **Town Hall** also com-petes for space on this square. The most noticeable building on Freedom Square is the **Protestant church** with a cupola in Classical style. Construction started in 1825 but the church was not completed until 1896. Not far from the square the **Kossuth Museum** exhibits such things as Kossuth's afore-mentioned oak table, his furniture, his clothing and other relics. A little further on, on **Széchenyi Street** is a 1200 meter deep spring, from which water at a temperature of 65 °C is drawn for the thermal baths and the open air swimming pool.

Nagykörös, 15 km south of Cegléd, was mentioned as far back as 1266. After the Tatar campaigns it increased its boun-daries by purchasing eight neighboring villages. In 1368 it was awarded the sta-tus of a market town. During the Turkish occupation the town was protected by the Sultan. This had the effect of further in-creasing the population and the size of the town. At this time its grazing lands stretched from Pest to the Tisza and was used by 8 to 11 thousand head of cattle. Together with Cegléd and Kecskemét its task was to supply the Turks guarding Buda Castle with money and provisions. For quite a time Nagykörös acted as a major economic rival ato Kecskemét.

The Sultan's Favorite: Kecskemét

It was far from easy to settle on the sea of sand which covered the area between the Danube and the Tisza. For this reason vines and fruit trees were planted here as far back as the Middle Ages. The garden town which you will find today was built up on this horticultural tradition.

On **Szabadság tér** (Freedom Square) in the town center you will find the **Prot-estant church**, built originally in the 15th century, but renovated and rebuilt many times since then. Its 52 meter high "Red Tower" was enlarged and given a helmet-shaped steeple in 1808. There is also a tall, narrow Classical **Roman-Catholic church** which dates from the

18th century. The Baroque erstwhile **Town Hall**, with its fire tower and protruding gable, was built around 1710. Its façade was rebuilt in 1811. Other interesting sights on this central square are: the statue of Kossuth, the old school built in 1830 where poet József Arany once tought and, on the southern end, a number of sturdy, patrician dwellings (A little aside here: Statues of Kossuth are not only to be found all over Hungary: The national hero has recently been granted a place in the Capitol in Washington. He is the seventh non-American to be awarded this honor.)

The **Protestant Cemetery** also calls for a visit for its strange, carved wooden grave markers recalling those ancient times when the Magyars were still nomads. For some restful activities a visit the the **thermal baths** is recommended. If you want to relax a while after your long walk, why not visit the thermal

Above left: Kecskemét, the Sultan's favorite town. Above right: Summer festivities.

swimming pool? The water is 34-35 °C and comes from a 950 meter deep well.

Kecskemét is the largest town between the Danube and the Tisza. Its name comes from the Hungarian word for goat (*kecske*). This explains the goat which can be seen on the omnipresent coat-of-arms. In the Middle Ages, Kecskemét was protected by a moat instead of a wall on which the present-day peripheral boulevard was built. This means that the course of the moat can still be traced.

Turkish rule determined the fate of the town for 150 years. Fortunately, however, Kecskemét appealed to the Sultans, who did not apply the same destructive measures as they did elsewhere. The surrounding plain, densely populated during the Middle Ages, was almost completely "cleared" during Turkish rule, and only the few towns which were protected by the Sultan were spared. In time Kecskemét became the third largest town in Hungary, mainly due to the waves of refugees who settled here from other parts of the land. Its inhabitants earned their livings primarily by small businesses and cattle trading. Industry began to develop around the turn of the century, based mainly on agriculture. Europe's largest **chicken farm** is one of the main local employers as is the second largest cannery in the country.

Its striking and colorful Majolika tiles come from the **Zsolnay porcelain factory** in Pécs. Opposite the palace stands the recently restored and onion-domed **synagogue**, built between 1864 and 1871 in Romantic-Moorish style by János Zitterbach and serving today as a center of science and technology, with exhibits illustrating these two fields. On Szabadság tér you will find the eclectic **New College**, built in 1913 serving as the towns music school. In front of the building are statues of the composers Béla Bartók and Zoltán Kodály who was born in Kecskemét. Szabadság tér joins **Kossuth tér**, which boasts a total of three churches. The first a Catholic one, was built by Gáspár Oswald between 1774 and 1805 in typical eighteenth-century style, the tower is of later date. The second, the St. Nicholas Church, was granted to the Franciscans in 1647 who later redid the interior in standard Baroque taste. They were also responsible for the neighboring house, which today houses the **Zoltán Kodály Music Institute**. The third church was already mentioned; it is the Protestant church with the "Red Tower" built originally in 1683 and enlarged in a century later. In the meeting room you will find frescoes from the last century depicting important stages in Hungarian history.

The large brick building with the Kecskemét coat-of-arms, the **Town Hall**, is the work of the great Secession architect Ödön Lechner. The frescoes inside were painted by the equally talented Bertalan Székely. Not far from the square, next to the former **Piarist School**, you will find the Baroque Piarist church, built in 1740. Inside it has a single aisle, its chancel is slightly raised over the crypt which it is supported on four pillars. On the unusual altarpiece you will find shepherds who are painted in Kecskemét traditional costume. The **József Katona Theater**, an imitation in small of the Comic Theater in Budapest, stands to the south of the Town Hall. It was built at the same time by the same Austrian architects Helmer and Fellner, responsible for at least sixty theaters in Europe.

Kecskemét has several museums to choose from. Visits to the **Museum of Naive Art** and to the private collection of traditional furniture, earthenware and religious paraphernalia relics are recommended to art lovers. On Kölcsej u. 3 you will find a museum documenting the sometimes gory aspects of medicinal history. On Szerfözö utca 19 stands the **Museum for Applied Arts**, displaying many items of local folk art. The so-called **Art Garden** merits an inspection. There is still a colony of artists working here today. But before leaving town, let us pay a visit to the **Windmill Inn** on the edge of the town on the road to Szeged. This is an ideal place to enjoy a *Pusztapörkölt* or a veal *paprikás*. And before eating, try the locally-produced *barack* or apricot schnapps.

Today the world of the individual farmsteads on the edge of the town has shrunk considerably, thanks to the planned economy of the old Communist government. The inhabitants of the villages preferred to move to the comfortable nearby towns such as Kecskemét and Kiskunfélegyháza, rather than continue living under unbearable conditions in the countryside. At the same time an exodus in the opposite direction began, with townspeople moving out to find peace and fresh air to escape the confines of living in concrete highrisis. It gradually became chic to buy an abandoned farmstead and turn it into a weekend country house. Finally, mention should be made of the **Go-Kart race track** that was built on the edge of town and which regularly hosts international competitions. Any tourist agency should be able to provide further information on the events taking place there.

Puszta Spectacles

The very name Hungary often conjures up clichées of gypsy music, paprika, schnapps, goulash and of course the puszta and the *csikós* (a Hungarian cowboy) cracking his whip. And no wonder, for such images are to be found in most advertisements of Hungary, whether they be for goods or holidays. But it is nevertheless amazing how many otherwise well-informed people will believe the reality of this kitsch, and are disappointed when they find out that Hungary is actually very different. The only way to find out more, of course, is to visit one of these events organized by the local travel bureau in such a place as Bugac, a few kilometers west of Kekskemét. With the firm knowledge of the theatrical nature of the shindig, one may even begin enjoying it for the skill of the riders.

Bugac, by the way, has been at the center of the Hungarian cattle industry for centuries. The wide variety of natural conditions in the sandy desert has been propilious for animal husbandry. Only in the 1930's did tourism increase considerably in this well- balanced quiet area, rich in ethnic tradition. But the rapid increase in farmsteads meant a decrease in pastureland available for cattle. Today only 2000 hectares of the 17.000 hectares of green pastures at the turn of the century remain. The sandy puszta and the massive Bugac area are part of the **Kiskunság National Park** today. Not only does breeding of the long-horned grey cattle still play an important role here, so does

raising white and black Merino sheep as well as Hungarian Mangalica pigs. These breeds which were developed over centuries but had almost died out, now form an important genetic base. In our modern world the shepherd leads a very different life, which is why his traditional utensils, once considered indispensible, have found their way into the museum opened in the National Park.

Tourists are still attracted to Bugac in great numbers. Visitors looking for the puszta should leave route 5 at milestone 107 and drive through the town of Bugac to their destination, the *csárda*. This inn with its thatched roof is the main goal of those seeking the promised oasis where true "Hungarian" culture can be found in the form of a gastronomic excursion. This is either followed or preceded by a ride across the puszta in a horse-drawn carriage and by look at a *csikós* show. Hunger, thirst and curiosity stilled by the hocus-pocus, one might be tempted to say "These are the Magyars." The answer is "caveat emptor".

Kiskunfélegyháza was razed to the ground in Turkish times and only really re-settled after 1743 when 219 families moved here from another town. Off main street is a house, built in 1733 and home today of the **Kiskun Museum**. It was renovated in the 18th century Baroque style and enlarged by a further story. It has a wide variety of objects on display from the time of the great tribal migration and also has an exhibition of local history. Part of its fame also rests on the **prison museum**. In 1860 one of the prisoners here was the Betyár Sándor Rózsa, a kind of Robin Hood loved by the people but feared by their overlords. In the courtyard is an old windmill. Szabadság tér (Freedom Square) and Petöfi tér mark the center of town, site of the **Town Hall**, built at the turn of the century and the **Hotel Kiskunság** next to it. Diagonally opposite is the **Swan House** (Hattyúház), built in 1819 where the father of the Hun-

Right: Long-horned grey cattle in the Bugac puszta, already prized in the Middle Ages.

gary's national poet Sándor Petöfi had his butcher's shop. Petöfi, who spent his childhood in this house, and regarded Kiskunfélegyháza as his birthplace, remains to this date the symbol of youth and revolution. Every year on 15th March – the day marking the beginning of the 1848 Revolution – the plinth of his statue in front of the building is adorned with colorful flowers and red, white and green flags. You may not be able to swim in this sea of flowers, but you can take a dip in the 47 ˚C water of the thermal bath. The population of Kiskunfélegyháza earns its living primarily from its gardens and geese – Europe's largest **goose farm** is located here.

Kiskörös was elevated to the status of a city in 1972 on the occasion of the 150th anniversary of the birth of Sándor Petöfi. The most important sight here is the **Petöfi House** with its thatched roof in the center of the town. This is where Petöfi was born on New Year's Eve 1822/23. Today the old house is of course a museum. The first **Petöfi statue** in the country was erected in Kiskörös in 1861. Today you will find a Petöfi statue, or at least a square named after him in almost every Hungarian town. The old one-party system mis-used Petöfi for their own purposes. But the Hungarian youth "freed" him and turned him into a passionate symbol of resistance to the regime. And so those who put flowers in front of his monuments or lit a candle for him on the 15th March, risked having a note made in their police file by doing so.

The development of Kiskörös has been typical of small towns in this area. The center consists of new buildings and a department store and hotel. Apart from the Petöfi Museum mentioned above, there are two further museums. The **Szent István Museum** is housed in a Slovak farmhouse, and there is also a **Museum of Transportation**.

Also worth a mention are the 58 ˚C iodic and bromic waters of the thermal bath. On the edge of Kiskörös you will find a nature reserve, the **Szücs Moorland Wood**.

157

To finish here is some advice for free. If you want to get to know the real Hungary, try and stay in private homes rather than in one of the neutral hotels. You will be well looked after, and will be able to see Hungarian life.

Lacemakers's Capital

Kiskunhalas is the home of the famous lacemaking industry. This old tradition was given a new lease of life in 1890 by the school teacher Maria Markovits with the aid of old drawings and lace works. And so the industrial manufacturing of Halas lace with its 56 different stitches began. You can admire all these enchanting details in the **Lace House**. In front of the building stands the statue of the tireless Mrs Markovits. The Lace Hotel is also worth a mention. In the center of the town is the **Hungarian Art Nouveau Town Hall**. Right next to it is a

Above: Peasant houses still defy the sterility of industrial norms.

museum named after the famous painter János Thorma with a large ethnographical collection as well as paintings by Thorma himself. You will also find the **Hotel Alföld** here (the name Alföld refers to the entire Great Hungarian Plain including Kiskunhalas). A **Museum of Local History**, which goes by the name "House of Collections" has also now opened its doors. The permanent exhibition here is devoted to the painter Tibor Csorba (1906-1985), who also taught in Kiskunhalas but moved to Poland. Near the station is the so-called **Kuruz Hill**, beneath which several hundred *kuruz* heroes were laid to rest. Who were these *kuruz*? The word usually refers to all the Hungarians who joined the War of Independence against the Habsburgs at the end of the 17th century. The war was started as a response to the attempt on the part of Leopold I to enforce his system of absolute rule. The monument erected in 1904 commemorates the battle which took place in 1702.

At the end of the last century, 87 windmills were still merrily grinding away, the first of which was built in 1799. Today only one of them works. A popular place of relaxation in winter and summer is the **thermal bath** with medicinal waters 49 °C hot on the former **People's Island**. But if you would rather not get wet go to the north of the town where you will find the pond (Sóstó) is considered, a paradise for anglers. Another pleasant activity in Kiskunhalas besides swimming and fishing is a browse through the local **flea market** held on Wednesdays and Saturdays which offers a vast array of items from useless junk at high prices to valuable antiques. With a little luck and a good eye you might become the proud owner of an Art Nouveau pocket watch or some genuine antique plates. And if your shopping bag stays empty, then at least consider the wealth of impressions you are carrying home in hour heart. The best time is in summer and before Christmas.

GÖDÖLLÖ AND HATVAN
Accomodation
Rooms can be found at the local tourist office. **Hatvan** has the budget **Park Hotel** on Kossuth tér 18, Zel (38) 11-861.
Restaurants
GÖDÖLLÖ: **Gödöllö étterem**, Szabadság tér; **Vadász étterem**, Dózsa György u. 30; **Patak vendéglö**, Blahané u.
HATVAN: **Aranyfácán**, Vörös Hadsereg u.; **Park étterem**, in the hotel; **Búzavirág**, Rákóczi út; **Sárga Csikó**, Horváth Mihály u.
Tourist Offices
Dunatours, Szabadság tér 6, Tel: (28) 20-977; **IBUSZ**, Szabadság tér 7, Tel: (28) 20-091.

JÁSZBERÉNY
Access: To Hatvan and route 32 south (27 km) or Route 4 to Üllö, Üllö to Gömrö then Rte 31 to Jászberény.
Accomodation
BUDGET: **Touring Hotel**, Serház u. 3, Tel: 12-051; **Lehel Gyöngye Hotel**, Neszüri Dülö, Tel: (64) 11-822; further inns and camping sites are to the east in Heves and in Jászszentandrás.
Restaurants
Lehel étterem, Lehel vezér tér 34; **Lehel Gyöngye étterem**, Fémnyomó u. 2; **Mátyás ételbár**, Déryné u. 2; **Rákóczi sörpince**, Réz u. 1.
Tourist Offices
IBUSZ, Lehel vezér tér 17., Tel: (64) 12-143.
Sightseeing
The **Jász Museum** (closed Mondays) documents the life of the Jász people and exhibits a carved horn allegedly belonging to Lehel, one of the leaders of the Magyars. Several baths in Jászberény, Jászapáti and Jászszentandrás.

KECSKEMÉT-CEGLÉD-NAGYKÖRÖS
Access: Rte 5 or M 5 from Budapest (ca. 80 km)
Accomodation
KECSKEMÉT: *MODERATE*: **Hotel Aranyhomok**, Széchenyi tér 2, Tel: (76) 20-011. *BUDGET*: **Hotel Szauna**, Sport u. 3, Tel: (76) 22-900; **Három Gunnár**, Batthyány u. 7, Tel: (76) 29-555. **Autó camping**, Sport u. 5, Tel: (76) 28-700. In addition there are several inns (tanya) in rural areas outside Kecskemét that offer pleasant and inexpensive accomodation.
Budget hotels in **Nagykörös** (**Központi**, Széchenyi tér 1, Tel: (20) 50-778) and in **Cegléd** (**Hotel Kossuth**, Rákóczi út 1, Tel: (20) 11-812).
Restaurants
At the hotels in **Nagykörös** and **Cegléd**. **KECSKEMÉT**: **Hotel Aranyhomok; Akadémia étterem**, Akadémia körút 19; **Hírös étterem**, Rákóczi út 3; **Szélmalom csárda**, Városföld 167.
Tourist Offices
KECSKEMÉT: Organizes tours out into the Bugac- puszta with Hungarian "barbecueing", folkloric programs and the rest: **Pusztatourist**, Szabadság tér 2, Tel: (76) 29-499; **IBUSZ**, Széchenyi tér 1-3, Tel: (76) 22-955.
Museums
The Medical and Medicinal History Museum: Kölcsey u. 3; **Museum for Hungarian Applied Arts,** Kölsö Szabadság utja 8; **Toy workshop and museum**, Gáspár u. 11; **Museum of Hungary's naive Artists**, Gáspár u. 11. **Ráday Museum of the Reformed Church District on the Danube**, Szabadság tér 7. (All museums are closed on Mondays, hours are 10 a.m. to 6 p.m.)

KISKUNSÁG (KISKUN REGION)
Accomodation
KISKUNFÉLEGYHÁZA: *BUDGET:* **Hotel Kiskunság**, Petöfi tér 4, Tel: (76) 61-751; **Borostyan panzió**, Szölö u. 1, Tel: (76) 61-427. **KISKÖRÖS**: **Hotel Szarvas**, Kossuth ú., Tel: (78) 11-125; **KISKUNHALAS**: **Hotel Alföld**, Lenin tér 6, Tel: (77) 21-140; **Hotel Csipke**, Semmelweis tér 16, Tel: (77) 21-455; **Malom panzió**, Malom sor 1, Tel: (77) 21-650; **Napfény-Termál camping**, Brinkus L. u., Tel: (77) 22-555/39.
Restaurants
KISKUNFÉLEGYHÁZA: At the **Kiskunság** hotel; **Halászcsárda**, Petöfi tér 2; **Arany Páva étterem**, Blaha Lujza tér 1; **Aranhegyi csárda**, Páka 118, on Rte 5 on the way to Kecskemét. **KISKÖRÖS**: At the **Szarvas** hotel; **Kurtakocsma**, József Attila u; **Fürdövendéglö**, at the baths, Erdötelki út. **KISKUNHALAS**: **Ezerjó étterem**, Szilády u. 6,; **Városi étterem**, Lenin tér 6; **Tölgyfa étterem**, Brinkus L. u. 1.
Tourist Offices
KISKUNFÉLEGYHÁZA: **IBUSZ**, Gorkij u. 2, Tel: (76) 62-045. **KISKÖRÖS**: **Pusztatourist**, Petöfi tér 14, Tel: (78) 11-349. **KISKUNHALAS**: **Pusztatourist**, Semmelweis tér 16, Tel: (77) 21-455.
Sightseeing
Kiskunfélegyháza has a museum detailing the Kiskun region. **Kiskörös** boasts the birth house of Sándor Petöfi. **Kiskunhalas'** reputation rests on its busy lacemakers.The latter two towns also have thermal waters. Kiskunhalas has a museum documenting the lacemaking craft (Kossuth u. 37/a). Also: Thorma János Museum on Köztársaság u.2 (closed on Mondays) and the workshop of the saddler Balázs Tóth Abonyi, Szász K.u.

THE SOUTHERN PLAIN

CSONGRÁD
SZEGED
HÓDMEZŐVÁSÁRHELY
BÉKÉSCSABA
GYULA

The districts of Csongrád and Békés in the southeast of Hungary are defined by the river Tisza and its tributaries, the three Körös rivers: the White, the Black and the Rapid Körös. They rise in Romania and flow into both districts from the south and the east before joining together near the town of **Csongrád** to form a single river, the Triple-Körös (Hármas körös), which later flows into the Tisza. The town from which the district of Csongrád took its name was formerly a Bulgarian town called Czernigrad (Black Castle). The old town center with its low thatched houses begins a few meters behind the **high school**, built in the Secession style typical of the turn of the century (Kossuth Square).

About 80 km to the south, near Szeged, the Maros river joins the Tisza. This is the lowest point in the country, lying only 79 m above sea level. The *kubikus*, poorly paid day laborers, used to wander from site to site with their barrows and spades leveling and securing the river banks. They played a significant part in the architectonic development of the Hungarian rivers. (For further information see the *kubikus* exhibition in Csongrád and in the "Black House" in Szeged.)

Left: Small-time and amateur farmers earn some extra income at the Szeged market.

All five rivers break their banks annually when the snows of the Carpathians melt and despite flood regulation measures and dikes, the land around them is regularly flooded. But a flood such as the one which destroyed Szeged on the night of the 11th and 12th March, 1879, belongs firmly to the past now. Despite its gentle sounding nick-name the Blonde Tisza turned into a snake, and with a terrible hissing "took possession of first the valleys and then even the hills", as writer Kálmán Mikszáth noted. According to official reports only 265 of the original 5723 houses still stood when the waters finally subsided. Since that night the inhabitants of Szeged have their own calender: before and after the flood.

Despite countless floods though, this stretch of land has always been inhabited. History tells of Asian horsemen, Roman legionnaires, marauding Huns, and of Bulgarians who settled the regions and were then forcibly driven from the land by the arrival of the Magyars under Árpád in 896. According to Anonymous, Hungary's oldest chronicler, he held his first assembly about 30 km north of the present-day town of Szeged: Today east of the E5 near Kistelek near the village of **Ópusztaszer**. The **Árpád Monument**, a Classical construction at the top of a broad flight of steps, symbolizes these

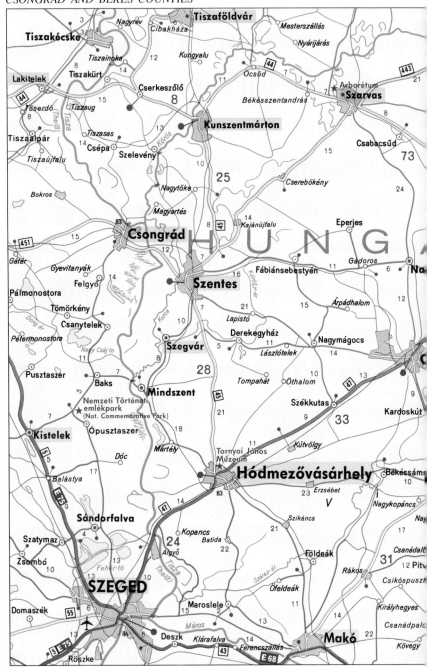

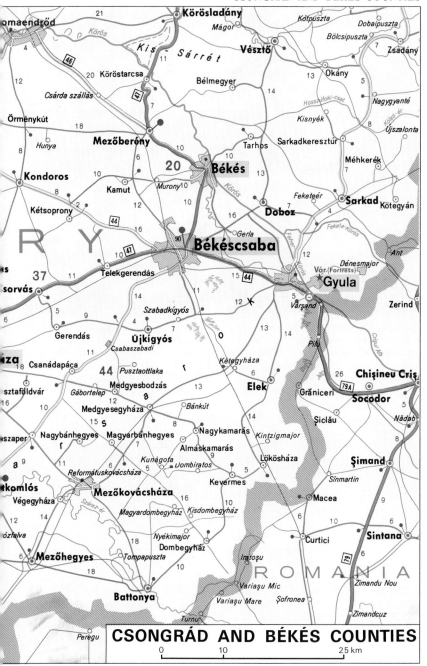

CSONGRÁD AND BÉKÉS COUNTIES

0   10   25 km

beginnings of the Hungarian State. The **National Memorial Park**, as this open-air historical museum is called, was begun in the year 1896, on the occasion of the Millenial celebrations of the Magyar arrival in the Carpathian basin. A few farms, a smithy, a coach builder's workshop, a cobbler, a general store, a lace maker's and a Classical village school offers a redolence of traditional Hungarian village life. A folkloric festival organized for tourists completes this nostalgic vision.

Szeged

Szeged was once a ferry port and depot for salt coming from Transylvania. In the 800 years "before the flood" despite frequent destruction and fires, it developed into an important center of trade and culture. As far back as the 12th century it was referred to in documents.

Above: The Szeged Cathedral. Right: The Bridge of Sighs in Szeged.

In the 13th century it aquired town privileges. Béla IV built a fortified castle on the banks of the Tisza after the Tatars invasion in 1241 but it was no defense against the Turks. Szeged only made a continuous recovery from its misfortunes after the invaders had been ousted once and for all in 1686. Then the Tisza destroyed it in 1879, leaving a pile of rubble in its wake. The inhabitants of Szeged built their town again using brand-new building methods.

The new Szeged, designed on the drawing board, has a balanced and yet eclectic feel to it. The layout is easy to memorize. Broad radial avenues intersect the two peripheral boulevards, the **Little Inner City Periphery** and the **Great Periphery**, which surround the city itself on both sides of the Tisza. The individual parts of the small **Boulevard** are named after the European capitals which contributed financially to the reconstruction of the town. When looking at the city map showing only the boulevards and the radial avenues, the pattern looks like a

simple sun as might be drawn by a child. It could act as the symbol for Hungary's "sun city", which basks in the warmth of over 2000 sun hours a year. No wonder paprika, fruit and grapes grow so well on the cultivated plains around the town.

It is not possible to establish who first introduced **paprika** to Hungary. But paprika dishes have been cooked in Hungary since Turkish times. The Christians improved on Turkish dishes when someone discovered that pork fat brings out the full flavor of the spice. Paprika was originally the spice of the poor, dismissed by those who could afford more exotic spices. This is why it is rarely mentioned in old Hungarian cookbooks. A small book published in 1775 mentions it for the first time. The author writes: "Paprika is grown in the garden. Then it is ground to a powder and used to add spice to a meal." Hungarian paprika, with its characteristic mild spiciness (or hot mildness) thrives best in the area around Szeged, where it has become an important export. The Hungarian scientist Albert Szent-Gy-örgyi (1893-1986) was even awarded the Nobel Prize for his work on "the isolation of vitamin C from paprika".

And while on the subject: Onions and garlic are two further important ingredients of Hungarian cuisine. The best in the country grow around the small town of **Makó** on the Maros, about 30 km east of Szeged. But it was not only onions and garlic which contributed to the fame of Makó. It was also the radioactive Maros mud, whose therapeutic effects are said to be greater than the other excellent healing muds of Hungary. If you want to take a mud cure in this little town, but think that your holiday will not be satisfactorily filled by cures, fishing, walking and visiting the two **Baroque churches**, you can commute between Szeged and Makó.

Szeged, which likes to call itself "a small-scale metropolis" has a number of treats for the tourist. These include architectural gems as well as cultural and gastronomic specialties. The most beautiful square in town is **Széchenyi tér**. The large trees on it have not always been

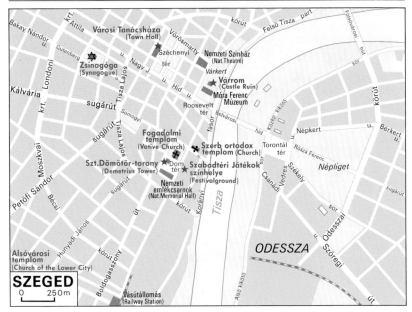

there. In the mid-19th century the town commander complained that they got in his way when he was practicing to shoot. Since then a new crop has grown up and endows the square with its special look along with a display of marble and bronze statues and, last but not least, the beautiful **fountain** allegorically depicting the dichotomy of the merciless and merciful Tisza river. The two buildings, joined by the **Bridge of Sighs** and adorned with a **tower**, is an enlarged and embellished replica by the Secessionist architect Ödön Lechner of the old Town Hall from "before the flood". Gyula Juhász called it "a wonderful Baroque Fata Morgana", and Mihály Babits compared it to a coquettish dancer.

Szeged's Churches

Dóm tér (Cathedral Square) is surrounded by buildings with arcades (the

Right: The little Gothic church of Óföldeák, pretty as a picture.

Bishop's Palace and the **University**, for example) and is Szeged's largest square. It is dominated by the imposing two-towered neo-Romanesque **church** (built in 1912-29). This church was the first building in Szeged to be constructed from red brick. The organ inside is huge, with 5 manuals and almost 11.000 pipes; its beautiful sound and the church's acoustics attracts organists from all over the world. Above the south portal stands a 3 m high Carrara marble statue of the Virgin Mary, the patron saint of Hungary. The 12 apostles stand by her side. The interior walls of the cathedral are painted white, blue and gold. It can seat many people, but has very little room for contemplation and quiet prayer. The painting over the ceiling of the chancel – by far one of the most restrained parts of the otherwise pompous surroundings – depicts Mary as the traditional peasant cloak and wearing typical Szegeder butterfly slippers. Thanks to its size and its wonderful acoustics, the square in front of the cathedral is used for the inter-

166

national renowned **Summer Festival**, which includes performances of opera, operetta, musicals and plays. The eight-sided tower in front of the cathedral, the **Demetrius Tower**, which dates from the 12th century, serves as a baptism chapel.

The Baroque-style **Greek-Orthodox church** with a particularly beautiful iconostasis stands on the corner of Somogyi utca and the northern side of the square.

But the most impressive church is the **Alsóvárosi templom** on Mátyás király tér. This simple building is purely Gothic in style with tall, narrow windows. The Romanesque window in the sacristy is the only relic pointing to the fact that a church once stood here at the time of the Árpáds. The interior, with its high altar and chancel, was redone in Baroque style like most Hungarian churches. The **Black Madonna**, a copy of the famous Madonna of Czestochowa, becomes the focus of the re-consecration of the church at the annual melon harvest. This folk festival is attended by the whole of Szeged.

The new **synagogue** in the Gutenberg utca, built between 1900 and 1903, is one of the finest and largest synagogues in Europe. The windows were conceived as illustrations for the book *The Flora and Minerals of the Jews*, written by the first Rabbi of the synagogue, Immanuel Löw.

The oldest witness to life in the town, the ruins of the fortified **castle**, built by Béla IV, form the border of **Móra Park** at the northernmost bridgehead of Szeged's central bridge. Before the castle was destroyed in 1880 it was the town prison. The Hungarian Robin Hood, the famous Betyár Sándor Rózsa (1813- 1878), for whose capture a reward of 10.000 florins was offered, languished in this prison for 12 years.

The **museum** at 1, Roosevelt tér boasts an archaeological collection and an interesting permanent exhibition of art from the Hungarian Plain. Like the park it is named after the writer Ferenc Móra

(1879-1934). He came from a very poor family and was a teacher at the Szeged high school.

Potter's Paradise

25 km to the east of Szeged is **Hódmezövásárhely**, once a typical agricultural town, which was mentioned as far back as the time of the Árpáds. In modern times a leather, fur and pottery industry developed here. As almost everywhere in Hungary, wars and revolutions have seen to it that there are few reminders of earlier times. Any architecture that is worth seeing is usually from the 18th century or imitations of earlier styles but also dating from the 18th century. One showpiece of the Secession is the restored **synagogue** on the erstwhile Tanácsköztársság tér. The farming museum is rather quaint and seems to hold the surrounding high-rise buildings at bay.

Overall Hódmezövásárhely, "the potter's town with an artesian well" is an attractive place to visit. Two interesting

items distinguish Szánto Kovács utca. The first is the **Greek-Orthodox church**, a lovely place to stay a while, the other is the **János Tornyai Museum**. The single-aisled Baroque church, built in the middle of the 18th century possesses a very valuable Nahum iconostasis from Mount Athos, consisting of a total of 16 icons. (Nahum was one of the 12 less well-known prophets who lived in the 7th century B.C.) The museum at no. 16-18 houses a collection of objects from the Stone Age, including a representation of the primal mother which probably dates from the year 3000 B.C. In the museum's collection of paintings one also finds works by the painter János Tornyai (1869-1936) who was born in Hód-mezővásárhely, and who gave the museum its name. Tornyai concentrated on painting the Plain and its dwellers. 700 of his paintings were recently dis-

Above: Travel Hungarian style. Right: The potters of Hódmezővásárhely exhibit their wares freely.

covered under the floorboards of a Budapest attic. A circle of fellow painters gathered around him in Hódmező-vásárhely around the turn of the century, and since then this town has been an important center of art in Hungary. The works of this colony of artists are not characterized by any similarities in style, but rather by a common love of the Plain which is reflected in their art.

Hódmezövásárhely is also a well-known pottery town, famous in particular for its black pottery. The black color is achieved through a special baking process. The oldest extant pieces demonstrating the use of this technique date from the Neolithic Age. The shapes of the jugs and other vessels today can be traced back to Turkish models.

The village museum in **Szegvár**, 20 km away (towards Szentes) has an interesting collection of old traditional objects and archaeological finds. The painting over the altar in the neighboring church, in a subdued modern style, was done by a certain Ferenc Purgel, who works in the local wine factory.

Békéscsaba and Gyula

Highway 47 and the railway track running parallel to it will take you via Oros-háza to **Békéscsaba**, the capital of the Békés district. This region, settled by Hungarians at the landtaking, was almost entirely depleted of human life during the Turkish Wars and the War of Independence against the Habsburgs. But new settlement brought Serbs, Slovaks, Romanians and Germans to this area. If you also count the Hungarians who remained or returned, this area witnessed the greatest variety of new settlers in Hungary in the 18th century. The most charming thing about Békéscsaba is a walk along the **Körös canal** on the "Promenade of Sculptures". The little **Árpád Wood** along the canal to the south has a pleasant and refreshing mineral

pool. The **Mihály Munkácsy Museum** contains an archaeological and ethnographical collection and several pictures by the internationally-known artist Mihály Munkácsy (1844-1900).

20 km south of Békéscsaba (Highway 44) is **Gyula**, the center of Hungarian vegetable growing and probably the most beautiful town in the Körös region. In the east of the town, on the banks of the White Körös, stands the only preserved brick **fortress** in Hungary, whose beginnings can be traced back to the 14th century. This massive construction with its 3 meter thick walls, equipped with all possible defenses available at the time, was nevertheless unable to withstand the Turkish assault. For almost 130 years the castle was in Turkish hands. After the Second World War it was completely renovated. Today it houses a museum and is the site of a Summer Festival. It is interesting to note that one of its owners at the beginning of the 16th century was Count Georg von Brandenburg who acquired it when he married the widowed daughter-in-law of King Mátyás. Other names are associated with Gyula which will also be known to non-Hungarians. The ancestors of Albrecht Dürer came from this town. This is where Ferenc Erkel, composer of the Hungarian national anthem, was born in 1810. The "Erkel Tree", an oak in whose shade the master sat while composing, still stands today in the **Harruckern Almássy Castle Park**. The former riding hall of this Baroque castle was turned into a covered swimming pool in 1960. Two years before that thermal springs were found on the castle grounds. In the years which followed more swimming pools were added and the large wooded park soon became a popular recreation center. Béla Bartók spent some time in Gyula collecting folksongs from this area. If he had been able to swim at the castle, he would surely not have written home in such a despair: "There is plenty of dust here and heat too." The small **patisserie** at 1, Jókai utca is an ideal place to take a quiet nostalgic break on your tour of the

town. It is the oldest patisserie in Hungary after the tiny Ruszwurm in Budapest's castle district. It is furnished in Biedermeier style and includes a little pastry museum displaying all the utensils of the trade. The old Town Hall, the Romanian-Orthodox church and the Roman-Catholic church, three Baroque buildings, all deserve careful inspection too, after the calory break.

The scenery in the districts of Csongrád and Békés has few spectacular sights to offer the traveler. But the plains reaching as far as the horizon, rivers that shrink to mere rivulets in their wide beds during the dry season, but swell into raging torrents in the rainy season, the alkaline steppes of the puszta, acacia groves and nature reserves with rare flora and fauna are all interesting places to visit in order to escape the towns and cities. A boat journey from Békés lasting several hours through the **Körös Nature**

Above: The 15th century fortress of Gyula today serves as a stage.

Reservation should not be missed. A visit to the arboretum in **Szarvas** on the left bank of the Hármas Körös (Highway 44) is also a must. Hungary has many arboreta, but this 84 hectare area in the north of town offers the richest variety. 1700 different plants grow here, with each species represented in great number. Count József Bolza (1780-1862) created this area on the model of Schönbrunn Castle in Vienna. He was nick-named Pepi, and his work was called Pepikert, or Pepi Garden. Here too you can take a memorable trip on a steamer departure on a dead arm of the Körös.

Highway 44 runs on to Kecskemét, crossing the Körös at **Kunszentmárton** and the Tisza at **Lakitelek**. This "land between the rivers" is one of the most beautiful parts of the region with countless picturesque spots where the fauna and flora have remained undisturbed since the rivers were regulated. The history and geography of the area is documented in the Museum at **Tiszaföldvár**, where there is also a large crystal collection.

CSONGRÁD
Accomodation

Hotel Erzsébet, Felszabadulás út 3, Tel: (63) 31-960. The camping site along the river is quite pleasant. Nearby **Szentes** also has the **Hotel Petőfi**, Petőfi u. 2, Tel: 255.

Restaurants

At the **Hotel Erzsébet**; **Bökény**, Muskátli u. 1; **Csuka csárda**, Szentesi út 1; **Halásztanya**, Kossuth tér 17.

Tourist Offices

Szeged Tourist, Felszabadulás út 14, Tel: (63) 31-232.

Sightseeing

Csongrád has nice natural surroundings and a beautiful old town. The **Kubikus museum** documents the hard life of the day-laborers who worked on straightening the Tisza.

SZEGED
Accomodation

MODERATE: **Hotel Hungária**, Komócsin Z. tér 2, Tel: (62) 21-211. *BUDGET*: **Hotel Napfény**, Dorozsmai út 4, Tel: (62) 25-800; **Hotel Royal**, Kölcsey u. 1, Tel: (62) 12-911. **Hotel Tisza**, Wesselényi u. 1, Tel: (62) 12-466. *CAMPING*: Dorozsmai út (**Hotel Napfény**).

Restaurants

Szeged is famous for its paprika and for its spicy dishes. Try *halászlé* or *halleves* (fish soup) at least once during your stay. **Alabárdos**, Oskola u. 13; **Hági** (very recommendable even with the odd obnoxious waiter), Kelemen u. 3; **Tisza Gyöngye**, Partfürdő; **Halászcsárda Fehértó**, Külterület 41.

Tourist Offices

Szeged Tourist, Victor Hugo u. 1, Tel: (62) 11-966; **Alföld Tours**, Bajcsy-Zsilinsky u. 28, Tel: (62) 12-070; **Express** (for youths and students), Kígyó u. 3, Tel: (62) 11-310.

Sightseeing

Szeged has one of the largest innercity areas and one of the prettiest in Hungary. Sites worth seeing are: **Széchenyi square**, the **Fekete Ház** (Black House), the **Cathedral**, the **New Synagogue**. Try for a tour on the Tisza or catch a performance at the openair festival on Cathedral square (in Summer). Excursion to national historic park at **Ópusztaszer**, north of the city. Swim in the thermal baths on Torontál tér.

HÓDMEZÖVÁSÁRHELY AND MAKÓ
Accomodation

Proximity to Szeged makes these two towns pleasant alternatives if Szeged is booked up. **HÓDMEZÖVÁSÁRHELY**: *BUDGET*: **Hotel**

Béke, Kossuth tér 2, Tel: (62) 42-019; **Hotel Fáma**, Szeremlei u. 7, Tel: (62) 44-444. **MAKÓ**: *BUDGET*: **Hotel Korona**, Lenin tér 10, Tel: (65) 11-384; **Camping Motel** (with camping site), Wekerle út 30, Tel: (65) 12-232.

Restaurants

HÓDMEZÖVÁSÁRHELY: **Akvárium**, Ady E. u. 1; **Alföldi**, Vidra u. 2; **Hódtava**, Hóvirág u. 2/b. **MAKÓ**: At the **Korona**.

Tourist Offices

HÓDMEZÖVÁSÁRHELY: **Szeged Tourist**, Szönyi u. 1, Tel: (62) 41-325. **MAKÓ**: **Szeged Tourist**, Lenin tér 10, Tel: (65) 12-384.

Sightseeing

Hódmezövásárhely is particularly well-known for its pottery, which can be viewed at the **Csucsi potter's house** (Rákóczi út 101) and at the **House of Folkloric Art** (Árpád u.). The **Farm Museum** in Kopáncs also exhibits several items of pottery. Local history and art can be seen at the **Tornyai-János Museum**, Szantó Kovács János u. 16-18. Paintings celebrating the entire Puszta hang in the **Alföldi gallery**. All museums are closed on Mondays.

BÉKÉSCSABA AND GYULA
Accomodation

BÉKÉSCSABA: *MODERATE*: **Hotel Csaba**, Szt. István tér 2, Tel: (66) 24-422; **Hotel Körös**, Kossuth tér 2, Tel: (66) 21-777.
GYULA: *MODERATE*: **Hotel Aranykereszt**, Eszperantó tér 2, Tel: (66) 62-057. *BUDGET*: **Hotel Park**, Part u. 15, Tel: (66) 62-622. Gyula has several camping sites offering small vacation homes for rent: Tel: (66) 62-690, (66) 62-240.

Restaurants

BÉKÉSCSABA: **Veszely csárda**, on the Veszely bridge; **Körös étterem**, Kossuth tér; **Lencési étterem**, Lencsési u. 17. **GYULA**: **Komló étterem**, Béke sgt. 6; **Park vendéglő**, Part u. 15; **Budrió vendéglő**, Béke sgt. 69.

Tourist Offices

BÉKÉSCSABA: **Békés Tourist**, Tanácsköztársaság útja 10, Tel: (66) 23-448. **GYULA**: **Békés Tourist**, Kossuth u. 16, Tel: (66) 62-261; **Gyula-tourist**, Eszperantó tér 2, Tel: (66) 61- 192.

Sehenswürdigkeiten

BÉKÉSCSABA: **Mihály Munkácsy Museum** (Széchenyi u.9), a painting gallery; Opposite is an exhibit of local minorities. Garai u. 21 is a Slovak house. On the road to Gyula is a grain museum with a windmill. **GYULA**: Kohán-Museum, Béke sgt. 35. The fortress also has a museum. All museums closed on Mondays). While having cake at the old coffeehouse, visit the pastry chef's kitchen museum!

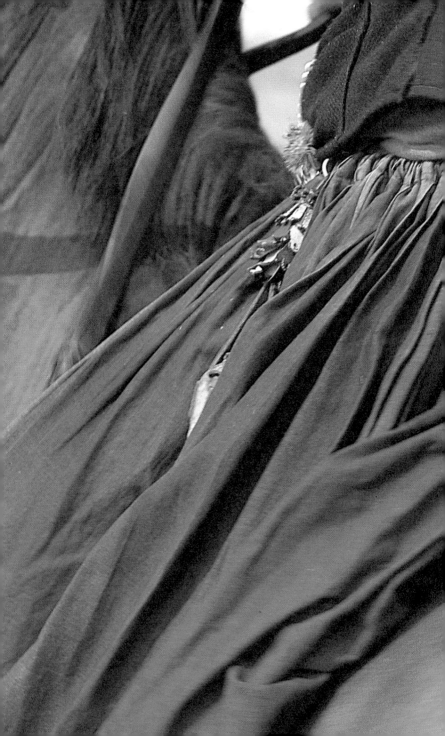

THE GREAT PUSZTA

ROUTES TO HORTOBÁGY
DEBRECEN
THE NYÍRSÉG

ROUTES TO HORTOBÁGY

No objective measurements can explain why poets and travel agents cheek-by-jowl, unanimously exalt Hungary's Great Plain, the *puszta*. Its flatness is excrutiating at times, its colors, seldom brilliant, cover various shades of brown, taupe and ochre, with the occasional spot of yellow or violet where sunflowers or the gentle wild asters bloom. In summer the sun stares down from a blue-grey sky, pressing through the humidity, creating mirages; everything shimmers in the heat and relief comes only from passing, violent storms. In winter freezing winds bluster unopposed across the great plain, driving icy rain and snow against the cowering steppes.

Puszta simply means "desert" in Hungarian and by and large applies to the entire area east of the Danube. But the region beyond the Tisza river has its own special quality. As the western borders fade from memory, some portion of genuine Hungary surfaces in the scent of sweating horses, melancoly looks and ribald laughter, houses behung with thick

Preceding pages: The csíkos were at the top of the puszta's social hierarchy. Left: Long hours on the puszta were spent doing this embroidery.

grapes, old men slumbering on their porches, the imagined sound of a nomads' cavalcade. This is where the Hungarians first arrived, this is where they settled all the tribes (Jazygians, Cumans, and Pechenegs) that followed, this is where they suffered most under the Mongols, Turks and Habsburgs, this is where they ferociously held on to their independence. Even when Maria Theresia seduced Hungary in 1740, she failed to get support from the eastern magnates whose Protestantism traced back in time and ideal to the very etymology and origin of the word. And so it is the sense that traditions have been maintained that has made the puszta so attractive to travelers from far and wide, even if the events advertized by local travel bureaus emit an unmistakably kitschy fragrance. By chance or through friends one sometimes comes across village marriages, traditional funerals, horse meets and markets and other celebrations, where some of the original flavor survives.

Two roads of very different quality lead to the great eastern plain from Budapest. The sign pointing toward Debrecen is the low road, so to speak, route 4, a lawless strip of tar, that carries all sorts of traffic from eighteen-wheelers to one-horse-power carts, and leads to the only automobile crossing into the USSR.

175

Szolnok

Szolnok, where route 4 crosses the Tisza, celebrated its 900th anniversary in 1975. The Turks built the first bridge over the river here. During the revolution of 1848-49, János Damjanich led one of several major victories against the Austrians in Szolnok. The local museum, housed in a beautiful Classical building, that was once a hotel, is dedicated to him. Today Szolnok combines fine architecture with the standard ugly modern highrises. It is a fairly important industrial center, producing paper, oil, gas, sugar and most of Hungary's pre-fab kitchens. but by no means without attractions for tourists, such as its thermal and medicinal baths (in a neo-antique building with colonade), the pleasant banks of the Tisza and the sights in the rest of the county. It even runs an artist colony since the

Above: Tobacco grown and cured in the puszta supplies the Debrecen and Nyíregyháza cigarette factories.

1930s, where the old defensive earth walls used to be, past the bridge over the Zagyva.

Barring some pretty neo-Classical and neo-Baroque façades, the following small towns, **Törökszentmiklós** and **Kisújszállás**, have little inherent visiting value, even less perhaps than some of the villages that squat in the emptiness to the right and left of route 4. The Catholic church in Tiszapüspöki, for example, has paintings by Kracker (see Eger), and Fegyvernek boasts the remains of an old tower standing in its cemetery. Advisable also is a detour through the swampy lands in the south (the Sárrét), through **Mezötúr** and Túrkeve. The first is famous for its potters, whose wares have been gathered and exhibited in the old synagogue, a sight in its own right. **Túrkeve**, smaller and with an air of permanent fatigue about it, has two famous sons, the Finta brothers, both sculptors who set out into the big world to make their fortunes. Sándor made it to Paris and Gergely, whose moving *Human Destiny*, a hand virtually sucking in a helples earthling, is among the displayed art works, moved to New York.

More Potters

Potters also make the reputation of the town of **Karcag**, a community of about 25.000 sprawled out in the midst of fertile fields and with a pleasant, laid-back atmosphere. Its central Kossuth square, dotted with statues and memorials, courageously mixes old and new architecture. Karcag was once a major Cuman center and to find out more about this nomadic tribe that arrived in Hungary in the early 13th century, there is the **Györffy Museum**, a rather rundown building, whose dedicatee, István Györffy (1884-1939) had been one of Hungary's major ethnographers. Somewhat more enjoyable for its hominess is the little peasant house on Jókai street, where one finds the

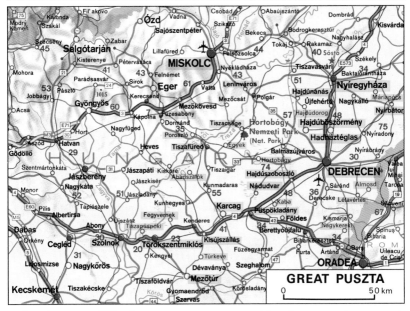

GREAT PUSZTA

0   50 km

entire microcosm of life of everyman on the puszta. Another traditional home is the one of Sándor Kántor on Ferenc Erkel street, the most famous of Karcag's potters. Besides plates, vases and jugs, the museum also exhibits those large, strange jugs shaped like puszta cowboys, and whose borderline taste will elicit expletives of dubious enthusiasm from your friends back home.

Back on route 4, the countryside races by in a shimmer of fields, telephone poles, trains, lonely farms battling collapse, with yards serving as coop, stall, stable and summer kitchen all at once. The road circumvents the bulk of **Püspökladány**, which can be avoided in all good conscience unless one is in search of fuel, food or lodgings. **Kaba**, a few kilometers eastward, has a small thermal pond that makes for agreeable refreshment. **Nádudvar**, 10 km north of route 4, is one of several sources of black pottery, a technique borrowed from the Turks, involving baking in an air-tight kiln. Designs, usually floral or abstract,

are carved into the wares using a smooth pebble. The soot and creosote etch their way into the clay and can later be polished, whereby the designs remain mat. Nádudvar offers courses in pottery during the summer, a courteous form of "gentle" tourism.

A glance at the map shows that a number of towns in this area are called Hajdú-something. The prefix goes back to the days when the Transylvanian nobleman István Bocskai, who, after successfully pushing back the Turks, was confronted with the Habsburgs. They sent in general Basta, a solid upholder of official Catholic theology, who sacked Protestant Transylvania. Bocskai forged an army out of dispossessed cattle ranchers the so-called Hayducks, and threw the Austrians out. The Hayducks were given settlements and exempt from taxes in return for military service.

The most prominent statue in **Hajdú-szoboszló** is that of Bocskai himself, and the museum in Bocskai street has been devoted to him and his Hayducks, but

177

most people come rather for local water, that was discovered in 1925. At the time it flowed into a disused clay quarry where it brought fun and health to the townees. The iodic and bromic waters helped heal wounds which later benefited the soldiers of World War II. Then pools appeared, bathhouses, inhalation rooms, mud baths, saunas, and a full-fledged medical infrastructure to tend to the over 1.5 Mio people who now visit the spa annually. Hajdúszoboszló has its own potter family, the Fazékás, who run a small operation with a little museum in a quaint peasant house with a porch supported by fat, squat columns. Otherwise the town's charm rests on its proximity to the Great Puszta, that is the Hortobágy National Park and its capital Debrecen. But let us backtrack at this point to the "high road" to and through the Puszta, which begins in Budapest with the signs pointing

toward the M 3 motorway and Miskolc. After riding in the shadow of Hungary's mountains for a while one comes to **Füzesabony**, where route 33 leads straight as an arrow, making every turn a danger, into the heart of the puszta. Except for the tar which has replaced the old basalt cobblestones, this is the same trail cattle drivers and salt carriers from Transylvania used in centuries past. At **Poroszló**, it crosses the wetlands surrounding the great Tisza river and finally, on a cantilever bridge, the Tisza itself.

The Tisza River

The Old Man of Hungary – for it is a kind of Mississippi – tends to the soul and body of the area. It provides fish of all sorts, notably carp, and water; its floods, until the straightening of its banks during the 19th century – which in turn led to a lethal drop in the great plain's water level – were devastating, but it has also inspired poets and painters. Today, together with several important canals, it

Above: A trademark of the Great Plain – the shadoof. Right: Sunflowers form a major part of Hungary's agriculture.

supplies the **Kisköre reservoir** referred to as the "little Balaton", probably for its holiday crowd rather than for the actual quality of the swimming. **Abádszalók**, about 21 km southwards, was recently "opened" to Western tourism. But it has already donned the garish colors of a holiday resort for a while now, with camping grounds by the water, a huge, wobbly slide polished by thousands of behinds of fun-screeching children. Gypsies lay out their wares on the road to the beach, wares that all look suspiciously similar, as if they came from the same factory, chess sets, painted boxes, shepherd flutes, wooden spoons ... The path along the beach has sprouted a myriad of *lángos* (fried dough) huts, *palacsinta* (pancake) huts, sausage mongers, soft drink peddlers, watermelon dealers and the like, all with long lines. Like the great lake in the west, it has its "Füred", **Tiszafüred**, a small but very pretty town of about 16.000 inhabitants, some industry, a fair amount of agriculture, a rapidly waxing tourist trade, a small but

pleasant thermal bath and, finally, a past, being as it were at one of the few crossing points on the river.

The gaudiness fades to the north in **Egyek** and Tiszacsege. The first has one *espresszó*, one gas station, a farm breeding the woolly Mangalica pigs, whose meat, according to the experts, far surpasses that of the garden variety pig and one of the most picturesque stork's nest, visited every year of course by the same family. In **Tiszacsege** one can take sustenance at the old Kadarcsi csárda, which also offers folkloric programs. (Not without reason do the csárdas in Hungary evoke some older and romantic times. Their appearance at regular intervals along route 33, for example, goes back to the heavy trade days when they cared for traveler and horse alike).

East of Tiszafüred the horizon gradually vanishes as if the earth had been ironed flat. The odd tree on the roadside disappears and with it all hopes of shadow. Great fish ponds glitter, herds of grey longhorns and Racka sheep with

long twisted horns move slowly across the still plain. Now and then a gaggle of geese in an enclosure brighten the onerous shades of burned grass. And the typical *gémeskut*, the shadoof, often the only source of water for the animals, stand out abstractly in the distance.

The Hortobágy Puszta

This is the famous Great Puszta, an enormous, continuous plain, the largest in Europe, fertile when it comes to interesting flora, useless for the farmer except in the case of animal husbandry. It ranges from 88 to 92 meters above sea level. The occasional bump in the glebe is a so-called Cuman hill, made by nomadic tribes of yore as a watch tower of sorts. The rest is all nature in pure form hanging in very delicate balance. Parts of the puszta have been declared off limits to all

Above: Life on the puszta – half the speed, twice the quality. Right: At the flower festival of Debrecen.

but the very special, while artificial fertilizers and other chemicals have been banned from other parts. The **Hortobágy National Park** serves as a home to a great variety of birds, many of which make a pit stop here during migration, and mammals, to strange flowers, an encyclopaedic variety of buzzing, whirring, chirping, crawling insects, and of course a very special people. The cormoran, almost extinct in Europe for lack of peace and quiet, has found a home here, there are bustards and egrets and other herons, cranes, ospreys and storks.

Novelists have used the puszta as a setting, poets drew inspiration from its forlorn wilderness, painters brought it to canvas and an army of biologists, ornithologists, entomologists and ethnographers have examined it, taken it apart, put it back together and drawn conclusions in books and treatise. Their work has been distilled into a bite-size portion at the **Hortobágy Shepherd Museum**. It documents the life of the puszta workers, the horse riders (*csikós*), cattle drivers (*gulyás*) and shepherds (*júhász*). Their individual costumes, marking the hierarchy, their beautiful felt coats especially made and embroidered as a particular honor all stand in the sterility of glass cases. Their dogs, faithful and hardworking companions, the Puli and the Komondor, to mention the two most famous, are also remembered. These people spent at least one half year out in the wilds tending to the animals, and they wiled away the lonely hours by carving pipes, sticks (which they would always take prophylactically to the csárda as it was considered rude to fight with ones fists), and tobacco pouches.

Hortobágy itself is an intersting place. One arrives on an ancient stone bridge supported by nine arches, built between 1827 and 1833. Just before it, however, a little road leads to **Máta** known principally for its Nonius horses. It is also the site of the yearly International Equestrian

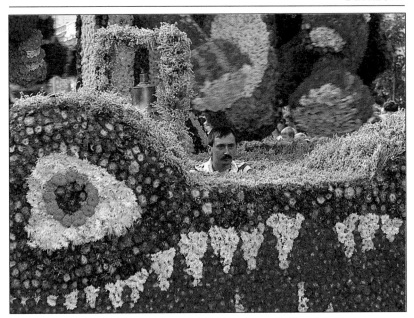

Days, where the creme of riders demonstrate their complete control over their animal, making it lie down, riding two horses at once by standing with a foot on each saddle, and so on. If you miss the June event, there are other opportunities to see more low-key events throughout the summer. The local tourist bureau also offers programs in the puszta that are enjoyable and accessible for the newcomer.

Another important local event is the *hídivásár* (bridge market), which has been held near the old bridge in Hortobágy on August 19 and 20 since 1892. What began as an agricultural fair has grown into a bustling shindig including a real fair with ferris wheel, shooting galleries and the like. Everything has its price, from the watermelons to the sheepskins, from baskets to chess sets, from Chinese back scratchers to braids of garlic. Newcomers to the market are the convoys of Romanians who sometimes have some genuine peasant antiques, especially plates, vases and woven and embroidered fabrics.

DEBRECEN

If Hungary possesses a second capital city then it must be **Debrecen**. Not nearly as beautiful as Pécs or Szeged, not as industrial as Miskolc, it nevertheless boasts a history of dignified independence, and, some point out, the largest surface area of any city in Europe. Indeed, the entire Hortobágy Puszta has belonged to Debrecen for centuries, even though the postwar Communist government *de jure* nationalized it. Renting out the land and having the csíkos, the gulyás and júhász care for its herds reaped enough revenue to pay off the Turks. The city's wealth also pushed the price of land well beyond the national norm. Debrecen's coat-of-arms tells much about its history. A lamb represents the religious element: In 1536 it embraced the Reformation and remained forevermore an eyesore for the Austrians, having earned the title "Rome of Calvinism". The palm trees honors its long mercantile tradition which stretched as far as the Middle East. Debrecen had,

for example, a fairly important leather trade, which kept tanners, shoemakers and the like busy already in the Middle Ages. The phoenix recalls the endless fires from which Debrecen had to recover. And the sun commemorates a 500 mm annual rainfall. Twice it served as a capital, once in 1849, when Kossuth proclaimed Hungary's full independence from the Habsburgs, and for a brief period at the end of World War II, when it became the seat of the provisional Hungarian government. Today its economy rests by and large on tourism, on meat processing, on textiles and on pharmaceutica.

Debrecen is in many ways a peculiar town. Locals point out the fact that the erstwhile Red Army Street, Piac u. today, leads straight to the majestic *Nagy Templom*, the Great Church in the middle of town, that Szabadság u. (Freedom street) leads to the big cemetery, and that Béke u. (Peace street) leads to the slaughterhouse. Furthermore Debrecen has no river, which exacerbates its dustiness. The water supply lies under the **Great Forest** (*nagy erdö*) in the north of town, where pools, modern thermal baths, a stadium, discos and restaurants such as the Vigadó and the Rozsakert play hide and seek in the trees with the august façade of the **Lajos Kossuth University**.

Debrecen revolves around the **Great Church** on the appropriately named Calvin square, a large, dignified, but simple building completed in 1823 after a fire destroyed the old wooden church of St. Andrew in 1802. Inside, the walls are pure white, offsetting the dark pews and ornate, guilded pulpit. It is an ideal backdrop for spiritual contemplation or to take in an organ or choral concert. It provided the setting for Kossuth's declaration of independence on April 14, 1849. The famous **Protestant School** stands behind the church, on the other side of a small park where the town erected two statues. One honors the great Bocskai and the

Above: The Great Church of Debrecen, a beacon of Calvinism in Central Europe.

other the 42 Protestant clergymen from Debrecen who were "invited" in 1675 by the Habsburgs to pull an oar on a galley. A little later a Dutch admiral named Ruyter took pity on those who had survived and released them in Naples.

The school with its motto *orando et laborando* (praying and working) bluntly written over the entrance has always stood here, though prior to 1538 it preached the Catholic gospel. Since then it has evolved into one of the main suppliers of pastors, teachers and school curricula for Hungary's Protestant communities and boasts many great names in its student body, such as the poet Csokonai Vitez. It also offered scholarships for children of poor families, thanks to subsidies from the city, and provided Debrecen with a necessary fire brigade, made up of those students strong enough to wield the 34 pound *gerondium*, an oak stick used to beat out fires. Maria Theresia prohibited all subsidies to Protestant institutions during the 18th century, and for a while the school lived from hand to mouth. The fire that ravaged the church in 1802 also took part of the school. Twice it played a historic role, when the revolutionary and provisional Hungarian assemblies sat in its oratorium in 1849 and 1944 respectively.

Students still use its ancient frescoed halls, but part of it has been reserved for a museum documenting student life, with an old class room, scientific gadgets to demonstrate phenomena such as electricity (1776 Leyden Jar and a Siemens-Halske generator, for example), the power of gravity and a meteorite that fell to earth not far from Debrecen in 1857. There is also an exhibition of sacral art showing leftovers of the old St Andrew's church, grave stones and parts of a coffered ceiling. The library has over half a million books including nearly 300 translations of the bible.

Next to the school stands the **Déri Museum** named after its founder Ferenc

Déri, a silk merchant with a great gift for antiquities and paintings. The collections from ancient Egypt, Etruria, Rome and Greece are of high quality as well as the gallery presenting Hungarian Romantic, which focusses mainly on the works of the great Munkácsy and Székely.

The center of town, that part presided over by the Great Church, bears the look of financial comfort. Here one finds everything from hotels to discos to new and used book stores. Its architectural lines hark back to the great movements of the 19th and early 20th century. The county seat at number is Secession as is Debrecen's most ancient inn, the **Arany Bika** (Golden Bull, thus named by one of its owners János Bika). Its restaurant and coffee house have a good reputation, but the hotel itself has, so it is said, started sliding during the past years. On Kossuth street the **Csokonai Theater** is in an exotic Romantic-Moorish style. The singular, newly restored tower at the corner of Széchenyi street belongs to the **Small Church**, which was erected in 1720. The original onion dome blew away during a violent storm.

Debrecen comes fully alive under the steamy summer sun, when the Jazz Days in July attract international crowds, and the Kossuth University opens, as it has been doing since 1927, its portals to students of Hungarian from around the globe. The climax comes with the great **flower festival** on August 20th, a parade of floats made from millions of flowers that ends at the Nagyerdei Stadium with a bustling folkloric festival. Other activities include horseback riding and especially swimming either in Debrecen itself or one of the ponds/lakes in the surrounding area (the Tisza is not so far off either). In the south the **Vekeri Lake** offers camping and the very fine Paripa csárda. To the northwest, on route 35 to Miskolc, is **Leninváros**, a modern eyesore whose "flag" is provided for by the smoke stack of the local chemical factory.

THE NYÍRSÉG

Barring the beautiful Hortobágy plain, the area immediately surrounding Debrecen has little to offer. **Nagykereki**, to the south, on the way to the Romanian border, has a castle where Bocskai once lived, with several exhibits devoted mainly to Bocskai and his wars. To the east near Létavértes in a more wooded and slightly hilly region is the quaint little village of **Almosd**, where the poet Kölcsey, author of the Hungarian national anthem, once lived in a small peasant house. Finally in northerly direction lie several old Hayduck settlements, **Hajdúböszörmény**, **Hajdúnánás**, and **Hajdúdorog** all of which have a either museums of local history or nice baths.

Immediately beyond the town line of the unpronounceable Hajdúhadháztéglás, is the border to Szabolcs-Szatmár, the easternmost administrative district of Hungary. As in the outer reaches of Hungary's mountains, one finds villages here by-passed by the 20th century, overlooked by mass tourism that has brought a certain dose of greed and corruption to, say, the Balaton region. Splendors have no place out here, the beauty of the region lies in modest charm. Churches in most cases are no larger than the communities they serve, and more often not much older than in western Hungary, castles are hardly more than big manors. Life itself moves along at a slower pace, whether by hard work or sitting in the shade munching away on sunflower seeds.

Szabolcs-Szatmár District

The first section of Szabolcs-Szatmár is known as the **Nyírség**, which stems either from the word Nyír, meaning birch, or Nyir meaning swamp, both of which play a fair role in the local land-

Left: The typical church towers of eastern Hungary (here in Csaroda).

scape. **Nyíregyháza**, has grown in the past two centuries from a relatively peaceful town, lazily sprawled out on the flatlands, to the busy capital of Szabolcs-Szatmár. Prosperity at the end of the 19th century accounts for the eclecticity of its architectural styles. The Catholic church on Kossuth square is neo-Gothic, the government's headquarters on once Tanácsköztarsaság square (names referring to Hungary's Communist past are being changed), as well as the **Zsigmond Theater** are the works of the Romantic-Secessionist Ignác Alpár.

Nyíregyháza's major industrial development took place during the 1960s with the establishment of a rubber factory and a paper mill, but the main source of income for the locals remains agriculture and the processing of agricultural products, including tobacco and apples. Those boom years endowed the town with long, broad avenues lined in uniformly sterile apartment silos.

Like Debrecen, Nyíregyháza has no river but a large natural water supply about 6 km north of town. The *sóstó* (literally salt lake) has a large swimming complex, with indoor pools, outdoor thermal baths and a host of little cook- and coffeeshops too counteract the effect of the healing waters. It has become the most important touristic center of the county. A **village museum** has been put together adjacent to the "salt lake" as well as a cultural park, as it is called, with an open-air stage and a rather uncultural exhibit of war machinery.

Nyíregyháza itself has several nice churches, a theological seminary of some repute, several streets of subdued beauty and a museum named after the multifaceted regional doctor András Josa with equally multi-faceted exhibits. One room features works by the Nyíregyházan painter Gyula Benczúr, another shows artifacts – including letters, a pen and furniture – from the life of the major modern Hungarian writer Gyula Krúdy.

Nyírbátor, about 37 km east of Ny-íregyháza has a stronger cultural flavor, thanks to its two churches. The name of the town recalls the great Transylvanian family of the Báthorys, and in fact both churches, one Catholic the other Protestant, were funded by them, a unique example of religious tolerance that so frightened the great Habsburgs. Both are also quite different in style. The **Protestant church** radiates austere simplicity, white walls, a groined ceiling and tall ogee windows hinting at its Gothic origins and a carved, painted pulpit. The red marble sarcophagus of the István Báthory, who had the church built, lies in a glass case. One of the most beautiful objects, an intricately decorated wooden, Renaissance, 14-seat stall has been moved to the National Museum in Budapest. Outside stands a 30 m high, majestic bell tower, the kind of which one sees very frequently in eastern Hungary.

Above: A casual dish rack. Right: How do you like them apples?

They are usually made of oak, have roofs looking somewhat like those high hats worn by the colonists of New England, whereby the "brim" protects the gallery. Each corner is decorated by another little tower. The church and its grounds serve as a site for a summer music festival, which accounts for the lonely bronze of Franz Liszt's head and the statue of the great Hungarian lutenist and balladeer Sebestyen Tinodi.

Nyírbátor's **Catholic church** is quite different, having been totally destroyed by the Turks, and then rebuilt by the Franciscans in full Baroque style. The Minorite monastery in the back serves today as a museum to the great Báthorys and to various aspects of local life.

A third interesting church is a few kilometers west of town in the village of **Máriapócs**. It belongs to the Orthodox faith and is the site of pilgrimages, for here, if we are to believe the message from the crutches and other symbols of illness hanging on the walls, miracles have taken place.

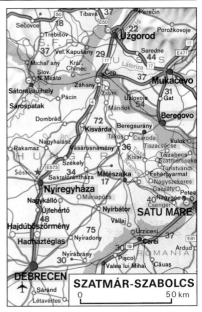

SATU MARE

SZATMÁR-SZABOLCS

0   50 km

The Eastern Domains

The rest of eastern Hungary can be roughly divided into three regions, Szatmár, Bereg and the Rétköz. The first begins east of Nyírbátor and reaches the borders with the USSR and Romania. Economically it is somewhat depressed, perhaps because it has been forgotten. Some villages, especially those along the borders, seem void of cars. Some roads indicated on the maps disappear into the muck of damp fields. **Mátészalka** itself has lost all its old character, but the museum on Kossuth street is worth a visit for its recording of local peasant life and fine collection of carts. **Fehérgyarmat** on the other hand has a pretty downtown area with a little park, at the entrance of which stands a typical arched Transylvanian portal of carved wood. To the south lies a gently hilly, forested landscape dotted with sleepy villages. Besides the houses, many of which are in disrepair but at least in original shape, with white-washed walls and thatched

roofs, there are usually only churches to visit, and each one clings to memory for some special quality. The brick Catholic church in **Csenger** has a beautiful painted coffer ceiling, those in **Nagyszekeres** and **Gacsály** have memorable bell towers. To see the insides of the churches one generally has to chase down either the pastor or the sexton. An excursion along the Tisza to the Russian (Ukrainian) border at Tiszabecs and back to Fehérgyarmat reaps more varied sites. **Turistvándi**, for example, has an old but functioning water mill. **Szatmárcseke** was the birthplace of the poet Kölcsey, who lived in Almosd (see above), and the local cemetery not only reveals a pretty mausoleum to him but also the so-called *kopjafa*, the wooden boat-shaped grave markers that still recall heathen Hungary. Finally, in **Tiszacsécse** stands a little white cottage, leaning from age under the weight of a thatched roof, where Moricz Zsigmond (1879-1942), one of Hungary's greatest writers and critics, was born. In the distance, through the mist

187

that seems to rise from the Great Plain, the Carpathians look down on Hungary.

The second region mentioned above lies north of Nyíregyháza. The **Rétköz** (the meadow area), sometimes also called*Tiszakanyár* (Tisza bend), produces a great deal of food, especially apples that are shipped to cool storage in Nyíregyháza. Route 4 leads directly to its heart, **Kisvárda**, a fumy, busy town with a history of past prosperity. Its 15th century castle has been revamped to serve as a theater, while the old synagogue, with its ornamented ceiling and simple, blue, yellow and clear glass windows, houses displays of life in the Rétköz. To the north route 4 begins collecting the disparate traffic heading to the Soviet Union. In late autumn, when the days are warm and nights cold, the Tisza frequently throws a thick blanket of fog over the region. The

Above: Sometimes, seldom something happens somewhere in eastern Hungary. Right: Sheep and shepherd have all the time in the world.

crossing, a single narrow bridge, is in **Záhony**. Neighboring Zsurk boasts a church with wooden bell-tower and painted ceiling. **Mándok** (a few kilometers southward) used to have a unique specimen of a 17th century wooden orthodox church, but it was transported to the open-air museum of Szentendre (see Danube Bend).

What lies beyond the border, Transcarpathia, used to be Hungarian, Ruthenian, Ukrainian, a jumble of nationalities living by and large in peace with each other. **Munkács** (Mukachevo) even played an important role in Hungarian history as the site of a last-ditch effort to resist the Habsburgs during the Kuruc war led by Thököly. And beyond the town, on the road across the mountains to L'vov, is the **Verecke Pass**, through which Árpád led his tribes of Magyars around 896. The Soviet Union adopted Transcarpathia after World War II, but for many Hungarians, this is only a temporary state of affairs at best, at worst it's their nomadic fate.

A part of Transcarpathia still within the confines of Hungary is called **Bereg**. It is cut off from the rest of the country by the Tisza which has only two bridges in the east, one in **Kisar** near Fehérgyarmat, the other in **Vásárosnamény**. When the borders were open for Soviet citizens, many of whom still consider themselves Hungarian here, the villages came alive with buying and selling, a sometimes exploitative trade that ultimately led to the borders closing again. Small businesses shot up around this clientele, like the Felicia Espressó in **Beregsurány**.

Up Route 41

Route 41 from Nyíregyháza leads straight to Bereg and offers the opportunity to drop by the Renaissance castle of Ádám Vay, one of the important military leaders (and a poet) during Rákóczi's War of Independence (1703-1711). **Vásárosnamény** offers modest lodgings and a museum to boot. Ancient agricultural tools including a splendid bark container, a forest of cast iron wood/coal stoves from Munkács, a room devoted to death and mourning in the region, as well as embroideries are just some of the displays that the curators have arranged for the visitor. Two local churches have achieved some fame in Hungary. In 1766, one Ferenc Lándor Asztalos painted the coffered ceiling and the pulpit of the Protestant church in **Tákos**. The floral frescos of the church in **Csaroda**, that were painted in 1642, covered a much older set of frescos depicting saints from the days when Hungary entertained fairly cordial relations with Constantinople. These are sights to savor quietly. They span generations, with their wars, their plagues, their revolutions, and they speak a language of simple devotion and humanity. The people out in the east, like their churches are simple and friendly; as you head westward, give an occasional wave to one of those eternal figures sitting on a bench watching. When they neither wave back nor smile, you will once again be in a civilized world.

SZOLNOK
Accomodation
MODERATE: **Hotel Pelikán**, Vízpart körút 1, Tel: (56) 13-356; **Hotel Tisza**, Marx park 2, Tel: (56) 17-666; **Hotel Touring**, Tiszaliget, Tel: (56) 12-928. *BUDGET:* **Motel Pelikán**, Vízpart körút, Tel: (56) 18-130. *CAMPING:* Tiszaliget, Tel: (56) 18-596.
Restaurants
Aranylakat, Tiszaliget; **Evezös csárda**, Vízpart körut 1; **Szolnok étterem**, Jubileum tér 2.
Tourist Offices
Tiszatour, Ságvári körút 32, Tel: (56) 11-384; **IBUSZ**, Kossuth u. 18, Tel: (56) 17-580.
Sightseeing
János-Damjanich Museum, recreational activities on the Tisza river, or a visit to the spa.

ALONG ROUTE 4
Accomodation
MEZŐTÚR: **Berettyó**, Kossuth tér 8.
TÚRKEVE: **Kevi fogadó**, Kenyérmezei út 27.
KISÚJSZÁLLÁS: **Kunsági Motel**, Felszabadulás u. 9-11; **Erdö camping**, Nagyerdö.
PÜSPÖKLADÁNY: **Hotel Árnyas** (with camping), Petöfi u. 62.
Restaurants
Route 4 being well-travelled, has spawned a good number of way-side eateries. Just in case, however, here are a few in the individual towns: **MEZŐTÚR**: **Akácfa vendéglö**, Erzsébet- liget; **Béke étterem**, Rákóczi u. 60. **KISÚJSZÁLLÁS:** Vadász étterem, next to the camping; Kisút étterem, Felszabadulás u. 9.
Museums
MEZŐTÚR: The town's synagogue ia a display room for local pottery. **TÚRKEVE**: The Finta brothers sculptures and drawings are exhibited in the museum on József A.u. **KARCAG**: Györffy Museum for local history and ethnography, Püspökladány út.

HAJDÚSZOBOSZLÓ
Accomodation
MODERATE: **Hotel Délibáb**, József A. u. 4, Tel: (52) 60-808; **Hotel Kemping** (as the name suggests, with a camping site), on the road to Debrecen, Tel: (52) 62-427. *BUDGET:* **Hotel Gambrinusz**, József A. u. 3, Tel: (52) 60-100.
Restaurants
The Délibáb's restaurant provides a nice meal as do: the **Gambrinusz'** restaurant and the **Magyaros étterem**, Lenin u. 3.
Tourist offices
Hajdútourist, József A. u. 2, Tel: (52) 60-440; **IBUSZ**, Hösök tere 4, Tel: (52) 60-070.

Sightseeing
It is possible to take tours into the **puszta** from Hajdúszoboszló. **Pottery** is an important part of the region as are the **Hayducks**, to whom a museum was dedicated, Bocskai u. 12. There is also a potter's house on Ady Endre u. 2, exceptionally its hours of visit are Mo from 8 a.m. to 4 p.m. Hajdúszoboszló has a well-tended spa.

DEBRECEN
Accomodation
MODERATE: **Hotel Arany Bika**, Piacutca, 11-15, Tel: (52) 16-777; **Hotel Thermal**, Nagyerdei körút 9-11, Tel: (52) 11-888. *BUDGET:* **Hotel Fönix**, Barna u. 17, Tel: (52) 13-355; **Hotel Debrecen**, Petöfi tér 9, Tel: (52) 16-550; **Hotel Sport**, Oláh Gábor u. 3-5, Tel: (52) 16-792. *CAMPING:* Nagyerdei körút 102, Tel: (52) 12-456; at Vekeri Lake ca. 12 km south of the city, Tel: (52) 13-500.
Restaurants
At the **Arany Bika**; **Gambrinusz**, Piacutca 28; **Szabadság** (rough place late nights, but the food is good), Piacutca 25; The ex-Lenin Park is the site of two good restaurants with dance floors: the **Rózsakert** and the **Ujvigadó**. For a late dinner try the **Nádas csárda** (open 24 hours) on Route 4 west of town.
Tourist Offices
Hajdútourist, Kálvin tér 2/a; **IBUSZ**, Piac u. 11-13, Tel: (52) 15-555; **Cooptourist**, Holló János u. 4, Tel: (52) 10- 770; **Express** (for youths and students), Kandia u. 1, Tel: (52) 14-393.
Sightseeing
See **puszta** below. Debrecen's reputation rests on its Calvinistic past: the **Great Church**, the **Protestant College** and the history that went along with the religion. Visits to these sights and the **Déri Museum** (Déri tér 1) are a must. Its collections include 19th century Hungarian paintings and items from ancient Egypt and Rome (closed Mondays). The Museum of the Protestant College (Kálvin tér 16) documents the trials and tribulations of Protestants in Hungary and in school. For some sportive activities walk through the Great Forest (Nagy Erdö), or visit the the thermal baths (Nagyerdei körút), the pools at Szávai Gy. u., Lake Vekeri south of Debrecen. Horseback riding is a major activity in the area.
Festivals
Summer brings a number of interesting events, the **Debrecen Jazz Days** in July, concerts in the Great Church and the **Flower Festival** on August 20. The Kossuth University also offers language courses for those interested in learning Hungarian and its culture.

THE PUSZTA
Accomodation

TISZAFÜRED: **Hotel Vadász**, Lenin u. 4, Tel (11-047; **Kemény Kastély**, Homokcsárda 1/1; **Patkós Motel** (with camping), Egyek (northeast of Tiszafüred). Camping sites also at the resort of Abádszalok, ca. 25 km southwards.

HORTOBÁGY: Several inns keep guest rooms for travelers here, the **Csárda Fogadó** which also maintains a camping site, Tel: (52) 69-139, the inn (fogadó) at Kossuth L. u. 1; the **Hotel Hortobágy**, Tel: (52) 69-071; and there is the **Puszta kemping**: inquire at the **Shepherd Museum** where the **tourist office** is located.

Restaurants

TISZAFÜRED: **Birkacsárda**, Poroszlói u. 10; **Vadász étterem**, Lenin u. 4; **Vendéglö étterem**, Somogyi Béla u. 8; There are pleasant *csárdas* all along the road to Debrecen at regular intervals. A drive north to Tiszacsege is worth a lunch or dinner at the **Kadarcsi csárda**.

Tourist Offices

TISZAFÜRED: **IBUSZ**, Somogy Béla u. 30., Tel: 11-047. The Hortobágy office at the Shepherd Museum organizes many tours and events out on the wide plain. You will also find out more about horseback riding and other sports.

Museums

Hortobágy Shepherd Museum (at the nine-arched bridge), closed Mondays and off season. A picture gallery has been set up on Petöfi tér.

Events

The Hortobágy Equestrian Days take place in July. August 19-20 is the so-called bridge market at the eastern end of Hortobágy's nine-arched bridge.

NYÍREGYHÁZA
Accomodation

MODERATE: **Hotel Szabolcs**, Dózsa Gy. u.3, Tel: (42) 12-333; **Hotel Krúdy**, at the Sóstó, Tel: (42) 12-424. *BUDGET*: **Hotel KEMÉV**, Bethlen G. u. 58-60; **Hotel Epitök**, Fürdö u. 51, Tel: (42) 10-075. Two camping sites, the **Fenyves** and the **Igrice**, have been set up near the Sós-tó.

Restaurants

At the hotels **Szabolcs** and **Krúdy**; **Aranyszarvas étterem**, Szarva u. 56;
Piaccsarnok étterem, Búza tér; **Tölgyes csárda**, Sóstoi u. 60; **Ungvá étterem**, Luther-ház; **Zöld Elefánt étterem**, Körút 1;

Tourist Information

Nyírtourist, Dózsa Gy. u. 3, Tel: (42) 11-544; **IBUSZ**, Lenin tér 10, Tel: (42) 12-122; **Express** (for youths and students), Arany J. u. 2, Tel: (42) 11-650.

Sightseeing

Among the main attractions in Nyíregyháza is the **Sós-tó** or salt lake a few kilometers north of town. Not far is a village museum (falúmúzeum). In Nyíregyháza visit the **Jósa-András Múzeum** on Benczúr tér 21. Excursions to **Nyírbátor** to visit the Catholic and Protestant churches there, and the Orthodox one in **Máriapócs**.

NYÍRSÉG
NORTHERN HALF
Accomodation

KISVÁRDA : **Strand,** Városmajor 37, Tel: 649. **ZÁHONY**: **Kemév fogadó**, Zalka Máté u. 1, Tel: (42) 60-153.
VÁSÁROSNAMÉNY : **Hotel Bereg**, Beregszászi u. 4, Tel: 71-764; **Camping**, Tisza-part.

Restaurants

Kisvárda: **Várda étterem**, Lenin u. 17.; **Kinizsi étterem**, Lenin u. 60. **Vásárosnamény**: In the **Bereg** hotel; **Vasúti étterem**, Lenin u.7.

Tourist Offices

KISVÁRDA : **Nyírtourist**, Lenin u. 2. **VÁSÁROSNAMÉNY** : **Bereg-Tourist**, Szabadság tér 9.

Sightseeing

Kisvárda has a local museum in the old synagogue and an ancient fort (with museum) where the town holds an annual theater festival. Vásárosnamény for its part has a very interesting museum with an enormous collection of castiron stoves. Beyond the Tisza river are some folk treasures, the churches of Tákos and Csaroda, and many typical wooden bell towers.

NYÍRSÉG
SOUTHERN HALF
Accomodation

MÁTÉSZALKA: **Hotel Szatmár**, Hösök tere 20.
FEHÉRGYARMAT: **Hotel Szamos**, Móricz Zsigmond út 8.

Restaurants

MÁTÉSZALKA: **Kossuth étterem**, Kossuth L. u. 36; In the **Szatmár** hotel; **Zöldfa étterem**, Bajcsy-Zsilinsky u. 19. **FEHÉRGYARMAT**: In the **Szamos** hotel; **Halászcsárda**, Kossuth tér 14.

Tourist Office

MÁTÉSZALKA: **Szatmár Tourist**, Bajcsy-Zsilinszky u. 30.

Museums:

MÁTÉSZALKA: Museum of the Szatmár region (closed Mondays) includes a very fine collection of carts. The birthplaces of author Zsigmond Móricz in **Tiszacsege** and of poet Kölcsey in **Szatmárcseke** are visitable on request.

THE HUNGARIAN MOUNTAINS

BÖRZSÖNY RANGE
MÁTRA RANGE
EGER AND THE BÜKK
AGGTELEK
MISKOLC
ZEMPLÉN RANGE

The flatlands cast a shadow on the hills in Hungary. The fame of the puszta, with its rambunctious riders, colorful festivals and deceptively laid-back lifestyle, coupled with the gaudier pleasures of the Balaton and Budapest, have attracted more attention than those foothills of the Carpathians that stretch all along the northeastern border. In its prime, Hungary possessed the spectacular Tátra and Fátra ranges in Slovakia and the densely forested Ukrainian Carpathians that are today in the USSR and Romania. What remains from these past glories can be roughly divided from east to west into the following ranges: Börzsöny, Mátra, Aggtelek, Bükk and Zemplén.

These mountains have always played an important role in Hungary's history. For one, they hold a fair reserve of coal and ore, which gave rise to several major industrial centers such as Ózd, Salgótarján, Kazincbarcika, and above all Miskolc. The great number of fortresses also testify to the strategic importance of the region. Most were built after the Mongol invasion of 1241 but, with a few notable exceptions, failed to offer any serious resistance to the Turks. If they all lie in

Left: Taking some home bread and grown off to market is a small but handy source of income.

ruins at the top of their lonely hills, it is thanks to demolition crews sent by the Habsburg emperor Luitpold I at the end of the 17th century, as a prophylactic measure against the Hungarian petulance when it came to Austrian expansion.

THE BÖRZSÖNY RANGE

The Ipoly river, flowing along the Czech border and into the Danube, marks the contours of the Börzsöny mountains, whose tame, generous valleys stretch eastward to the Cserhát and Karancs-Medves hills, past Salgótarján. The highest peak, the **Csóványos**, stands at 938 m, right on the dividing line between Pest and Nógrad districts. These erstwhile volcanic slopes exude a certain warmth and fertility propicious to a limited wine industry. Much of local life and culture has been preserved in museums. In **Szob** on the Danube, for example, the local museum documents the life and times of the denizen of the Börzsöny. Further to the north off the road to Kemence, is an old mining village called **Nagybörzsöny** where the trials and tribulations of the local miners is on display. Of particular interest here is the unassuming miners' church (*bányásztemplom*) whose portal is ornated with the miners' coat-of-arms.

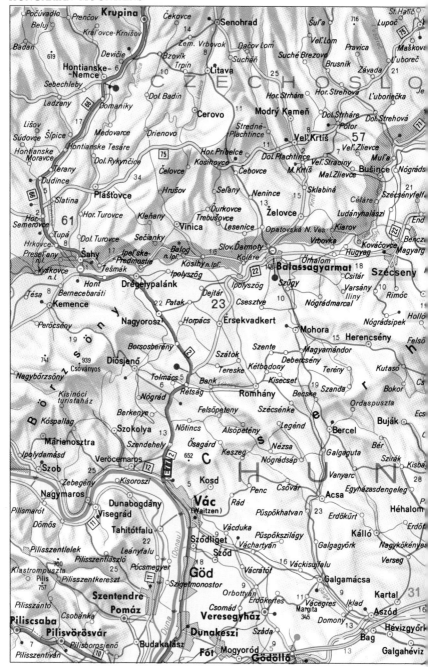

THE MOUNTAINS

0   10km

The bulk of the Börzsöny is taken up by **Nógrád district**, named after an extremely modest village, guarded by the fierce-looking ruins of a fortress. St. István himself, when dividing Hungary into counties, chose the spot to house the administrator of surrounding area. It changed hands several times during the Turkish Wars, and was finished off by lightening in the year 1685.

To the northeast of Nógrád, in a comfortable valley of the Cserhát range, lies **Balassagyarmat**, a town about 20.000 strong. Its main road recalls a relatively wealthy past, when Germans, Slovaks and Czechs mingled with the remains of the Hungarian population after the Turkish Wars to create a fairly important market town. Even the great Maulbertsch deigned come in the 18th century to participate in decorating the newly-built church. Everything seems a little more quiet now, as if covered in a thin layer of dust. Its claim to fame is the **Palozan Museum**, with one of the finest ethnographic collections documenting that peculiar tribe of uncertain origin (some say Slovak), that settled in the region. The building itself, designed by Gyula Walder in 1914, and recently restored, is a fine example of Hungarian eclecticism. The park surrounding it has its own share of sights, including Hungary's oldest open-air museum and an open-air stage.

The neighboring town of **Szécsény**, though a degree smaller than Balassagyarmat, is by far richer in sights and history. It was here, in 1705, that Ferenc II Rákóczi summoned the Hungarian Diet that ultimately elected him king. The Franciscan church and monastery, once upon a time in Gothic style, became one of the finest Baroque churches in the region. Of the two bastions remaining from the old fortress, the northeastern one used to serve as a prison and those with a

liking for penal paraphenalia may enjoy the exhibits. In the mid-18th century the Forgách family had a pretty castle built where the fortress once stood. Today this architectural jewel of burned yellow in the pastel landscape surrounded by an intricate wrought-iron fence, serves as a multi-purpose museum devoted to hunting and archeological findings in Nógrád district. A surprise awaits in the little house where the concierge once lived, something looking like a Buddhist shrine with various religious artifacts from the Asian sub- continent. Local authorities used the space to honor one Sándor Csoma Körösi (1784-1842), a linguist and orientalist, author of a Tibetan-English dictionary and grammar (1834).

Szécsény also boasts a cooperative selling Palozan artifacts and folk art. The Palozans, it soon becomes clear, have become something of a trade-mark and attraction for the western mountains. In particular the village of **Hollókö**, about 16 km southeast of Szécsény, where a Palozan community consisting of about 50 houses and a chapel were declared part of the world heritage by UNESCO in 1988. Many of the houses are inhabited by "normal" people, generally fairly elderly women who still – one suspects by decree – wear their traditional costumes and sell hand-stitched neckerchiefs and bookmarks.

When the little church bell tinkles at vespers, they are the only ones who appear in the dusk to go about their religious duties. The whitewashed houses themselves are typical for the Hungarian countryside, with a kitchen serving as an entrance flanked by two rooms. A small museum has been arranged in one of them, others serve as restaurants or offer modest lodgings for the weary traveler. The gloomy fortress overlooking Hollókö, once owned and operated by the Illés family and demolished in 1718 by the Austrians, is one of the most complete specimens of this kind in the country.

Right: The volcanic ground in the Börzsöny mountains is good for wine.

The capital of Nógrád county since 1950 has been a town pooh- poohed in many travel guides as a drab industrial center. True, **Salgótarján** is not beautiful, having grown into an kind of 7 km- long polyp along the Zagyva valley. Its wealth lies in coal mining and iron casting. It was for a while at least a stronghold of the workers' movement in Hungary. Some feeling of the old solidarity still seeps down from the town's famous statue, an oversized metal partisan holding an old Lewis machine gun, and from the exhibits in the mining museum, which proudly documents centuries of back- and soul-breaking work. One can also take a little trip down into disaffected diggings. For its part the fairly recently completed **Sándor Nógrádi Museum** offers a wider selection of artifacts from life above ground. The surrounding area is particularly beautiful with romantic ruins and such geological curiosities as basalt cliffs (in Somoskö). To the north of Salgótarján stands the 720 m Karancs peak known as the "Palozan Olympus".

THE MÁTRA RANGE

The dramatic Mátra, a small, steep, and densely-wooded range, lies to the south of Salgótarján. Its northern edge has only few important attractions. The Catholic church in the tiny village of **Nádújfalu** has an interesting painted coffered ceiling, and in **Pétervására** the onetime castle of Count Keglevics has become a technical school, so the amusing frescos in the main meeting room are out of reach of the general public.

The Mátra's sightseeing route connects Gyöngyös to Eger, passing by Hungary's highest peak, the **Kékestetö** (1015 m) by Mátraháza, site of a ski jump, skiing slopes and a secession-style hotel built in 1927. The **Paráds** (Parádsasvár, Parád and Parádfürdö) constitue a line of pretty villages tucked away in a narrow valley. The great Hungarian architect Miklós Ybl designed two castles here, one in **Sasvár**, that grows out of the woods as if it had grown along with the trees, the other in Parád itself. It is here that Count

197

Károlyi tried to set an example for other nobles in 1919 by freeing his serfs. Parád also boasts a little Palozan house with a simple kitchen, barn and yard, and a very fine coach museum showing coaches and the tools of the coach-making trade as well. Finally, Parádfürdö consists mainly of an old and beautiful spa.

The landscape around **Recsk** appears beautiful to the innocent traveler, but to Hungarians the name is inevitably associated with a Stalinist concentration camp that was located in the hills somewhere nearby. It, and all records or mention of its existence, were eliminated after Imre Nagy came to power in 1953. Its survivors were not permitted to talk about it in public or private.

Another way to reach Eger is along the southern slopes of the Mátra through Abasár and Markaz. The great smokestack that dominates the foothills belongs

Above: The Turks – headache and trademark of Eger. Right: Romantic encounter on the way to Eger's fortress.

to the lignite-fired **Gagarin power plant**, which, besides electricity, provides Hungary with a sizable portion of its air pollution. The area once belonged to the powerful Aba family that supplied Hungary with a king in 1041- 1044, Samuel Aba. His grave is in the beautiful 12th century crypt of the parish church of **Feldebrö**. The frescos here are unique examples of Romanesque art in Hungary (if not in Europe) and well worth a little detour. And finally, before reaching Eger look for the hot springs of **Egerszalók** that burst free when a team of drillers was looking for oil.

EGER AND THE BÜKK RANGE

Eger, one of Hungary's urban pearls if one disregards the standard highrises that litter the northern end of the city, lies in a wide valley between the Mátra and **Bükk mountains**. Bükk in Hungarian means "beech", and an excursion into its hills, where charcoal burners still ply their trade, reveals generous slopes replete with their silver trunks. The colors are particularly ravishing on a sparkling fall day, when the foliage turns bright orange and yellow.

Eger's history began when St. István made it one of the ten bishoprics in his domain. The remains of the old bishop's residence up in the **fort**, a plain building with a harmonious Gothic arcade, is among the surviving architectural treasures. In 1552, a year in which numerous fortresses surrendered to the Turks without much struggle, István Dobó, commander of Eger, held off a large Turkish army for 39 days. Even the women chipped in by pouring boiling peat on the infidel beneath the castle walls. This victory, sung by Hungarian bards, became the subject of a famous novel by Géza Gardonyi, *The Stars of Eger* (1901). Gardonyi even purchased a little house behind the fort where he lived from 1897 until his death in 1922.

In the years following the great siege, Italian builders hastily reinforced and enlarged the fortress using stones from the ruined churches in the town, which accounts for the almost surrealist appearance of isolated lancet window frames and other carved stones in the middle of otherwise prosaic walls. In spite of the preparations however, the Turks finally took the fort in 1596. The history of the town, the fort and the bishops, including remains from its military and civilian life, has been collected and displayed in several interesting museums up in the ruins of the fort.

After the Habsburgs resumed control at the end of the 17th century, the bishops of Eger, in their infinite wisdom, provided an agreeable climate for artists, architects and craftsmen to work in. As a result Eger possesses a great wealth of Baroque buildings. No lesser talent than Giovanni Battista Carlone moved to Eger, where he had a house built for himself (Széchenyi u. 15). He redesigned the **basilika**, which had been used by the Turks as a mosque, though it was later completed in Classisitic style by József Hild. The virtuosic sculptures are by Mario Casagrande. The great **Minorite church** on Dobó square, where two bronzes commemorate Dobó and the struggle with the Turks, was built by Christoph Dientzenhofer from Prague, with frescoes and paintings by Martin Raindl and J. L. Kracker, among others. 160 houses in downtown Eger, including most of those on Dobó u., where German artisans settled in the 18th century, have been declared monuments. On Kossuth Lajos u., one house after the other begs a moment of contemplation. Number 9 is the seat of the county council, beyond its portals one finds two wrought-iron gates, two gems of the trade by Henrik Fazola.

The pride of the town is the **Lyceum** opposite the basilika. Two enlightened bishops of Eger, Bárkóczy and Esterházy, had contemplated endowing Eger with a university in this building, but Vienna refused. Thus it remained merely a school possessing today an excellent library of

199

130.000 volumes and a ceiling fresco representing the council of Trent painted by Kracker. The creme of its current collection consist of scientific works from the 16th-18th centuries. Another smaller lending library in the ex-chapel features frescos by Maulbertsch.

91 years of Turkish occupation also left its mark, however: one minaret, the northernmost Turkish relic in Europe, two Turkish baths, and indirectly the beautiful Serbian church (Széchenyi u. 59), sponsored by Serbian merchants who moved to Eger during the Turkish occupation. Of course, for today's merchants of Eger, the once feared crescent now serves as an attractive logo for such establishments as a Turkish coffee house, a Turkish bazar, a hotel Minaret, a restaurant Talisman.

Eger produces one major export article. Take a cab when you visit the

Above: Charcoal makers still ply their trade in the Bükk mountains. Right: The Lipizzaner horses, raised in Szilvásvárad.

Szépasszony völgy, the Valley of the Pretty Woman, for it generates one of the finest Hungarian wines, the famous, dark red, strong and lively *Eger Bull's Blood* (*Egri bikavér*). It consists of a mixture of red wines, the Hungarian Kadarka, a Burgundy and a Médoc. Eger also produces several other nice wines, which are all available in the Valley in special wine saloons that growers have arranged at the entrance of their cellars.

Excursions around Eger also reap a fair share of sites. The Matyo people, who are known for their beautiful embroidery, live mainly in **Mezökövesd**, southward, on the border of the puszta. Their name goes back to King Mátyás Corvinus, who gave the town market rights. To the east is **Noszvaj** with a beautiful castle, **Bogács**, where one may benefit from the smelly, sulphurous waters, and finally **Bükkzsérc** where Kracker took a break from his work in Eger to do the altar paintings in the Catholic church.

The road to the north is by far the most interesting however, One of the last Ro-

manesque churches in Hungary stands in a lonely spot a few kilometers east of **Bélapátfalva**. It was begun in the 1230s by the Cistercian order, but only completed after a new crew arrived in the wake of the lethal Mongol invasion of 1241. All that remains of the adjacent monastery is a knee-high wall, but its stones are a little west of Bélapátfalva. They were used to build a small church on the road to **Bükkszentmárton**, on the place where a village had stood before the Mongols.

The next town northwards, **Szilvásvárad**, is by reputation a one-horse town: Its breeding stables, museum, track, even hotel, is devoted to the rare and world-famous Lippizzaner horses. The Szalajka Valley to the east of town meanders on well-marked hiking trails up toward the highest peak in the Bükk mountains, the **Istallos-kö**, past a waterfall gently tripping down several steps. Along the way are numerous open-air exhibits detailing the sometimes stark life of the Bükk timbermen and charcoal burners.

FROM AGGTELEK TO MISKOLC

The wildest, remotest and most dramatic country in Hungary lies due north of Szilvásvárad, the dolomitic slopes of the **Aggtelek Range**. With its sleepy villages and peaceful valleys, it is an ideal place for those with a taste for being far from the maddening crowds. **Aggtelek** itself is a tiny village, where such wonderful things as single-digit telephone numbers still exist. Near the eastern town line is a clear lake resting in the midst of a striking rocky landscape. In spite of its size though, Aggtelek draws large crowds during the high season. Most come to explore Europe's largest **cave network** that winds its stalagmitic, stalagtitic way for over 22 km. The tallest stalagmite in the world stands a full 25 m high in the Baradla cave which has an entrance in Czechoslovakia (where it is called Domica), in Aggtelek and in neighboring Josvafö.

One road back to civilization, that is, to Miskolc, carves its way through the

201

wooded slopes of the **Cserehát hills**, by Szin and Szinpetri, and then down to **Szalonna**, where the artless little protestant church reveals a surprise, the remains of 13th century frescos and a wooden choir decorated with typical floral folk motives. **Rakaca**, to the east, boasts the country's largest reservoir.

Miskolc is Hungary's second largest city, with a population of about 240.000, and one of the worst reputations as far as tourism goes because it is also Hungary's second largest industrial center. Poisonous air from the iron works sometimes sits without budging in the valley, sirens from the factories low day and night. Arriving from the northeast and particularly from the south one is greeted by an army of grim highrises. Only the tortuous trip from Eger over the Bükk mountains provides for a somewhat more memorable welcome. In **Lillafüred**, the old palace hotel pitturesquely stands on

Above: The cellars of Tokaj have produced fine wines for centuries.

the bank of the Hámor Lake. Nature offers all her splendors here for the hiker, including two caves. Then shortly past the town line on the right the four remaining towers of the **Diosgyör Fortress** seem to beckon. It enjoyed the favors of such kings as Lajos the Great and Mátyás Corvinus and after its destruction at the end of the 17th century, of local builders who used it as a source of stones.

As expected, of course, in Miskolc there is more to actually see than meets the eye. The Protestant church in town breathes a simple charm, with its pure white walls. The other Protestant church, in the sea of graves on the Avas hill, reminds us with its pointed shingle roof and separate bell tower, that we are in eastern Hungary. Inside, the walls display paraphenalia such as weather vanes and steeple stars from other no longer existing churches. G. B. Carlone, from Eger, built the Baroque Minorite church on Heros' square. Behind it, in a small rather tousled garden, is the Classical Greek orthodox church with a fine iconostases by Miklós Jankovich. Icons, bibles and religious objects from other orthodox Hungarian parishes have been gathered in a small museum. Miskolc still has a functioning synagogue in the middle of town, and when walking up toward the TV tower to catch a veritable bird's eye view of the city and the puszta, one passes close to a forlorn Jewish cemetery, where the grass needs mowing and the keeper's laden clothesline hangs from grave to grave.

Like most Hungarian towns, Miskolc also has its spa. In **Miskolctapolca** naturally radioactive waters are used to treat lung ailments, and they can be enjoyed in the setting of a natural cavern. In summer, after swimming and healing, one can take a pleasant walk in the park, have a bite and refreshments at one of the many little cafés, and even go rowing on an artificial pond.

THE ZEMPLÉN RANGE

The last mountain range on our trip through northeastern Hungary, the **Zemplén**, is the most colorful in many ways. Its southern end consists of warm and fertile hills, the northern part ressembles the Bükk in overall character, with the Nagy-Milic summit reaching the 894 m mark.

By far the most interesting trail to the Zemplén is on route 37 from Miskolc through the town of **Scerencs**, where in 1605 István Bocskai, leader of the Hayducks against the Habsburgs and the Turks alternatively, was officially chosen to lead the country. The castle where this took place belonged to the Rákóczi family and harbors today not only a museum of Zemplén history, but a large collection of postcards. Northwest of Szerencs is **Monok**, a community of about 2000 souls that has succeeded in producing two of Hungary's great leaders-for-hard-times. The first was Lajos Kossuth, whose birth house has naturally been turned into a museum, and

the second is of more recent date, socialist Prime Minister Miklós Németh who took the helm in the decisive year 1989.

"The wine of kings and the kings of wine" it has been called. Once upon a time it served as a solvent for the medical preparations of medieval witch-doctors, later it made its way to royal tables, then it was sung by poets and musicians, today **Tokajer**, the wine that grows around a promontory on the southern tip of the Zemplén, is considered if not the finest, then at least a unique wine. The region, named after a small, once wealthy village, lies more or less to the right of route 37, where the Tisza and Bodrog rivers meet. Tokajer comes in various forms, is generally more pungent than normal wines, and as such tends to ressemble sherry. A vicious philloxera threatened the further existence of Tokajer (and other wines in Hungary) at the end of the 19th century, but thanks to resistant strains donated by America, the industry picked up again after a temporary hiatus. In Tokaj itself one can find ample infor-

mation on the wine and its history, especially in the cellar museum on Petöfi street, and in the Tokaj museum on Gábor Bethlen u. If by car, keep in mind that Hungarian law does not permit any alcohol for the driver. Bottled Tokajer is available throughout most of Hungary at a reasonable rate. If you chose to purchase some wine directly from the growers, bring your own containers.

Further north in **Sárospatak**, the mood turns more serious. The **Protestant College** here, where such great Hungarians as Kossuth, Kazinczy and Csokonai Vitez studied, opened its doors in 1531 and became something of a Calvinist beacon for Europe. The library contains even more books than that of Eger, but its fresco by a local artist fails in its attempt to give the illusion of a domed ceiling. A number of rooms have been commandeered for an

interesting exhibition documenting aspects of student life over the centuries.

The **castle** within the old walls of the fortress represents a curious mixture of styles, beginning with Renaissance and ending somewhere closer to the Baroque. Its core, the square, five-storied **Red Tower**, which overlooks the flatlands, with its feudal coarseness, existed already before the year 1526. Originally it belonged to the Perényi family. Later it was purchased by the Rákóczis, a particularly rebellious dynasty who made it (in)famous. In 1670, Ferenc I Rákoczi and accomplices conspired against the Habsburgs in the so-called *sub rosa* room in the northeastern corner; and his son Ferenc II, leader of the War of Independence against the Habsburgs (1703-1711) held the last Hungarian assembly here in 1708. The castle was later purchased by the Austrian Windischgraetz family. The bulk of the exhibits consists of flags, weapons, military garb, and a collection of 16th to 19th century Hungarian furniture.

Above left: Folk art exhibited in Telkibánya. Above right: Detail from the fresco in the Sárospatak library. Far right: Another day goes by in Gönc.

Across from the castle is the **Hotel Borostyan**, once upon a time a Dominican cloister, whose cells became rooms and whose chapel serves as a restaurant and periodically as a disco (something to know if booking a room). And down the street, in this otherwise purely Protestant center, stands the Catholic church, across the street from a small museum with Catholic church paraphernalia.

Sárospatak commissioned one of Hungary's foremost architects to design the cultural house, and it has become something of a site in its own right. Iván Makovec, in his usual style, built something obviously modern, but at the same time using primeval, organic shapes, truly a pleasure to the eye considering the number of townscapes destroyed by ugly, impractically utilitarian and drab official buildings.

Sárospatak, as it is known locally, is by no means the last stop on this journey. An excursion through the higher Zemplén reaps quite a number of small gems. **Sátoraljaújhely** has focussed its atten-

tion on its great son Ferenc Kazinczy, the "renewer" of the Hungarian language, with a museum and mausoleum in his honor. The road west leads to **Füzér**, where the Perényi's fortress stands like a single tooth atop its volcanic pedestal, exhibiting the elongated windows of what used to be its chapel. **Hollóháza** has a reputation for its ceramics, and a tour through the factory (with museum) reveals that many of the older patterns and colors were certainly more attractive, though the new ones also appear to have found their own market.

Older maps have not marked the brand new road that connects to Kéked and **Gönc**, a village whose reputation rests on its production of oak barrels in which Tokajer ripens. Here the road forks either back to Sátoraljaújhely over **Telkibánya** where the local museum possesses a fine collection of pottery, ceramics and local minerals, or south to **Vizsoly**. In the church of this unassuming community is a copy of the first Hungarian-language bible.

BÖRZSÖNY-KARANCS RANGE
Accomodation
BALASSAGYARMAT: **Hotel Ipoly**, Bajcsy-Zsilinsky u. 1.

SALGÓTARJÁN: **Hotel Karancs**, Tanácsköztársaság tér 21, Tel: (32) 10-088; **Hotel Salgó**, Eresztvény, Tel: (32) 10- 558; Camping, Tel: (32) 11-168. **Special**: Inquire at the tourist office in Salgótarján about rooming in **Hollókö**.

Restaurants
BALASSAGYARMAT: At the **Hotel Poly**; **Balassa étterem**, Rákóczi u. 34; **Palóc étterem**, Rákóczi u. 23.

SZÉCSÉNY: **Rákóczi étterem**, Rákóczi út 95.

HOLLÓKÖ: **Vár étterem**, Kossuth L. u..

SALGÓTARJÁN: At the **Karancs**; **Salgó étterem**, Lenin tér; **Fekete Gyémánt**, Tanács út.

Tourist Offices
BALASSAGYARMAT: **Nógrád Tourist**, Köztársaság tér 7/a; **IBUSZ**, Rákóczi fejedelem u. 48. SALGÓTARJÁN: **Nógrád Tourist**, Palócz Imre tér 3.

Sightseeing
The mountains offer good opportunities for hiking around a little. Do not miss the **Palozan Museum** in Balassagyarmat with its open-air museum nearby, the **Castle** and its museums in Szécsény, devoted to a variety of subjects: Hunting, literature, archeological finds and to the great orientalist Sándor Csama Körösi (closed Mondays). The old part of **Hollókö** where Palozan houses have been placed on the UNESCO list of protected monuments is also important. A small Palozan museum has been placed in one of the houses. Also take a walk up to the old fortress; and if in **Salgótarján** see the **Mining Museum** (Bem u. 4) which offers excursions down into an authentic mineshaft. The Sándor Nógrádi Museum on Rákóczi út shows aspects of local culture past and present (closed Mondays).

MÁTRA
Accomodation
Being a fairly important attraction, the Mátra mountains have no dearth of lodgings, mostly in the form of inns and bed-and-breakfasts.

GYÖNGYÖS: **Hotel Mátra**, Mátyás Király u. 2, Tel: (37) 12-057.

MÁTRAFÜRED: *MODERATE*: **Hotel Avar**, Parádi út 5, Tel: (37) 13-195. PARÁD: Hotel Palóc, **Kossuth u. 332;** Motel Túra **(including a camping site), on Rute 24 near Parádsasvár.**

Restaurants
GYÖNGYÖS: In the **Hotel Mátra**; Kékes étterem, Fö tér 7; **Kedves kisvendéglö**, Arany János u. 1; **Olimpia étterem**, Olimpia u. 2;

Huszárkert **Kisvendéglö**, Rózsa u. **PARÁD**: Muflon étterem; at the **Hotel Palóc**.

Tourist Offices
GYÖNGYÖS: **Mátratourist**, Szabadság tér 2, Tel: (37) 11-565; **IBUSZ**, Kossuth u. 6..

Sightseeing
The Mátra range is one of the few places in Hungary that keeps on running in Winter owing to the skiing opportunities it offers, including ski-jumping. Summer is for hikers and water enthusiasts who can enjoy baths at Mátrafüred and Parádfürdö in particular. **Museums:** In Paràd you will find stables and a coach museum in the middle of town with coaches and coachmaking tools.

EGER
Accomodation
MODERATE: **Hotel Eger**, Szálloda u. 1-3, Tel: (36) 13-233; **Hotel Park**, Klapka György u. 8. *BUDGET:* **Hotel Unicornis**, Dr. Hibay K. u. 2, Tel: (36) 12-886; **Tourist fogadó**, Mekchey u. 2, Tel: (36) 11-724; **Ködmön fogadó**, Szépasszonyvölgy, Tel: (36) 13-172; **Fortuna panzió**, Kapási u. 35/a, Tel: (36) 16- 480; **Panzió Kökút**, Kökút u. 11, Szépasszonyvölgy, Tel: (36) 10-292. *CAMPING:* **Autocamping**, Rákóczi u. 79. Other lodgings can be found in Noszvaj-Síkfökút to the east: **Hotel Síkfökút**; and to the north in Szilvásvárad: **Hotel Lipicai**, Egri út 14.

Restaurants
In the hotels Eger, **Park** and **Unicornis**; **Belvárosi étterem**, Bajcsy-Zsilinsky u. 8; **Vadászkürt étterem**, Marx u. 4; **Mecset étterem**, Knézich u. 8; **Várkapitány étterem**, Fazola Henrik u.; **Tálisman**, Kossuth Lajos u.; Tulipánkert, Szépasszonyvölgy.

Tourist Offices
Egertourist, Bajcsy-Zsilinsky u. 9, Tel: (36) 11-724; **Express**, Széchenyi u. 26.

Sightseeing
Some of the important sites in Eger are: the **Fort** and its historical and religious exhibitions. the **Gèza Gárdonyi memorial museum** (Gárdonyi u. 28) in the house where Gárdonyi wrote his famous *Stars of Eger*. Several interesting **churches**: The Basilica with its treasure chamber, the Minorite Church, the Lyceum with its library and frescos, and last but not least the **minaret**, which can only be seen from the outside. The **Szépasszonyvölgy** is the nicest place to enjoy Eger's wines and of course there is a museum here too documenting the wine. Excursions to **Mezökövesd**, to Bélapátfalva to see the ancient church; and a visit to the horse-town **Szilvásvárad**, where one can take a beautiful walk into the Bükk mountains.

AGGTELEK
Accomodation
Hotel **Cseppkö**; the camping near the Baradla cave also has vacation homes. The **tourist office** is on the camping site. The only restaurant in town is in the Hotel Cseppkö. Further lodgings, including a camping site are in the next village **Jósvafö**, where the **Hotel Tengerszem**, also has the restaurant monopoly.

Sightseeing
Visitors to Aggtelek enjoy dramatic countryside and must have a penchant for caves: Europe's longest is here, the **Baradla cave**. It contains an impressive collection of stalagmites and stalagtites. Also worthwhile: a visit to the chapel Szalonna, a swim in the Rakaca reservoir and a look at Szendrö.

MISKOLC
Accomodation
MODERATE: **Hotel Pannónia**, Kossuth u. 2, Tel: (46) 88-022; **Hotel Juno**, Csaba u. 2-4, M'tapolca, Tel: (46) 64- 133; **Hotel Park**, Bak Dénes u., M'tapolca, Tel: (46) 60-811.
BUDGET: **Hotel Aranycsillag**, Széchenyi u. 22-24, Tel: (46) 35-114; **Hotel Avas**, Széchenyi u. 1, Tel: (46) 37- 798; **Hotel Lido**, Kiss J. u. 4, M'tapolca, Tel: (46) 69-035; **Ozon fogadó**, Erzsébet sétány 7, Lillafüred, Tel: (46) 51-299.
CAMPING: **Autocamping**, Iglói út 13, M'tapolca, Tel: (46) 67-171.

Restaurants
MISKOLC: **Hági étterem**, Zsolcai kapu 5; **Halásztanya kisvendéglö**, Mélyvölgy 15; **Matyó étterem**, Klapka György u. 27; **Pálos vendéglö**, Árpád u.1; **Vár étterem**, Vince u. 2. LILLAFÜRED: **Vadászkürt étterem**, Palota 80.

Tourist Offices
Borsod Tourist, Széchenyi u. 35, Tel: (46) 35-946; **Cooptourist**, Arany János u. 35, Tel: (46) 36-591; **Express**, Széchenyi u. 56, Tel: (46) 36-560.

Sightseeing
Four churches, two Protestant, one Catholic and a Greek Orthodox (incl. a museum of the Greek Orthodox faith in Hungary) are among the treasures of Miskolc. The Diósgyör fortress is the site of concerts during the summer. Lillafüred has its own share of natural splendors, a lake, caves, hikes into the **Bükk mountains**. Not to be missed is a swim in the caves of Miskolctapolca with its radioactive waters. On the way to Tokaj, stop off at the **Rákóczi castle** to visit the historical museum and the display of old postcards. In **Monok** is the birthplace of Lajos Kossuth.

TOKAJ
Accomodation
Hotel Tokaj, Rákóczi út 5; a camping site has been arranged on the banks of the Tisza.

Restaurants
At the **Tokaj** hotel; **Halászcsárda Tiszavirág**, Münnich F. u. 4; **Rákóczi étterem**, Bethlen Gábor u. 35.

Tourist Office
Tokaj Wine Tours, Rákóczi u. 39

Sightseeing
One comes to Tokaj not to breath fresh air, but to taste the wine, visit the wine museums in Tokaj and Tarcal and see a few cellars. If you are driving remember at all!

SÁROSPATAK
Accomodation
MODERATE: **Hotel Bodrog**, Rákóczi u. 58, Tel: (41) 11-744; **Hotel Borostyán** (in an old cloister), Kádár Kata u. 28, Tel: (41) 11-611.
CAMPING: **Tengerszem**, Herczeg u. 2.
SÁTORALJAÚJHELY: **Hotel Báév**, 'Árpád út 10/a, (41) 22-143; **Hotel Zemplén**, Széchenyi tér 5-7, Tel: (41) 22-522; **Kossuth camping**, Várhegy u. 10, Tel: (41) 21-164.

Restaurants
In the hotels **Bodrog** and **Borostyán**; **Otthon étterem**, Zrínyi u. 45; **Kisvendéglö**, Szabadság tér 2; **Vadászkürt étterem**, Kossuth L. u. 57.

Tourist Offices
Borsod Tourist, Kossuth u. 46, Tel: (41) 11-620.

Sightseeing
Sárospatak has a particularly well-preserved fort and a visitable **Protestant College** with a museum of student history. The library should also be seen. The **Fort** itself has several exhibits, one detailing the War of Independence (1793-1711), with military paraphenalia, costumes and the like, and with furniture from the 16th - 19th centuries. Excursions to northern Zemplén, in particular to **Hollóháza**, where ceramics have been produced for centuries.
On the way stop off at the new museum (local history) on Ràkóczi u. in Sátoraljaújhely. After Hollóhaza comes **Gönc** with a house museum, whose guide (in 1990) was born there. Further, in **Telkibánya**, is a little museum of local history with a nice collection of ceramics and crystals. The first Hungarian translation of the bible is south in the Protestant church of **Visoly**. All museums are closed on Mondays. Out in the small villages, however, it is sometimes possible to find the keeper or parson nearby and have a short tour for a small obolus (this applies to churches in particular).

WINTER IN HUNGARY

It is the end of October. The trees have already shed their yellow and red foliage. The rivers cast off thick billows of fog that drown the landscapes in the morning. To relieve their loneliness the taller trees try to catch a low cloud with their dark, bare boughs. The chattering harvesters have long left the vineyards, the vines hang barren on their wires and song has given way to the whispering winds. The puszta's subtle coloring has melded into a few grey and brown hews, the riders have gone home, the shutters on lonely houses are closed. Winter is coming to Hungary, and hardly any tourists venture into this dying country.

A cold wind also sweeps through the streets of Budapest but not everyone is hurrying back to the warmth of the comfort of their homes. There is music, laughing and talking coming from the city park where the boating pond has been turned into an ice rink. Old and young meet here, staying until late in the evening to skate under the bright lights, to dance and occasionally to drink hot tea with their friends.

Many people also travel to their summer retreats to go skating on frozen lakes. On weekends Lake Velence near Budapest is usually very crowded. Many travel further to Lake Balaton to escape the crowds. This lake, the largest in central and western Europe freezes quickly in winter and remains frozen for a long time. It is often covered with a 20-30 cm thick layer of ice. The record was in 1929 when the layer measured 70 cm. In extremes of temperature the ice contracts and tears apart. This phenomenon is accompanied by strange sounds. When the temperature rises again the ice expands and piles form along the beaches. This

movement of ice can cause serious damage to the buildings near the bank. And it can be dangerous to skate on the ice at this time too.

The Balaton in Winter has an almost sinister charm. Just when the air is at its most still, a storm often blows up without warning in the Lake Balaton area. When the fishermen hear the storm rustling in the trees far away, they no longer have enough time to take shelter on the Zala shore. "The oncoming storm drove a snow" cloud from behind the mountain, from which shot icy crystals as sharp as needles. The cloud blocked off half the sight and blanketed the entire area around Tihany, the rocky peninsula and gloomy church included the darkness, while the clayey eastern shore sparkled in the light of the moon. The storm howled through the tops of the trees of the Arác Valley. The windvanes on the old Summer Villa shrieked like dammed souls crying for their lost lives, and as the storm swept over the ice of Lake Balaton a supernatural sound whistled out from the piles of ice on the lake. It was as if one could hear ghosts following each other, howling and weeping all at once. Now and again one of them screamed in anger. Was it he who was chasing the others?"

What the Lake Balaton connoisseur Jókai portrayed in his work *Timár's Two Worlds* is thankfully a rare occurrence. But precisely because it is so rare, it is important to know that this lake is not always harmless and idyllic.

In good weather most of the visitors put on their ice skates and let themselves be blown along in the wind. Others make themselves a sledge or a wind surf board, with which they can cruise along at 70-80 km an hour. Some even take a chance and drive their cars onto the lake.

What to Do

If despite all this movement you are chilled to the bone, why not visit the

Preceding pages: A German folk dance. Caught in the act at Kaposvár. Left: Hungary dies once a year.

Hévíz, Europe's largest warm water pool. 86 million liters of thermal water rise daily from a depth of 36.5 meters. In winter the water is 23-26°C and you can swim in the open air or under a glass roof.

Hungary is not only a large, flat puszta, but has its own share of mountains too. They are not all that high but they are well suited for winter sports – assuming there is snow of course. The **Kékés** with an elevation of 1015 m is the highest point in Hungary. According to statistics the sun shines for 275 hours here in the winter months, and this is enjoyed by hikers, skiers and the patients at the local sanatorium alike. There is a fine panorama from here and two slopes of usable length: One is 2400 m long and runs to Mátraháza, the other, more difficult and steeper runs north. This is recommended only for experienced skiers.

Another hibernal activity of course is sledding, which can be practiced on any

Above: By now the wine has already been pressed and bottled.

smooth slope or forest path. Jósafö, all the way in the north near Aggtelek, has prepared trails for this purpose. Even if you are staying in Budapest, however, you will find opportunities to ski. From the 477 m height of the village of Normafa you will find a wonderful view of the city itself and a pleasant skiing area with two jumps and a lift.

Customs

Winter is also the time when pigs are slaughtered. This usually takes place in December, for pork is the traditional New Year's Day dish. The pig is supposed to bring good luck into the house. Chicken should not be eaten, for chickens are supposed to act counter to good luck.

These events have grown into family festivals when relatives come together. Slaughtering takes place early in the morning, and then there is work to be done. The men prepare the sausage meat, pickle or braise the bacon, and the women do the rest. But this communal work soon turns into a binge of eating, drinking and endless chattering. At the end each participant takes back a sample for those who had to stay at home.

A number of originally religious festivals at which unique ceremonies take place are part of this cycle of the year. Most of them are associated with the New Year. Until the 16th century the New Year began at Christmas in Hungary. "Lucia Day" (December 13) was the most important day for girls and women in December, and they were not allowed to work on this particular feast. Countless stories tell of how Lucia punishes those who dare to spin, sew or wash clothes on her day. Lucia hurls the spindle at the woman, turns her yarn into tow, or sews up the chickens so that they can't lay any more eggs. On Lucia's Day the so-called Lucia chair is begun. This helps the people to recognize witches on the day of fasting before Christmas. There is hardly a village without its own stories about the Lucia chair.

The "Shepherds of Bethlehem", who wore their sheepskins inside out, are the focal point of Hungarian Christmas plays. The participants in this scenario sing and carry the crib with the baby Jesus or a church-shaped Bethlehem. Today it is usually children who take part in these processions. The words of the nativity plays vary from area to area.

"Regölés" is the Hungarian variation of the greeting found all over Europe at Christmas and New Year. Children, young lads and men go from house to house wishing good luck and a good harvest for the coming year. Hungarian linguists have discovered that the expression *regölés* and the refrain of the *regös* song, "hey regö rejtem", is of Finno-Ugric origin, and is one of the earliest expressions of Hungarian religion and poetry. It is reminiscent of the old Shaman chants.

On 26th and 27th December all men and boys called István (Steven) and János (John) in Hungarian villages celebrate their name-days. Because both names are common in Hungary, the name-days of these two saints play an important role in the Christmas cycle. This is also a time when friends and relations are visited and festive meals are prepared.

The second most important celebration in the New Year is Three King's Day, whose Hungarian name "vízkerest" (blessing of the water) goes back to the Greek concept *Hagiamos*, although most Catholic peoples know it by the name Epiphany. A source from 11th century reports that the 6th January was celebrated "in the Greek fashion" when water was blessed according to Byzantine rites.

Historical sources tell more about Hungarian Lenten traditions than any other custom. This was one event upon which both secular and religious authorities could wholeheartedly agree. "Carnival" was one of the "bad" customs, because of the noise, nonsense and rioting it fomented, and it had to be forbidden. However carnival was and still is celebrated with the same enthusiasm.

Perhaps the most famous and spectacular of Hungary's carnival celebrations is the "Busójárás" procession down south in Mohács on the Danube and surrounding villages. Whether derived from an ancient custom to chase out the winter or from the expulsion of the Turks is not certain. It involves dressing up in outlandish clothing and donning frightening masks, whereby the animal masks are particularly remarkable, especially the bears, horses, goats and storks. Brief sketches combining mime and dialogue are part of the procession. For example, the horse or goat is brought to the market and while the owner and the dealer argue about the price the animal falls dead to the floor. It comes alive again when the music starts. And, of course, there is a bonfire to rid the world of the old spirit, and a fair deal of drinking the usher in the new.

HEALING WATERS

Moses struck the rock with his staff and immediately water gushed forth to refresh his thirsty flock. The Hungarians bored holes in the ground and immediately thermal waters gushed forth to heal the sick. The more than 500 mineral and healing springs in the country produce water with temperatures ranging between 35 °C and 90 °C constituting one of Hungary's most important resources. More than 150 million cubic meters of water is used every year from an estimated 300 billion cubic meters.

People settled here far back in time to be near these medicinal and thermal waters. And besides washing and healing, the springs have also been used to heat entire housing projects, notably in Szeged. Archaeological finds prove it.

The greatest concentration of baths is today in Budapest. According to legend it was a hermit living alone at the foot of the Gellért Hill who first recognized the healing powers of the sparkling spring nearby and who first used the water for therapeutic purposes. He quickly gained a reputation as a miracle healer. We won't go into the question of whether he earned any money from his miracles! Later the Knights of Saint John of Jerusalem founded a "Bath House" on the very spot where St. Elizabeth healed lepers using the salubrious waters.

The Turks occupied the country from 1526 to 1686 bringing with them not only want and destruction, but coffee, new arts and crafts and their own bathing culture, for the prophet says: "Cleanliness is half of belief." The Turks were most impressed by the medicinal springs and the medicinal mud available in their new dominions. Even sick or injured horses and mules were brought to the springs. And

Left: The Széchenyi Bath's impressing entrance in Budapest is a place for a cure and a good time.

the Hungarians followed suit. Miklós Oláh (1493- 1568), archbishop of Esztergom wrote of the peasants and vintners who came to Buda to swim in the hot water in the open air: "Only their heads poke out of the water. They look like the pictures of the resurrection found on numerous church murals."

The Celts, and later the Romans, also used the sorings of Buda in a big way. *Akink*, which means "lots of water" became *Aquincum* under Roman rule (1st-4th century), the capital of the province Pannonia Inferior. The ruins of the formerly splendid bath houses reveal that they were fed by a system of canals and had floor and wall heating, massage rooms and communal relaxation rooms.

The medicinal waters did not fall into disuse after the fall of the Roman Empire and the decay of *Aquincum*. But it was not until the Magyars arrived that their use was recorded again. Saint István built a hospital next to the mineral-enriched thermal spring in 1006 in Pécsvárad (Southern Hungary). It employed six bath masters and four nurses. Géza II gave the spa of Pásztó near Esztergom to the Cistercians in 1142. András II gave his daughter, who would later become Saint Elizabeth, a silver bath tub on the occasion of her marriage to Ludwig IV., son of the landgrave of Thuringia. The first bathroom (with a toilet, incidentally) was built by Count István Széchenyi in his castle at Nagycenk (south of Sopron) in 1840. King Mátyás (1458- 1490) had a bath room built for his "Black Army", a permanent troop of mercenaries in every one of his 700 battle ships. This must be unique in military history.

Hungary soon became famous for its excellent spas. As far back as the end of the 17th century a book was published in Venice called *On Hungarian Mineral Waters*, and by 1860 there were as many as 20 travel guides in German which encouraged their readers to take baths and cures in Hungary. Today some of the

medicinal waters in the country can be purchased in bottles. Extracts of medicinal herbs are added to "Bük bitter water" to improve its taste and healing powers.

The bath houses were used for different reasons at different times in history. In Roman and medieval times they were not only used for ablutionary or for therapeutic reasons but were also a meeting place for people, merchants, politicians and lovers too. A medieval chronicler reported that "any sense of shame disappeared". The Turks put an end to this amorous behavior in their splendid baths with their green and red cupolas. Men and women had to bathe and take cures separately from then on. The health consciousness of recent years and a vacation in Hungary can be combined as a cure under medical supervision. You may wish to check with your insurance company to find out if it will at least foot the bill for treatments. A holiday in Hungary

often works out cheaper than other places. You can swim in closed baths or romantic caves (**Miskolctapolca**). Or you can splash about in open-air swimming pools or in thermal lakes.

Hévíz is the largest European lake of this kind, with a surface of 47.000 square meters and average water temperature of 35 °C. Doctors have been recommending its therapeutic effects since 1730. A steady stream of over 80 million liters of water annually have accounted for the fact that the lake's water was changed three times by the year 1980. But since then the cave fountainhead (36 m underwater) has only been working at half strength.

This means that the lake may well cool down and its ecological balance will be destroyed because the replenishment of the water is now too slow. The cause of this misfortune is the bauxite mining taking place in Nyirád, about 40 km north east of Hévíz, which pumps away the karst water. Hungarians will have to begin asking themselves whether they

Above: Waiting for the water to take effect.
Right: Another dimension of chess.

would rather do without the medicinal effects of the lake, a lake in which millions of people have taken successful cures over the last 200 years, or whether they would prefer to do without the bauxite mines, which safeguard many of the jobs in the large aluminium industry.

The spa of **Zalakaros** which has blossomed since 1964 and which lies 30 km south of Hévíz may well replace the lake. In any case it will always be there for tourists, anglers and water sports. The Old Lake in **Tata** (70 km west of Budapest), reclaimed from the swamps in the 18th century and fed by numerous springs, is near to being rescued. A deposit pool has been dug out at the mines of Tatabánya, where pollutants are collected. Visitors can safely swim in the Old Lake, and they can enjoy the shores of the lake as the famous German author Karl May once did when he was a guest at Esterházy castle.

A spa town in Hungary is recognizable from its name, generally. It will contain the suffix *fürdo* or *füred*, as in Parádfürdö

or Balatonfüred and Mátrafüred. Each spa has one or more specialities: Arthritis is treated in **Bükfürdö** near Köszeg, for example. On the other hand, postoperational or open wounds are quickly healed in **Hajdúszoboszló**. The above mentioned caves of Miskolctapolca seem to do the lungs a world of good. In short, no illness, be it bone, nervous, gynecological, skin- related, stomachal, and so on, lacks a spa in Hungary.

Your doctor should decide on the most suitable place to take a cure. For although the waters are medicinal, they can be harmful under certain conditions. There are countless brochures to help you choose between a drinking, bathing or even a radioactive mud cure. You can also choose which area you visit – the mountains or the plains or Budapest. Suffice to say, you can benefit from the waters at any time and place. Depending on available funds you can choose to stay on a camp site, in a spa hotel or in one of the old baronial castles which have now been turned into hotels.

EATING IN HUNGARY

When thinking of Hungarian food, I inevitably recall my Hungarian father's long battle with various elusive stomachal disorders resulting in a steady intake of pre- and postprandial medicines from plain old bicarbonate of soda to sophisticated wizard oils of modern pharmaceutica. Notwithstanding his abdominal agues he still delights to this day in heavy *pörkölts*, spicy *páprikáses* and juicy portions of stuffed cabbage. With a special glint he can nibble at *töpörtyü* (pork crackling), impale a *dobos* cake or bite into a *csabai* sausage red enough to seer your eyebrows. He can also prepare meals recalling some of the glory of medieval Hungarian cuisine.

Hungarian cuisine has maintained its reputation for tastiness to this very day, but the cost to its consumer's health is not to be underestimated. Daily 10.5 million Hungarians plunge their flatware into dishes that make the taste buds burst and the heart stop in its tracks so that one could almost say that eating in Hungary is a most agreeable form of suicide. The ingredient behind the scenes, giving both taste and weight, is simply pork lard or *zsír*. It is used to oil pans and cake forms, it gives strudels (*rétes*) their fluffiness, it fries onions and replaces butter on bread. The equivalent of the American barbecue in Hungary is called *sütés szalonna* and consists of heating pork fat over an open fire, catching the drippings on a piece of white bread bedecked with onions and indeed eating it. If profuse doses of wine and beer fail to wash it all down, there is always Hungary's reputed *barackpalinka*, apricot brandy.

It is hardly any wonder then, that Hungarians form the bulk of the patients at spas, where the waters are used to treat

Left: Gulash tastes best in Hungary, its home country in a cauldron and with a hint of smoke and ashes.

stomach dysfunctions. Barring a few concessions to "jóga és müzli" by the odd fitness magazine, or the rare vegetarian restaurant, nutritional consciousness that has descended upon the rest of Europe has not reached the Hungarian hearth. Furthermore the average meal hardly provides some of the checks and balances its Western counterpart might offer: Fresh vegetables are seldom available even in season (exept in the more expensive places or private homes), and under salad (*saláta*) a Hungarian menu usually means pickled cabbage, peppers, pickles or the like. *Fejes saláta* refers usually to a head of lettuce cleft in twain and sprinkled with a mixture of vinegar, water and sugar.

By no means does this imply that eating out in Hungary will be a problem. István Lukacs, chef at the Atrium Hyatt gives advice sounding rather like a sports trainer prepping athletes: "Begin with lighter foods, a broth, some fish if it's being offered, chicken, beef, and after a few days, as your stomach gets accustomed to the new food, you can begin trying the heavier dishes." The test for the gold is something called *csülök*, pigs knuckles prepared with onions, peppers and sometimes peas and beans. Also if digestion appears to be slow and unwieldly, Hungary has some excellent remedies: The famous *Unicum*, a stomach bitter is available in most bars, and supermarkets and pharmacies usually carry some type of mildly purgative bitter water (*keserü víz*) to be ingested in homoeopathic doses.

Fortunately there is a good deal of relatively light foods available to begin your culinary journey. Among the soups are various broths and the delicious, cold fruit soup (*gyümölcs leves*). The *Jókai bableves*, a bean soup named after the writer Mór Jókai, is closer to an entrée, with its supplements of smoked sausage and slabs of pork. Advisable too at the beginning in the manner of entrées is

anything marked *rántott* indicating something fried in batter, such as chicken or turkey breast (*pulykamell*). *Pecsenye*, literally "roast", also suggests a lighter preparation of meat; *brassoi pecsenye* is a pleasant mixture of strips of pork, potatoes and onions. In the chapter "meleg elöételek" one sometimes finds *Hortobágyi palacsinta*, a thin pancake stuffed with *pörkölt* (see below). Further down the menu, buried amongst the desserts (*tészták* = pastry), is a dish called *túros csusza* consisting of flat noodles with farmers cheese, sometimes garnished with cracklings (*töpörtyüvel*) or flavored with dill.

Hungary also has a fair amount of fish, albeit the most famous one, *fogas* from Lake Balaton, tends to be more readily available in Vienna where it is sold for much needed hard currency. Low supply and high demand of this delicacy has in addition pushed its market price at times

Above: Garlic, paprika and a myriad of pickles counteract the pork fat.

into the ionosphere. Carp (*ponty*) from the Tisza and the Danube is more affordable and wide-spread, and forms the basis of the spicy Szeged fish soup (*halászlé*), a specialty of the Szeged restaurant Hagi. While traveling along the Danube or the Tisza, keep an eye out for fish restaurants (*halászcsárda* or the like), for they always have something interesting to taste.

Hungary's national dish, if there is such a thing, is what is generally referred to as goulash. At its heart, besides the usual *zsír*, onions and optionally garlic, lies red gold, the famous paprika, red peppers ranging from sweet to very hot. The peppers grow on Hungarian soil, mainly around Szeged and Kalocsa, and no attempts at duplication in other countries have ever been successful. They not only give food a special flavor and a characteristic red color but also provide a considerable amount of vitamin C, as Nobel Prize winner Albert Szent-Györgyi discovered in his laboratory. For centuries paprika, dried and pulverized, graced the tables of Hungary's poor unable to afford the real pepper from the colonies. Then it slowly made its way up the social ladder and established its dominion on the spice shelf. Ask for "goulash" and you will be served a reddish broth with a few chunks of meat and some vegetables in it. The stew-like dish known in most countries as goulash is called *pörkölt* in Hungarian and has two saucier variations: *páprikás* and *tokány*. *Székely-gulyás*, named after the writer József Székely, lying somewhere between the soup and the stew, includes sauerkraut. (Nota bene: Sour cream is often used to provide goulash-type recipes with additional flavor and texture). These dishes are generally served with small dumplings called *galuska*, rice or *tarhonya*, a small, round pasta.

Desserts in Hungary are nothing to mess with in terms of calory intake. The coffeehouses throughout the land offer a vast palette of rich, nutty, chocolatty, creamy cakes and a pleasant sortment of coffees, from the powerful expresso to *café au lait*. The celebrated Dobos cake you can tell from the burnt sugar wafers covering each portion.

Another sweet specialty is *somloi galuska*, a tasty combination of dough, whipped cream, nuts, raisins and other ingredients the sum of whose parts defies description. Those partial to chocolate mousse may wish to try the Hungarian version called *Rigó Jancsi*, named after a famous Gypsy baron. Most places offer a very tasty fruit or cheese strudel generically called *rétes*. Finally, there is the *palacsinta*, a thin pancake filled with jam, farmer's cheese, chocolate or with dried fruits and nuts and covered in chocolate sauce and whipped cream (Gundel-palacsinta). In spring, summer and fall markets and privateers sell the abundant gifts from the land itself – cherries, plums, apricots, peaches, grapes, watermelons....

A fast-food tradition also exists in Hungary parallel to that certain American import. In summer every beach or local fair attracts sausage and pork-hamburger mongers, but the longest queues will inevitably be at the *lángos*-lady, who peddles plate-size portions of fried dough optionally spiced-up with cheese, sour cream and onions. This item must be eaten hot otherwise it looses its crispiness like a potato chip in damp weather. Another favorite is corn on the cob which you find under the sign saying *kukorica*.

To conclude, a word about liquids. The country is a major producer of quality wines the most famous of which is probably the dark and powerful *Bull's Blood* from Eger (*egri bikavér*) and Tokajer. The latter comes from a small region around a town called Tokaj in the southern foothills of the Zemplén mountains. Originally these rather heavy, pungent wines were used in homoeopathy alone but gourmets soon discovered them. They have since earned the distinction: "Wine of kings and king of wines." Some, such as the *Furmint* or *Hárslevelü* are relatively light and aromatic. *Szamorodni* indicates a procedure whereby the grapes are picked and pressed pell-mell relatively late in the season. *Aszú* wine is made from the latest crop in the season, pressed and soaked in a young wine, in casks made of oak from Gönc. The number of baskets of grapes soaked in every cask determines quality, cost and sweetness.

Other excellent wine regions are around the Balaton, in the Villány hills south of Pécs, along the Danube south of Kalocsa, and around Sopron. A word of caution: If you are driving, steer clear of any alcohol as the limit in Hungary is a strict 0,0 pro mille. Which leads us to our last tip: Hungary produces some fine fruit juices, especially apricot, peach, grape, cherry and tomato. Adventurers might want to give pumpkin juice a try. Lastly Hungarian bottled water tastes a little peculiar at times, but there is no denying its salubrious qualities.

FOLKLORIC TRADITION

When speaking of folklore or folk art in general one usually is referring to the art of the peasantry. In Hungary it played a major role in the national reawakening during the 19th century. Peasant songs, for example, had a major influence on the poetry of Sándor Petöfi, and young writers and intellectuals already began collecting folksongs in the first half of the 19th century. By the 1860s a generation of specialists was at work investigating folk art. In 1885 and in 1896, the 1000th anniversary of the Hungarian state, two major folk art exhibits were held.

Music collecting proceeded in earnest under the aegis of Béla Bartók and Zoltan Kodály. The characteristic traits of the Hungarian Secession, a by-product of the Jugendstil, comes from its folk influence. Architects, painters and craftsmen went

Above: Folk music using traditional instruments is back en vogue. Right: Wine dancing on the puszta.

into little villages to urge their own inspiration to new heights. Examples of this can be seen throughout the country, in Budapest in the zoo, on Károly Kós square in the XIXth district, the city hall of Kiskunfélegyháza, or of Kecskemét. The ethnographical museum and the museum of applied arts opened their doors, as well as several open-air museums in Balassagyarmat, in Szentendre, in Nyíregyháza, in Szombathely and the little town of Szenne, where typical farm houses and even churches were gathered from all parts of Hungary. Nowadays they also serve as centers for folkloric events or as schools to revived old and almost forgotten handicrafts. Numerous museums throughout the country document the rich folkloric tradition of the land, among them the Déri museum in Debrecen and the Janus Pannonius museum in Pécs. On special festival days too many villages don a traditional atmosphere and the people accordingly don their ancestors' clothing and exhibit traditional crafts such as lace-

making, embroidery and weaving. One way to get acquainted with Hungarian folk art is to visit the Közmüvelödési Informaciós Vállatat on Miklós square, a pretty Baroque building possessing an excellent video library with several hundred tapes on the subject.

Hungarian folk music is probably the most famous element of Hungarian folk culture. The untrained ear however will often confuse the music played by gypsies in restaurants, gypsy music itself and Hungarian folk music. The first is in fact a kind of mish-mash usually aimed at a particular audience, thus if you are an American the gypsy band will play selections from *West Side Story* or Perry Como hits. Real gypsy music seldom leaves the gypsy circle itself. As for Hungarian folk music, it sometimes is performed by gypsy bands, but seldom in the restaurants catering to Western crowds. To capture its special tonality and lilt, it is worth listening to some of Bartók's *Microcosmos*. Hungarian folk music can be divided into several categories, including Transylvanian, Transdanubian, Highland, Mainland and Moldavian, and along with them come special dances.

Simultaneously to a world-wide movement, about twenty years ago, folk music in Hungary experienced a revival. Furthermore, as its newly acquired popularity as a stage offering grew, pressure also mounted for direct participation. This so-called dance-house movement, whereby the audience is the performing body, has maintained its popularity till today. Almost each day in Budapest one of the dance houses keeps its doors open and hosts one of the popular bands: Muzsikás, Téka, Méta, Ökrös Banda, Kalamajka or Jánosi.

The **Spring Festival**, by the way, held around the third week in March, usually includes a fair deal of folk music including the **Dancehouse Day** with folk songs, traditional dances, a crafts market offering baskets, dresses, records, toys and all the frills – in the Sports Hall in Budapest. The festivities last throughout the entire day. For the neophyte, a small

schooling session usually takes place at the beginning of the day so as to allow for greater participation.

Another interesting folk music festival is in Miskolc, the **Kaláka Folk Festival,** which also allows for some comparison with folk music and dance from other peoples: Irish, Dutch, Swedish and French. The Városi Müvelödesi Központ, Árpád u. 4, 3534 Miskolc, has more information. A smaller event, but equally interesting and especially for those with a little pioneer spirit, is the **Téka Camp** in Nagykálló, a little town east of Nyíregyháza. Information is available from Téka Együttes, P.O.Box 287, 1370 Budapest. If you are seaking information about folk music and dance events, you will find all you need at the Szakmai Ház, I. Budapest, Corvin tér I.

A new phenomenon has arisen in the past few years under the influence of

Above: The floral ornaments of Kalocsa are done by hand. Right: Stencils with complex designs.

Rock music, a kind of hodgepodge between pop and folk using guitars, accordions, saxophone and drums. The popular name for this stew is wedding- or espresso-rock, which suggests its place of origin and practice. In spite of an unspoken boycott by radio and TV stations, this musical form has achieved an incredibly high degree of popularity thanks to private studios that put out hundreds of cassettes. The Rózsavölgyi Zenemübolt (a music store) on Martinelli square has one of the best collections of records and cassettes on sale.

Several places have earned special fame for their embroidery and folk costumes. Just east of Budapest in the towns of Kazár and Galgamácsa in the Zagyva river valley, it is not unusual to see older women donning their traditional dress especially on Sundays when going to church. Galgamácsa also has a little museum devoted to a local textile artist, Mrs. Juli Dudás Vankó. And a little further eastwards is Mezökövesd, the center of the Matyóföld, famous for its lively and colorful embroidery, which is very much on display in town. Another famous embroidering town is Kalocsa, south of Budapest on the Danube, where the diligent *pingaló asszonyok* (painting women) have covered everything from blouses to the town's welcome sign with highly naturalistic and brightly-clored floral designs.

A newer old folk art is felt-making, which originated in Central Asia. The material itself was used at one time to cover tents, Hungarian herdsmen made coats out of it, bags, gloves and stockings. The center of this craft is in Kecskemét, on the Gáspár A. v. 11, where one also finds a small, but interesting museum. Lace-makers still practice their trade in the town of Kiskunhalas.

Traditional craftspeople have been fairly well organized into cooperatives where they are able to get their goods, be it basketry, pottery, leather work, or even furniture out to the public. Internally they also formed mutual help association about ten years ago to improve their working conditions. The resulting Népmüvészeti Egyesület (Folk Art Union), seated on Corvin Square in Budapest, also organizes exhibitions, summer workshops and tours.

One of the best workshops is in the village of Velem near the Austrian border in Vas county. Here, in pretty wooden houses, you can learn some of the art of weaving, wood carving, smithery and pottery. Another possibility is in the picturesque village of Magyarlukafa in Baranya county (near Pécs). An old peasant house has been redesigned to fit various ateliers, that also include papermaking, textile and an exhibition hall displaying some of the finest samples of the local art works. Further workshops are held in Ocsa near Budapest and in the Káli Medence, one of the most beautiful areas of Hungary, especially as far as landscape and folk architecture are concerned.

This leads us finally to the markets where one can find these items, if you do not wish to make them yourself. A kind of folk carneval with a market takes place August 18-20 on the Tóth Arpád sétány on Castle Hill in Buda. The flea market in Budapest is also a good source, albeit the prices have gradually become outrageous. Pécs holds a major fair on the first Sunday of every month, where everything from Mercedes Benz's to lace doilies trade hands. The first Sunday of the month is also a market day for nearby Kaposvár, and there is also the century-old Hídivásár, with its the **Bridge Market** held near the Hortóbágy bridge every August 19-20. If your wallet allows, there are several antique shops in Budapest that sell used folk items such as plates, clothes, embroideries and shirts: Folk Art, V. Budapest, Régiposta u. 7-9; Burg Folk Art , I. Budapest, Tárnok u. 3; Ládafia Folk Art, V. Budapest, Régiposta u. 12. Try to distinguish between truly valuable antiques and pretty, but ordinary items.

HUNGARY'S MINORITIES

Hungary is a small country even by European standards. The national pride of the Hungarians, however, is very large, matching the former size of their territory. Hungary has always been a multi-ethnic country. After the First World War the country was forced to give two thirds of its territory and a third of its Hungarian-speaking population to neighboring states. Today approximately five percent of the population of Hungary belongs to an ethnic minority. Communist policies of standardization intended to dissolve the small ethnic groups and assimilate them into the gray mass of socialism, but they were only partially successful. In fact, during the 1980s the state enacted reforms whereby attempts were made to actually increase support for each group's cultural independence.

Above: Gypsies – mercurial, talented, but despised. Right: A calvary in a German community.

As regards minorities, Hungary seems to have set an example to its neighbors, where many Hungarians themselves live as minorities, in particular to Romania, where their numbers are estimated at between 2 and 2.5 million. Romania's anti-minority policies have for years been forcing a growing wave of refugees of Hungarians from Transylvania to the mother country. This emigration has not decreased since the downfall of the dictator Ceausescu, albeit owing to less stringent emigration formalities crossing the border is no longer a potentially life-threatening matter.

In contrast, the Slovaks, Serbs and Germans living in Hungary rarely emigrate. The fact that their numbers are continuously decreasing is due to modernization which brings about assimilation. The ethnic minorities in Hungary live almost only in villages and urbanization is resulting in the usual disintegration of the village cultural communities, where only the old people maintain their traditions. Only a relatively closed community with

its own institutions can preserve an individual language and culture, its schools and religion and an infrastructure accomodate graduates of higher education too. This is not the case in the Hungarian provinces. Although Hungary is by no means an urbanized society, the cultural and economic life of Budapest dominates the country. All vital institutions of the country are concentrated in the capital, and no less than 20 percent of the total population lives there. The melting-pot effect hardly leaves much room for preserving a national minority's cultural identity.

The Hungarian capital was not always a Hungarian-speaking town. Like most of the towns in Hungary it had a predominantly German population until the 19th century and was called *Ofen*, a term meaning stove and referring to the lime burners who eked out a living in the hills to the north. The German influence has made itself felt in one form as the other, latently or openly, on Hungarian history and culture right up until the present day.

There have always been historical links, too, with German-speaking Austria. Since the change in the regime in 1990, for example, contacts with Germany have been re-established, thanks in part to the many German-speaking Hungarians who were forced to leave the country after the Second World War. These so-called Danube Swabians, who have created a sound existence for themselves over the last 40 years in Germany, are very conscious of their origins, and are spurred on by the desire to help their homeland, as well as by the possibilities of opening new markets in Hungary. And there are still 230.000 Germans in Hungary itself. They are now seen as potential trade partners for their German brothers in the West. German aid in periods of restoration has a long tradition in Hungary. After the storms of the Tatars in the 13th century, and after the defeat of the Turks at the end of the 17th century, German settlers were brought into the country to repopulate the regions devastated by the wars.

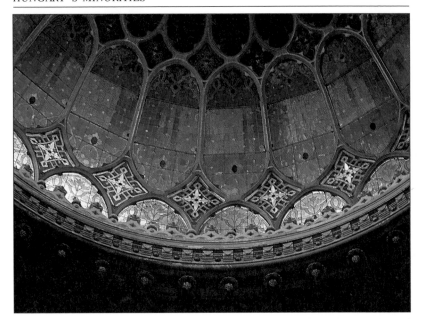

The Germans have also been an important civilizing factor in Hungary. The streams of people brought European culture to the Pannonian Plain too. Christianization in the 10th century was carried out with the help of German monks. Lutheran and Calvinist Protestantism also came from beyond the Alps. The presence of the Turks in Hungary at the time of the Reformation even helped spread the gospel of Protestantism, partly because the Catholic Church could not oppose the Protestant preachers in those areas occupied by the Turks. To this day the majority of Protestants still live in the eastern section of Hungary.

The largest Church was and still is the Catholic Church, followed by the Protestant Church. The third largest Church is the Lutheran Church. Romanian or Serbian ethnic groups usually belong to the Orthodox Churches, while the small Unitarian community is made up mainly of Hungarian peoples and is mainly located in Transylvania. The various other smaller Protestant communities – Adventists, Baptists and Methodists – who have joined together in the Council of Hungarian Free Churches, are comparatively small in number and significance.

Whether Catholic or Orthodox, Hungarian-German or Southern Slavic, almost all the people add the adjective "Hungarian" before their names, or before they speak of their religion or mother tongue. In every population census you come across people who write, for example, that their mother tongue is Slovakian, but their nationality is Hungarian. Loyalty to the state is hardly ever called into question, an attitude which has its roots in the Middle Ages when all who were subordinates of the Hungarian king were called "hungarus", regardless of their confession or ethnicity. Only with the rise of nationalism in the 19th century and the historical need for self-identification as an ethnically or

Above: The synagogue in Szeged – the beautiful remains of a tragic fate. Right: At a typical Gypsy market.

politically homogeneous nation did national tensions arise. But the Treaty of Trianon, which had such sad and negative results for the Hungarians who lived outside today's territorial boundaries, have almost made such problems obsolete in present- day Hungary, or have at least reduced them considerably, with the exception of the German-Hungarian conflict resulting from the Second World War. These were in any case brought about from outside the country.

The same tragic historical epoch resulted in the reduction of the once half a million strong Hungarian Jewish population to only 100.000. In the early summer of 1944 almost all Jews living in the provinces were taken to German concentration camps. Only the Jewish quarter in Budapest survived the war more or less intact. For this reason most Jews still live in the capital today. There is a rabbinical school here, the only such place in the whole of eastern Europe. The liberalization policies of the last years of the eighties led to the revitalization of Jewish self-awareness in Hungary. New cultural organizations and periodicals were founded, which are attempting to rescue the surviving structures of a dying culture from the ashes of two dictatorships. Among the great witnesses of the flowering Jewish culture in Hungary are the beautiful surviving synagogues in – for example – Budapest, Pécs, Szeged, Kecskemét and Gyöngyös.

The largest minority in Hungary, the gypsies, have found themselves in a situation which is in many ways similar to that of the Jews. Theirs is only partly a language or religious unit. Despite their numbers – ca. 500.000 – they live on the fringe of Hungarian society. They usually work in badly paid jobs, because they rarely have qualifications. Many work in construction or in industry and have to commute long distances to their places of work. They always remain foreign, whether in the towns or in the country-

side. They live a rootless life and many seek refuge in alcohol or gambling. What is thought of as typical and relatively well paid gypsy employment as musicians, is in reality only practiced by three percent of all gypsies. Whether they are made of poor huts or sad new buildings, the gypsy settlements on the edges of towns and villages are clearly separate ghettos, whose daily laws are not necessarily those of the rest of Hungarian society. Gypsies are today the poorest and socially weakest group in Hungary. And we must remember that they comprise almost five percent of the population.

The great changes which came in 1990 opened up whole new opportunities for Hungary's people, regardless of their religion or mother tongue, to develop their own culture. Religious schools are now being re-opened. The minorities, especially the Germans, are beginning to rebuild links with their homelands. And everyone is hoping that their Hungarian homeland will eventually become an integral part of Europe.

HORSES AND RIDERS

Hungary and horses: two apparently inseparable partners. Árpád himself is said to have led the Magyars across the Carpathian range on the back of a martial horse, a white one if we are to believe the legends. Admiral Horthy, Hungary's regent between 1920 and 1944, ushered in the era riding a white palfrey, an era that ultimately dragged the nation not into glory, but rather into a devastating war.

In the millenium and more that has elapsed between Árpád and Horthy, Hungarians have repeatedly taken to the saddle in order to conquer, to defend themselves and to let themselves ultimately be conquered. Their fast mounts carried them all the way to the countries on the North and Aegean Seas. They rode cavalcades during the wars against the Ottoman Empire, they joined the ranks of

Above: The Hungarian and his horse have developed a perfectly symbiotic relationship.

the imperial armies of Frederick the Great and Maria Theresia and served in the hussar regiments of the Austro-Hungarian monarchy right up until the First World War.

The original mounted warriors known as hussars already existed in the days of King Mátyás (1458-1490). The name "hussar" comes from the Hungarian word for "20" (*húsz*), because every twentieth household had to provide a rider. Towards the end of the 17th century, these heavily armed and armored regiments gave way to a light cavalry wearing the typical showy *dolman* (a jacket without tails) and the *shako* (a fur hat). They still look like this during equestrian meets or on the plates and vases on sale in souvenir shops. But hussars were not alone in the service of the monarchy until the Great War. Whole herds of so-called remounts (young and yet unschooled horses) were taken from the Great Puszta and pressed into military service.

The hussar is honored to this very day even by his modern mechanized counterpart. The hussar memorial on Disz tér on the Castle Hill in Budapest is every now and then the site of wreath-laying ceremonies.

In contrast to the loyal work horse, you can only breed fast and reliable military horses with carefully planned programs. Count István Széchenyi, who recognized the backward state of his country and introduced many reforms, also revived interest in horse-breeding with international recognition. Unlike the villagers of Rátó, who believed that a noble stallion could be hatched from an egg, Széchenyi did not believe in miracles. He bought tried and true pedigree horses, mainly from England. In order to finance his plans, he held races, a source of income that still supports horse breeding in Hungary today. It is not surprising that breeders strive for the highest quality as verified by the studbooks. Achievement alone is not sufficient, as the tale of the little mare *Nyiana* testifies. She broke all records in trotting, but lost out to bureaucracy. Her pedigree could simply not be proved. The famous stallion *Imperial* had a very different fate. Between 1962 and 1964 he raced from one brilliant victory to another. Then he suddenly retired from active sports, and bearing his stardom with pride, spent the following twenty years siring over 300 offspring.

It has been a long journey from the original Hungarian horse, supposedly a cross between Italian wild horses and the Mongolian horses introduced by Árpád, to the breeds they have today in the many stud farms scattered all over the country. The Lipizzan horse is known to all hippophiles, a gracious and strong breed with great stamina. Who can fail to admire the provettes, the bows, the caprioles and other forms of obedient behaviour with which the horse supports the rider?

The Lipizza stud farm was founded by the Austrian archduke Carl in 1580 near Trieste. Its horses were brought to safety in Mesöhegyes in southern Hungary in 1802 when Napoleon's troops were moving in. Part of the herd returned home, but the rest was used to found Hungary's own Lipizzan stud farm. After many misfortunes the animals finally found a permanent home in Szilvásvárad, in the romantic surroundings of the Bükk hills, a landscape which is reminiscent of their home in Trieste. This is one of the five Lipizzan stud farms in the world.

Another stud farm which has achieved great fame amongst horse lovers is in Mezöhegyes. Mainly Nonius and Gidrán horses are bred here. Joseph II founded a stud farm here for military horses, but it only achieved its present importance in 1810 with the arrival of the horse *Nonius*, born in Normandy. This was the original sire of a very handsome and resilient strong riding and carriage horse. The stud farm in Bábolna, south of Györ has also become famous through its thoroughbred and crossbreed Arabian horses. There are countless farms with great reputations all over Hungary, with names from A (Apaj-puszta) to Z (Zalakaros). At most of them you can spend a pleasant riding holiday, which includes tuition, rides and carriage rides. Travel agencies will give you further information and provide advice and brochures on the subject.

Hungarian horses in general are beautiful and have a good combination of temperament and gentleness. They enjoy a good life – they are revered and respected. Of course they are no longer buried after their death, as was the case with the Avars' favorite horses (as proven by richly decorated horse graves found in Pécs), instead memorials are erected to them. These are not only made of bronze or stone. The park belonging to the stud farm in Szilvásvárad has entire shrines and shamanic columns, evoking the time of the land-taking. It is dedicated to the memory of the mare *Zánka*, the farm director's favorite horse, who died of a heart attack while out riding.

INTELLECTUAL LIFE

Foreign visitors to Hungary often feel that they have not only arrived in a foreign country, but in a non-European continent. This is due not to the exotic nature of the country nor to its inhabitants, but to its language. There is hardly a written word which foreigners can understand. The Hungarians may use the Latin alphabet, but this is where the similarities with other European languages end. Who speaks Hungarian? Only the Hungarians and God almighty, is a common answer which, though it might seem a bit arrogant, also reveals the isolation felt by the people of Hungary.

And it is true – Hungarian is only spoken by the approximately 15 million Hungarians who live in the country and outside it. Finns, Estonians and a sprinkling of other tribes living out in the wilds of the Soviet Union also speak a related

Above left: Sándor Petőfi in Gyula. Above right: The College library in Debrecen.

language, albeit they cannot understand each other mutually. Moreover there is no sense of community arising from the very distant relationship. Hungarian has a great number of idiomatic expressions suggesting its cultural isolation in foreign waters. By the same token Hungarians like to point out with barely concealed pride, that they have nevertheless survived in this foreign sea. We are a small people, they say, but a great nation. During the Middle Ages the Hungarian kingdom was a powerful state on the level of other European states. All of that came to an end after the defeat at Mohács on August 29, 1526, sealed a fate that had been deteriorating for a while already.

The so-called "great" Nations, the French, British and Germans, feel no need to explain their achievements to foreigners. They are understandably proud of them and don't think them at all extraordinary. Only their failures have to be justified. The British five-pound note years ago, for example, arrogantly exhibited the Battle of Waterloo, a slap in the face of unifying Europe. The Hungarians – some note sadly – only exhibit people who died in exile or as martyrs on their currency. The Hungarians always assume the worst will happen, and are surprised when they actually achieve something great. And because their tumultuous history has left few monuments intact, these achievements are often overestimated. A curious mixture of arrogance and self-pitying modesty dominates in this country, which should not disconcert the visitor. And this attitude is by no means particular to the Hungarians. This proud feeling of inferiority is found all over eastern Europe, where all peoples see themselves as victims of history and of the careless actions of the so-called great nations.

The reason for this attitude lies in history, and it is important to know that Hungarians are very conscious of their history. Their national pride rests on the past. This is the case today as it was one hundred years ago when the millennium of the land-taking was celebrated with great pomp and ceremony. The architectural reminders of this national awakening can be admired all over the capital Budapest where nothing seems to be linked with the present.

Today everyone, regardless of political leaning, speaks with reverence and recognition of the founders of the state, and once again St. István's crown is proudly displayed on the flag of the new Hungarian republic. Only historians talk about the fact that the christianization of Hungary at the time of István led to violent reaction and bloody internecine battles. Instead it is regarded as a golden age which lasted until the battle of Mohács. And no one seems interested in the fact that there were countless internal battles, the storm of the Tatars, and various uprisings during the 500 years between the foundation of the state and the defeat by the Turks. The main thing is that everything took place in an independent state.

But the situation changed in the fateful year of 1526. Whereas previous battles had been fought between equals, from this date on a continuous war of independence was fought. Whether against Turks, Habsburgs or Soviets, it never led to success or victory. The Hungarians see only a chain of defeats, events which have left their mark on the national psyche. The fact that they have remained a nation, one people, despite this situation is apparently not enough to satisfy their national pride.

Hungarians are always chewing over their history and their fate. At the end of the 20th century the country at last seems to be freeing itself from Soviet colonial rule, just as it ultimately did from the Turks and the Habsburgs. And this time without armed conflict. Yet the population is suspicious, almost unable to believe it. For it is not easy to forget the myth of a Hungary in the grips of an armed style. The militant tradition is so strong and progress through reform has never been very popular. The division of society into politicians willing to make compromises and enthusiastic freedom fighters is a feature of Hungarian history, at least since the 18th century. It is reflected in the war of independence of Rákóczi, the Széchenyi-Kossuth dichotomy, in the negotiations with Austria about the 1867 compromise, and the split in the anti-communist opposition in the 1980s. Parallel to this division, though by no means identical to it, there have always been two cultural orientations in Hungary. Some hold up the authentic roots of Hungarian culture as examples, hoping to use them to create a new culture. Others believe that Hungary should be following western European models. This division broadly corresponds to the division between the supporters of the present conservative party in government, the Democratic Forum, and the supporters of the opposition, the Liberal Free Democrats. The division is by no

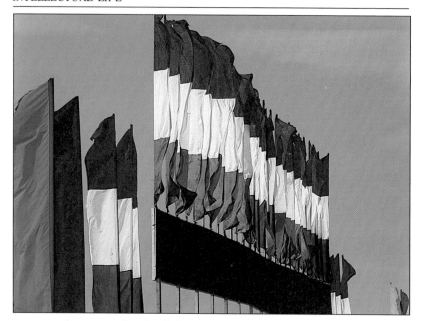

means as clear cut as that, but it has a clear influence on the intellectual and political life in the country.

Hungary feels like a border state between east and west, and to a certain extent this is what it is. Geographically it is on the edge of western Christianity. The Hungarians like to say that Europe ends where the Gothic churches end, and they are actually found in Hungarian settlements on the eastern border of Transylvania. Their eternal aim is full assimilation into the circle of European culture, whilst retaining their unmistakable Hungarian characteristics. Again and again it has been pointed out that Hungary and Europe are not two contradictory entities, yet even the fact that the subject has to be discussed reveals the deep insecurity of the country. Europe is synonymous with civilization, wealth, security, but also of democracy and cultural values. Europe is

Above: Piros, fehér, zöld – red, white and green, three colors thousands of Hungarians have fought and died for.

the epitome of good – the dark side of western European societies are never mentioned. This is not social analysis, but self-esteem. One Hungarian argument for their Europeanness is their Christian culture, which is seen as their chance to associate themselves with the western European democracies. In this debate literature is held as the trump card, as an example of Hungarian achievement on an equal footing with the literatures of other western European countries, including that of the "great" nations.

This is true even though the Hungarians have never managed to export their literature, despite the fact that it has received recognition. But this is not a question of esthetics, but access to the language and the political state of the country.

Hungarian literature followed European models faithfully and achieved works which were altogether equal to western European counterparts. Baroque extravagence is found in the great epic poem by Miklós Zrínyi, playful Rococo in the lyrics of Mihály Csokonai Vitéz. Classical severity pervades the works of Dániel Berzsenyi. Romanticism found a particularly fertile ground in Hungary: Poets such as Mihály Vörösmarty, János Arany, Sándor Petőfi are still devoured today by Hungary's reading public. The great novels of Mór Jókai were not only translated into all European languages, but even found interested readers in America and Asia. The 20th century brought with it the end of Romanticism, as is seen in the sober realism of the works of Zsigmond Móricz. The lyrics of the generation of poets between the wars, which included Dezső Kosztolányi, Mihály Babits, Attila József and their direct ancestor Endre Ady, was based on western European models. And how bleak is the life of a child who has the *Muppet Show* but never read Ferenc Molnár's *Boys of Paul Street*!

Hungarian writers have always found themselves forced to use their quills for social and political ends. Their names have often been associated with a political movement. This politicization of literature became particularly intensive after the Communists took power. In the absence of a political opposition, literature took on the role of social criticism. Its methods, which allow for several interpretations, its metaphors, symbolism and allusion presented the best opportunity for the discussion of forbidden topics. Hungarians have always read a great deal. Modern media do not dominate society to the extent found in the west.

After the events of 1989 this collaboration of the political and the esthetic has started to dissolve. But the works of authors such as Gyula Illyés, János Pilinszky, Péter Nádas, Miklós Mészöly and Péter Esterházy, to name but a few, are of great esthetic value despite their political content.

Political discussion is today no longer confined to political journals. It is found on television and in the daily newspapers.

There are also many new socio-political periodicals, popular amongst the intellectuals in the country. The broad mass of readers is probably more interested in the new publications on the subjects of psychology, parapsychology and pornography. With the abolition of censorship, almost everything which had previously been forbidden is now flooding the market, rubbish and quality publications alike. Publishers and periodicals are popping up like mushrooms. On the street corners and in subways everything is on sale. This is one phenomenon which will probably change with the "Europization" of Hungary.

Information on Europe and democracy is not only circulated in print, but is on television and radio too. Hungarian TV broadcasts the BBC every weekday evening, with the exception of Wednesdays, when German TV is aired. But it is not only due to these broadcasts that dozens of language schools are springing up all over the country, where high school pupils and pensioners learn their western European vocabulary alongside representatives from all possible professions. It is the feverish attempt to complete the union with Europe as quickly as possible, albeit according to one's own abilities.

This union is discussed everywhere. Not only in the formal framework of the media, but in the student clubs, cafés and bars that are rapidly taking over the courtyards and cellars of the old town of Budapest. Environmentalists, feminists, globetrotters, jazz fans, punks, artists, musicians, writers, would-be politicians, all meet here in the evenings, often in the same rooms, discussing God and the universe over a bottle of wine or a glass of juice. And if the visitor should still be astonished that this nation has managed to preserve itself, despite the events of fate in "foreign" Europe, he or she will soon realize that this love of discussion has proven to be one of the decisive factors in national survival.

Nelles Maps ...the maps, that get you going.

Nelles Map Series:

- Afghanistan
- Australia
- Burma
- Caribbean Islands 1/
  Bermuda, Bahamas,
  Greater Antilles
- Caribbean Islands 2/
  Lesser Antilles
- China 1/
  North-Eastern China
- China 2/
  Northern China
- China 3/
  Central China
- China 4/
  Southern China
- Crete
- Hawaiian Islands
- Hawaiian Islands 1/Kauai
- Hawaiian Islands 2/
  Honolulu, Oahu

- Hawaiian Islands 3/
  Maui, Molokai, Lanai
- Hawaiian Islands 4/Hawaii
- Himalaya
- Hong Kong
- Indian Subcontinent
- India 1/Northern India
- India 2/Western India
- India 3/Eastern India
- India 4/Southern India
- India 5/North-Eastern India
- Indonesia
- Indonesia 1/Sumatra
- Indonesia 2/
  Java + Nusa Tenggara
- Indonesia 3/Bali
- Indonesia 4/Kalimantan
- Indonesia 5/Java + Bali
- Indonesia 6/Sulawesi

- Indonesia 7/
  Irian Jaya + Maluku
- Jakarta
- Japan
- Kenya
- Korea
- Malaysia
- West Malaysia
- Nepal
- New Zealand
- Pakistan
- Philippines
- Singapore
- South East Asia
- Sri Lanka
- Taiwan
- Thailand
- Vietnam, Laos
  Kampuchea

HUNGARY
©Nelles Verlag GmbH, München 45
  All rights reserved
  ISBN 3-88618-374-2

First Edition 1991
Co-Publisher for U.K.:
Robertson McCarta, London
ISBN 1-85365-231-8 (for U.K.)

Publisher:	Günter Nelles	**DTP-Exposure:** Printshop Schimann, Pfaffenhofen
Chief Editor:	Dr. Heinz Vestner	
Project Editor:	Amalia Morgenstern	**Color**
Translation:	Ch. Banerji	**Separation:** Priegnitz, München
Editor in Charge:	Marton Radkai	
Cartography:	Nelles Verlag GmbH, by courtesy of Freytag-Berndt, Wien	**Printed by:** Gorenjski Tisk, Kranj, Yugoslavia

TABLE OF CONTENTS

PREPARATIONS

Climate

Both the Atlantic and Mediterranean exert their influences on Hungary which helps counter some of the colder eastern winds that might blow in from Russia. If planning to travel in winter bring warm clothing and a good rain coat. The chill remains in the air from about mid-October to mid-April, one can safely say, with exceptions confirming the rule. Out east where hardly a hedge or a hill provides the wind with an obstacle, the weather can become rather bone-chilling. Suffice to say the mountains offer skiing, snow permitting. Late spring and summer are generally marked by a great deal of sunshine (especially in the south and east), temperatures average about 20 ° C in June, July and August. Evenings become chilly at times. The air can be quite damp and in the east violent electrical storms are not unusual. Fall, particularly October, sometimes offers beautiful weather, with the crisp, sunny days of a true Indian Summer.

Clothing

Warm clothes are necessary from about mid-October to April, rain protection, waterproof shoes, head gear, ear muffs and gloves included. A light coat should be brought along during late spring and fall, especially if visiting the mountainous regions. Hungary boasts many beautiful old castles, forts, churches and peasant houses that have been turned into museums, and they tend to be rather cold, so packing some wool socks is a good idea. In summer evenings can be chilly, so remember to bring a jacket or a few light sweaters. You can always leave them in your suitcase if a heat wave strikes. Don't forget swimming apparel! This applies to winter as well, when a number of thermal baths keep indoor and outdoor pools operating.

Currency

Hungary's currency is the Forint. It divides up into 100 Fillér. Bills come in the following sizes: 1000 Ft, 500 Ft, 100 Ft, 50 Ft. 20 Ft and rare but there 10 Ft. A 5000 Ft bill was being talked about for a while. Coins come in the following denominations: 20 Ft, 10 Ft, 5 Ft, 2 Ft, 1 Ft; and 50 f, 20 f, 10 f.

No compulsory exchange exists in Hungary. But it is prohibited to import or export more than 100 Ft, so it is always considered wise to only change as much money as you foreseeably need. If you want to change excess money back to your own currency again, you will need the original exchange receipts. That is why it is advisable to always change money at some official place such as a bank, a travel agency and a post office during business hours, or in large hotels and camping sites. Besides traveler's checks, it is also possible to draw 9000 Forints on a Eurocheck at locations displaying the Eurocheck logo. Major credit cards, including American Express, Diner's Card and Eurocard can be used at a growing number of outlets from restaurants to department stores.

The Forint not being a convertible currency, you may be pestered relatively frequently by private money changers in the street, searching for a coveted hard currency and willing to give better than the official exchange. Please note, that inspite of tempting offers, this activity is illegal and often practiced by shady characters well-trained in the art of sleight-of-hand. If you are cheated, you will have no legal resort.

Arrival Formalities

Citizens from all European countries (except those listed below), the USA and Canada, no longer need a visa to travel to Hungary.

Citizens from Portugal, Greece, Turkey, Albania, Australia, New Zealand, Japan, the Koreas, India, Thailand, and other Asian nations, Latin America (except Argentina), South Africa, Israel and all Arab nations will have to purchase a visa from the nearest Hungarian embassy or consulate (a list follows). The visa currently costs in the region of US$25 and takes a day to complete, or ca. US$ 40 for speedy completion. If you are a citizen of an Arab nation, you will have to wait at least two weeks. Furthermore, if you intend to purchase a visa from a country other than your own, you will need an official residence permit of your host country.

If traveling to Hungary by train, you will have to get your visa prior to your trip. Otherwise they are usually available at border crossings. To save time and nerves during the peak season, try and get at least the two necessary passport photos before your trip. The airport's visa office is also notoriously slow. It is therefore advisable to acquire your visa prior to departure. Registering with the police is no longer necessary.

Albania: Ruga Skander beg, Tirana, Telex: 2004. **Algeria**: 18 Avenue de Frères Oughlis El-Mourandia, Algiers, Tel: (213) 600- 921. **Australia**: 79 Hopetown Circuit, Yarralumbla a.c.t., 2600 Canberra, (62) 82-32-26; Consulate: 351/a Edgecliff road, Edgecliff N.S.W. 2027 Sydney, (2) 328-7859. **Austria**: Bankgasse 4- 6, 1010 Wien, Tel: (0222) 63-26-31. **Belgium**: 54, rue Edmond Picard, 1180 Bruxelles, Tel: (2) 343-67-90. **Canada**: 7 Delaware Avenue, Ottawa K2P 0Z2, Ontario. Tel: (613) 234-83-16. **Egypt**: 36 Mohammed Mazhar Street, Zamalek, Cairo, Tel: (2) 34-62-215. **Finland**: Kuusisaarenkuja 6, Helsinki, Tel: (0) 48-41-44. **France**: 5 bis, Square de l'Avenue Foch, 75016 Paris, Tel: (1) 45-00-41- 59; Consulate: 7, rue Talleyrand, Paris, Tel: (1) 45-55-23-82. **Germany**: Turmstr. 30, 5300 Bonn 2, Tel: (0228) 37-57-97. **Great Britain**: 35 Eaton Place, London S. W. 1, Tel: (71) 235-52-18, Consulate Tel: 491-2952. **Greece**: 16,

Kalvou Psychico, Athens, Tel: (1) 671-48- 89.Consulates: Sachsenring 38, 5000 Köln, Tel: (0221) 37-67-97; and Vollmannstr. 2, 8000 München 81, Tel: (089) 91-10-32; Reifträgerweg 27-29, 1000 Berlin 38, Tel: (030) 803-50-63. **Holland**: La Haye Hoheweg 14, Den Haag, Tel: (70) 500-405. **India**: 2/50 M-Niti Marg, Chanyakyapuri, New Delhi 110021, Tel: (11) 618- 414. **Indonesia**: Jalan Rasuna Said, Block X/3 Kuningan, Djakarta, Tel: (21) 58-75-21. **Italy**: Via del Villini 16, Roma, Tel: (6) 85- 87-72; Consulate: Piazza Girolamo Fabrizio 2, Roma, (6) 85-04-51. **Japan**: 3-1, Aobadai 2-chome, Meguro-ku., Tokyo(3) 476-60-61/3. **Marocco**: 190. o.l.m. Soussi II., Rabat, Tel: (7) 507-57. **Norway**: Sophus Lies gt. 3, Oslo 2, Tel: (2) 56-46-88. **Portugal**: Calcada de Santo Amaro 85, 1300 Liboa, Tel: (1) 63-03-95. **Spain**: Calle Angel de Diego Roldan 21, Madrid 16, Tel. (1) 413-70-11. **Sweden**: Strandvägen 74 L, 11527 Stockholm, Tel: (8) 61-67-62; Consulate: Laboratoriegatan 2, 11527 Stockholm, Tel: (8) 63-66-39. **Switzerland**: Muristrasse 31, 3006 Bern, Tel: (31) 44-85-72; Consulate: Eigerplatz 5, 3007 Bern, Tel: (31) 45-13-55. **Thailand**: No. 28 soi Sukchai soi 42, Sukhumvit Road, Bangkok, Tel: (2) 391- 79-06. **Tunisia**: El Menhaz i. 8, rue Al-Jahed, Tel: (1) 233-338. **Turkey**: Gazi Mustafa Kamal Bolv. 10, Ankara, Tel: (40) 118-62-57; Consulate: Poyaracik Sokak 35, Texvikiye Istanbul, Tel: (90) 40- 42-75. **USA**: 3910 Shoemaker Street N. W., Washington D.C. 20008, Tel (202) 362-67-30; Consulate: 8 East 75th Street, New York, NY, 10021, Tel (212) 879-41-26.

Health and Sanitation

You are not expected to have any specific vaccinations before traveling to Hungary. Sanitary conditions are by and large good, even though the spas, especially the older ones, tend to look run down. Watch out for sunburn.

Health care in Hungary has been one of the state's priorities and it covers the province as well. Hospitals may not reflect the Western standard per se, but no hospital is pleasant in spite of its aim to cure. If you are very sick you may wish to be flown home for treatment. Make sure you are properly insured for this eventuality. Otherwise, for small problems, headaches, heartburn and the like, go to the local pharmacy. Medicine is fairly inexpensive in Hungary, the country produces its own patents. (Under Hungarien Language you will find a few important words and expressions concerning health).

Miscellaneous notes: Women may want to make sure they are properly equipped for menstruation, as the Hungarian paraphenalia leaves something to be desired. Secondly: AIDS knows no borders and Budapest is rapidly becoming known as a Western Bangkok as far as prostitution goes. Condom dispensers are proliferating but not at the same rate as the disease. Thirdly: Toilets are often in miserable condition and lacking proper paper. Keep a roll handy, even if you are in a multi-star hotel! Fourthly: Hungarian food may give your digestive system something to think about. Apply caution to your eating habits, bring along a mild purgative, an antacid if you tend toward heartburn, or equip yourself with the land's own medicine, a purgative bitter water. Watch out for Tokajer wine, it is generally to be stronger than most others.

Customs

Like everything in the country, regulations concerning customs are continuously changing. The best bet is to ask a representative of the Hungarian travel agency IBUSZ or the nearest consulate for the latest information. Not permitted are, for example, drugs, over 100 Forints and firearms (the latter have to be declared). There are certain limitations placed on CBs, and auto telephones have to be declared. Exports are also limited especially where food and beverages are concerned. Taking more than 100 Forints out of the country is prohibited. **Note**: Hungarian customs officials tend to let people through the road borders in bulk, but they do spot check vehicles. Stick to the law and enjoy your visit is the rule of thumb.

TRAVELING IN HUNGARY

Arriving

By plane: A number of international carriers fly to Budapest directly from major cities on a regular, even daily basis. This means that Hungary is easily accessible, even indirectly. The Hungarian airline MALÉV has direct flights to most European and several Middle Eastern capitals and pools with PanAm for the Budapest-New York route. Airliners flying to Budapest (and MALÉV pool flights) land at the Ferihegy terminal 1 about 20 km from the center of Budapest. The second terminal is used exclusively by the Hungarian airline MALÉV. The airport has a visa office and offers tourist services such as car rentals, hotel reservations, a duty-free and so on. Taxis are readily available to take you into town: Make sure the meter is running. In early 1991 the cost for a ride till the Danube was ca. 1000 Ft, but inflation is rapidly pushing the price up. A bus will take you until Erzsébet tér (erstwhile Engels tér) for a fraction of that price.

By train: You have to obtain a visa before traveling by train. Budapest is connected by rail to all major European cities.

By car: The six border crossings to the West are open all night and offer visa offices and limited tourist services. These are from north to south: Nickelsdorf / Hegyeshalom (the biggest), Klingenbach / Sopron, Deutschkreutz / Kóptremaháza, Rattersdorf / Köszeg, Schachendorf /

Bucsu and Heiligenkreutz / Rábafüzes. The same applies generally to the other crossings into Yugoslavia, Romania, Czechoslovakia and the USSR (for the latter you will have to have a valid visa!). Waiting at the borders can last quite long if you are traveling during the peak season.

By ship: Regular service has been established between Vienna and Budapest, and there are a number of cruises on the Danube. All passport and visa formalities take place an hour prior to departure in Vienna. Otherwise there is an official border crossing where the ships tie up on the Belgrád rakpart in Pest. Two more crossings are in Szeged and Mohács, for travelers crossing to or from Yugoslavia on the Tisza and Danube respectively.

Transportation

General: Hungary being relatively small any trip will be relatively short. There is no air travel within the country. Busses and trains are the main forms of transportation. There are enough filling stations to go around. Its flatness makes it very appropriate for bicycle riding.

By train: The national train company is called MÁV and it keeps several offices named MÁVTOURS open around the country in addition to the train stations. General number for inland travel in Budapest: 122-7860, and for trips abroad: 122-4052. Telephone numbers of the Budapest train stations: Eastern (keleti) station: 113-6835; Western (nyugati) station, 149-0115; Southern (déli) station, 155-8657.

MÁVTOUR addresses in Budapest: District 5: Guszev u. 1, Tel: 117-3723; in district 6, Andrássy út 35, Tel: 122-8438.

A selection of MÁVTOURS offices in the rest of the country: **Békéscsaba** on the erstwhile Tanácsköztársaság útja 6, Tel:(66) 26-856. **Debrecen**, Rózsa u. 4, Tel: (52) 14-606. **Eger**, Lumumba tér 1, Tel: (36) 15-264. **Györ**, Révai u. 6, Tel: (96) 12-831. **Kecskemét**, Horváth Döme

u. 10, Tel: (76) 26-145. **Miskolc**, Széchenyi u. 103, Tel: (46) 37-767. **Nyíregyháza**, Dózs György u.3, (42)11-544. **Pécs**, Lenin tér 1, Tel: (72) 24-523. **Siófok**, at the train station, Tel: (84) 13-217. **Szeged**, Boros J. u. 4/b, Tel: (62) 23-130. **Székesfehérvár**, Béke tér 5, Tel: (22) 12-139. **Szolnok**, Kossuth Lajos u. 18, Tel: (56) 12-836. **Szombathely**, Mártirok tere 1, Tel: (94) 12-348.

The trains themselves are not reputed for their comfort, but they are a good way of getting to know people. They are relatively inexpensive too, even though inflation has affected this branch of the economy as well. Steer clear of the so called Black Train that runs from Budapest to Matészalka on Friday evenings: It is not only filled to the point of bursting, but the riders tend to be particularly rowdy fellows who work weekdays in the capital and head home on weekends.

By bus: Going by bus is not as cheap as by train, but it offers a way to see a lot of the country. The tiniest villages in Hungary have a bus stop. The central bus station on Erzsébet tér in Budapest gives all information concerning international and national bus travel at least to the larger destinations. For international trips: Tel: 118-2122; for national trips: Tel: 117-2966. Find out locally where and when to catch a local bus.

By ship: Trips on the Danube, the Tisza, Lake Balaton and Lake Velence are generally organized in the form of special tours. Information is usually available at the local travel agency. One central office is MAHART, Belgrád rakpart, Budapest V, Tel: 118- 1704. On the Balaton MAHART runs an office in the port of Siófok, Tel: (84) 10-050.

Local transportation: As mentioned under the rubric "bus", just about all little villages in Hungary are on the bus network. Budapest has a good public transport system involving an underground network (the *földalatti* and the *metro*), a streetcar network and a bus network. A suburban train system also links the main downtown area with the outlying areas including the Danube Bend. Taxis are an experience as far as driving style of the cabby goes (barring the size difference, New Yorkers will feel perfectly at home in one of them), they are relatively inexpensive and generally available night and day. Make sure the meter is running.

PRACTICAL TIPS

Accomodation

Hungary offers a wide range of accomodations from 5-star hotels to youth hostels. The prices vary from Western levels for Western standard to Eastern level for Eastern standard. If planning to travel to Budapest during an event such as the Formula 1 races in August or the Spring Festival at the end of March, be sure you book a room well in advance. Several international chains operate luxury hotels in the city, notably the Hilton, Novotel, Ramada, and others.

An alternative to hotels is staying with private families, for which reservations can be made abroad at a branch of IBUSZ, the Hungarian travel agency (see under Tourist Offices), or at any major agency within the country. Finally there are a variety of bed-and-breakfasts, vacation huts and camping sites of differing caliber that cover a variety of needs.

The quality of hotels varies greatly, especially out in the provinces and in the moderate price categories. The main problem lies generally in poor sound insulation and generally low standards.

Private rooming can be very pleasant and cheap. They frequently give some insight into how Hungarians actually live. However, the room can also be inadequate and expensive, especially around Lake Balaton where the demand often exceeds the supply and free enterprise has started running wild.

IBUSZ runs an all-night office in Budapest, on Petöfi square 3, on the Pest side of the river. Another source of information is the TOURINFORM office on sütö utca 2, in Pest, Tel: 117-9800 (foreign languages are spoken here).

Driving

Driving through Hungary is one interesting way of discovering the country. Several companies operate a car rental service with connections abroad, so you can reserve a car before beginning your trip. Your local travel agency or car rental (AVIS, HERTZ or EUROPCAR) will have more information. Rentals made within Hungary are not necessarily cheaper. **Hertz/Fötaxi**, Kertész u. 24, Budapest VII, Tel: 111- 6116. **Avis/ Ibusz**, Martinelli tér 8, Budapest V, Tel: 118-6222. **Europcar/Volántourist**, Vas–kapu u. 16, Budapest IX, Tel: 133-4783.

Road quality ranges from fairly good to miserable. Highway 1 from Györ to Budapest is supposed to be completed and extended to Vienna by 1995. Until then that stretch will remain known as "Death Road" for its accidents. Another dangerous ribbon of tar is route 4 that connects Hungary to the only automobile and truck crossing into the Soviet Union. Take care when intending to cross a river: Frequently this is only possible using a ferry that does not run at night or at all during spring floods.

Speed limits unless otherwise indicated, are as follows: 120 kph on highways, 100 kph on main roads, on normal roads 80 kph and in towns and villages 60 kph (50 kph for motorcycles). No drinking at all is allowed on Hungarian roads and the police do enforce the law. Any fine incurred must be paid in Forint.

Hungary has not had any fuel shortages these past years and gas stations offering lead-free have been proliferating, though more remote sections of the country may pose a problem in this area. In order to buy diesel you will have to purchase coupons at a major travel agency or at the border crossings.

All accidents have to be reported to the police (Tel.: 07). A subsiduary of the Hungarian insurance company (Hungária Biztosító) must be alerted on the following work day or within 48 hours at the latest. In Budapest the address and telephone is: Hungária International Vehicle Office, Gvadányi u. 69, 1144 Budapest; 163- 3079 or 183-6527. Outside the capital ask the police or local travel agency to give you the number of the nearest office.

In the case of a breakdown, the Hungarian Automobile Club works together with most foreign clubs. Its number in Budapest is 169-1831 or 169-3714. Emergency telephones have been placed at regular intervals on the highways.

Caution: Hungarian drivers are reckless, to say the least, and the situation has worsened ever since more powerful Western cars have been made accessible to the general public. Many seem undeterred by the sharp anti-drinking legislation and they are convinced of their ability at the wheel in spite of the staggeringly high accident rate in Hungary that gives evidence the contrary. Moreover, the road often has to be shared with horse carts, pedestrians, sheep and cattle and bicycle riders with no proper lighting.

Electricity

Hungary operates on 220 Volts. If you are coming from a country with different voltage, check whatever appliances you have to see if they have built in converters, or bring one with you.

Holidays

Januar 1: New Year.

March 15th: Hungary's current national holiday, celebrates the beginning of the revolution of 1848.

Easter Monday.

August 20th: A national holiday celebrating the death of István I, Saint István, Hungary's first king and founder of the Hungarian state. Fireworks are the order of the day in many towns. Debrecen

offers the Flower Festival. Forget driving in Budapest.

October 23rd: Celebrates the beginning of the revolution of 1956.

December 25-26: Christmas Day and St. Stephen(István)'s Day, December 26.

If a holiday falls on a Tuesday or a Thursday, the day bridging it with a weekend also becomes a holiday.

Newspapers and Periodicals

Hungary is more directed toward German tourism and therefore most international media are in that language. This applies in particular to *Radio Danubius* that broadcasts mainly in the western half of the nation on 100,5 and 103,3 megahertz. It broadcasts English-language headline news during the peak season at 7 p.m. At noon *Radio Petöfi* in Budapest offers the same service. *Voice of America* has been broadcasting on the FM band too. Furthermore, most major hotels have cable television, with *Skychannel* and other English-language networks. As for print, you can buy a number of English-language newspapers and magazines (*Herald Tribune*, *Time*, *Newsweek* etc...) at better newstands and in hotels. The English/German *Daily News* is a good source for local events. A monthly program guide appearing in English, German and Hungarian covers the whole country. It is most often found in hotels (at the reception) and in travel agencies. In the further reaches of the republic information becomes sparse. If you are interested in international news only, any shortwave radio will do.

Shopping

The basic business hours are 7 a.m. to 7 p.m. weekdays and 7 a.m. to 2 p.m. Saturdays for stores selling foodstuffs.

Otherwise the hours are: 10 a.m. to 6 p.m. weekdays (until 8 p.m. on Thursdays) and 9 a.m. to 1 p.m. on Saturdays. In the wake of Hungary's return to free enterprise, a number of shopkeepers tend to stay open at other times, especially on the touristically well-trodden paths. Budapest – and other towns to a far lesser extent – is gradually becoming like New York with its all-night delis that are marked either "non-stop" or *éjjel-nappal*. The major routes to the West are often lined with late-night stands.

Prices at night are 10 per cent higher. Favored souvenir items are pottery, embroidered clothing, cloth, leather goods, lace and wine. Regarding clothes and cloth, they are often sold by street peddlers at touristic spots; prices vary as does quality, the rule is use your judgement. Shops on such streets as the Váci utca in Budapest tend to be expensive. Check the list of prohibited export items carefully before considering the purchase of an antique.

Spas

Hungary is known for its healing waters. You will find everything from plain baths to fully-equipped spas, including hotels and therapy facilities, all across the country, from Bükfürdö and Balf in the west to Nyíregyháza, Debrecen, Hajdúszoboszló and Kisvárda in the east. The baths are generally clean and well-tended to. They are also inexpensive, and often include mud baths, saunas, steam rooms and massages. Some of the spas may not be good for you, especially if you have heart problems. Do find out before taking your waters.

Telecommunications

The telephone system in Hungary is a national trauma, as locals and experienced visitors know. It is often simpler and cheaper to write a quick telegram. The problems include poor telephones often placed on loud streets, and a clearly shaky network.

Phoning from post offices does not always guarantee success and trying from some of the big hotels in Budapest can be very costly.

Essentially there are three types of telephones in the booths. The red ones are for international and national calls and take 2, 10 and 20 Ft coins unless otherwise indicated. The yellow telephones are generally only for national calls and take only 2 and 10 Ft coins (sometimes only 2 Ft coins, in which case they only serve a local network). Little metal telephones taking only 2 Ft coins and typical of Budapest, are for local calls only. It is cheaper to call between 6 p.m. and 7 a.m..

To call abroad dial 00, wait for tone, then dial your country code, area code and number. Phoning within Hungary: dial 06, wait for the tone, then dial the area code and local number. For the international information service in Budapest, dial 117-2200. The normal information number is 09, but do not expect the operator to speak a foreign language. If there is a telephone book hanging near the phone, do not expect it to be up-to-date either.

Telexes are still in use throughout the country, but telefax is on the rise, especially with hotels, tourist bureaus and travel agencies.

The normal opening hours for the post office is 8 a.m. to 6 p.m. weekdays, and 8 a.m. to 2 p.m. Saturdays. The post offices next to the western (nyugati) or eastern (keleti) train stations (Erzsébet körút 105 and Baross tér 11/c respectively) stay open 24 hours a day, seven days a week.

Tipping

It is customary to leave a tip in restaurants, bars, hotels and gasoline stations (not the self-service ones of course). The amount is not fixed. Round out a bill to the next highest round figure at your discretion. Toilets cost money in Hungary anywhere from 3 to 10 Forint. They are frequently rented by the woman or man sitting there with the soap, towels and sometimes the toilet paper. They keep the place clean as a visit to a non-guarded toilet usually shows.

ADDRESSES

Airlines

MALÉV, the Hungarian airline, has offices in several countries: . **Belgium**: 32 Ravensteinstraat, 100 Bruxelles (02) 511-18-78. **Danemark**, Vester Ferimagsgade 6, Copenhagen, Tel: (1) 125-042. **Finland**, Yrjönkatu 25, Helsinki, Tel: (0)646-116. **France**: 7 rue de la Paix, 75016 Paris, Tel: (1) 42-61-57-90. **Germany**: Baselerstr. 46-48, (069) 234-043; Salvatorstr. 2, 8000 München 2, Tel: (089) 293-434; Budapesterstr. 10, 1000 Berlin (West) 30, Tel: (030) 261-48-67, at the Dresden airport, Tel: 0037-(51) 58-41-43. **Great Britain**, 10, Vigo Street, London W1X 1AJ, Tel: (71) 439-0577. **Holland**, Noortse Bosch, Vijzelgracht 52, 1017 HS Amsterdam, Tel: (20) 23-43-36. **Italy**, Via P. da Cannobio 10, Milano, Tel: (02) 872-373. Via V. E. Orlando 75, Roma, Tel: (06) 48-55-42. **Norway**, Dronning Maudsgt. 11, Oslo, Tel: (2) 42-62-08. **Spain**: S. A. Intelco, Sagusta 22-5 15, 28004 Madrid. **Sweden**, Sveavägen 17, Stockholm, Tel: ((8) 11-46-46. **Switzerland**, Pelikanstr. 37, 8000 Zürich, Tel: (01) 211-65-65. **United Arab Emirates**, 68-B Sheikh Rashid Building, Al-Maktoum Street, Dubai, Tel: (4) 22-41-59. **USA**,Rockefeller Center, 630, 5th Ave., Room 1900, New York, NY, Tel: (212) 757-6480

Within Hungary, most travel agencies will be able to take care of business with MALÉV. In Budapest the airline runs in addition several offices: District I, Krisztina körút 41-43, Tel: 166,6860; District III, Laktanya u. 3-5, Tel: 188-6942; District 5, Roosevelt tér 2, Tel: 118-6614. Here is a list of representatives of some foreign airlines operating offices in Budapest: **Air Canada**: Sziklai S. u. 1, 1012 Budapest I, Tel: 175-4618. **Air France**: Kristóf tér 6, 1052 Budapest V, Tel: 118-0411, at the airport: 157-1163. **Air India**: Vörösmarty tér 6, 1051 Budapest V, Tel: 118-4804. **Alitalia**: Ferenciek tér 1, 1053 Budapest V, Tel: 118-6882. **Austrian Airlines**: Régiposta u. 5, 1052 Budapest v, Tel: 117-1550, at the airport: 167-4374. **British Airways**: Apáczai Csere János u. 5, 1052 Budapest V, Tel: 118-3041. **Finnair**: Váci u. 19-21, 1052 Budapest V, Tel: 117-4022. **Iberia**: Baross tér 20, 1077 Budapest IV, Tel: 122-0096. **KLM**: Vörösmarty tér 2, 1051 Budapest V, Tel: 117-4522. **Lufthansa**: Váci u. 19, 1052 Budapest V, Tel: 118-4511, at the airport 157-0290. **PanAm**: Apáczai Csere János u. 4, 1052 Budapest V, Tel: 118-7922. **Sabena**: Váci u. 1-3, 1052 Budapest, Tel: 118-4111. **SAS**: Váci u. 1-3, 118-5582. **Varig**: Bécsi u. 8-10, 1052 Budapest V, Tel: 117-1654.

Embassies/Consulates in Hungary

Australia: Apáczai Csere János u. 12-14, 1052 Budapest V, Tel: 118-8100. **Austria**: Benczúr u. 16, 1068 Budapest VI, Tel: 122-9467. **Belgium**: Donáti u. 34, 1015 Budapest I, Tel: 115-30-99. **Canada**: Budakeszi út 32, 1021 Budapest II, Tel: 176-7711. **Danemark** and **Finland**: Vérhalom u. 12-16, 1023 Budapest II, Tel: 115-2066. **France**: Lendvay u. 27, 1062 Budapest VI, Tel: 112-8268. **Germany**: Nógrádi u. 8, 1125 Budapest XII, Tel: 155-9366; Consulate: Izsó u. 5, 1146 Budapest XIV, Tel: 122-4204. **Great Britain**: Harmincad u. 6, 1051 Budapest V, Tel: 118-2888. **Holland**: Abonyi u. 31, 1146 Budapest XIV, Tel: 122-8432. **India**: Búzavirág u. 16, 1025 Budapest II, Tel: 115-3243. **Indonesia**: Gorkij fasor 26, 1068 Budapest VI, Tel: 142-8508. **Italy**: Népstadion út 95, 1143 Budapest XIV, Tel: 142-8722. **Japan**: Rómer Flóris u. 56-58, 1024 Budapest II, Tel: 115-0044. **Norway**: Határöör u. 35, 1122 Budapest XII, Tel: 155-1729. **Sweden**: Ajtósi Dürer sor 27/a, 1146 Budapest XIV, Tel: 122-9880. **Switzerland**: Népstadionút 107, 1143 Budapest XIV, Tel: 122-9491. **Spain**: Eötvös u. 11/b, 1067 Budapest VI, Tel:

142-8580. **USA**: Szabadság tér 12, 1054 Budapest V, Tel: 112-6450.

Tourist Offices

The oldest and most important Hungarian travel agency IBUSZ operates offices throughout the world, where prospective visitors can find much of the information they might want concerning special tours, programs and other events going on in Hungary. IBUSZ also books accomodations and takes care of visas. IBUSZ was one of the first large companies in Hungary to be privatized.

Austria: Kärntnerstr. 26, 1010 Wien, Tel: (01) 51-555; Pfeiffergasse 5, 5020 Salzburg, (0662) 84-22-97. **Finland**: ISO Robertinkatu 48-50/B-21, 00120 Helsinki, Tel: (0) 17-99-22. **France**: 27 rue du Quatre-Septembre, 75002 Paris, Tel: (1) 47-42- 50-25. **Germany**: Baseler Str. 46-48, 6000 Frankfurt 1, Tel: (069) 252-018; Großer Burstah 53, 2000 Hamburg 11, Tel: (040) 37-30-78; Mauritiussteinweg 114-116, 5000 Köln 1, (0221) 21-91-02; Dachauerstr. 5, 8000 München 2, Tel (089) 55-72-17; Kronprinzstr.6, 7000 Stuttgart 1, (0711) 37-30-78; Karl Liebknechtstr. 9, in East Berlin, Tel: 0037-(2) 212-35-59. **Great Britain**: Danube Travel Ltd., 6 Conduit Street, London W1R 9TG, Tel: (71) 493-02-63. **Holland**: World Trade Center Toren B-14-E, Strawinskylaan 1425, 1077 XX Amsterdam, Tel: (20) 64-98-51. **Italy**: Via V. E. Orlando 75, 00185 Roma, Tel: (6) 48-65-15. **Japan**: Ambassador Roppongi Building 403, 16-13 Roppongi 3-chome, Minato-ku, Tokyo 106. Tel: (03) 584-75-35. **Spain**: J. A. Mendizabal 1, 28008 Madrid, Tel: (01) 241-25-44. **Sweden**: Beridarebanen 1, Stockholm 10326, Tel: (8) 232-030. **Switzerland**: Freigutstr.5, 8002 Zürich, Tel:(01) 20-11-760. **USA**: Rockefeller Center, 630 Fifth Avenue, suite 2455, New York, NY 10111, Tel: (212) 582-74-12.

HUNGARIAN LANGUAGE

Hungarian belongs to the Finno-Ugric family of languages, meaning those spoken in such distant places as Finland, Siberia and Estonia. Note, that by and large, speakers of these languages do not mutually understand each other as might a Spaniard and an Italian. The first-time visitor will immediately notice that it is difficult if not impossible to even recognize the words written or spoken in every-day public life. A hotel is called *szálloda*, the police *rendörség*, restaurant becomes *étterem, vendéglö*, or *csárda*, in other words, nothing vaguely ressembling the words used in other western countries.

Hungarian is a so-called agglutinative language, meaning that prepositions and various qualifiers, plurals, possessives and the like, get stuck onto the ends of words.

For example, the word for hero is *hös*. Its plural becomes *hösök*, our heros becomes *höseink* and finally, seen on war memorials, the word *höseinknek*, to our heroes. Get it? Thus one can positively say, that whereas most languages gather words together to make sentences, Hungarian sweeps letters together.

Before provide some basic words and sentences, here is a vital list of specifically Hungarian pronunciations:

Vowels:

a = a closed "a" as in not
á = an open "a" as in pad
e = "e" as in exit
é = a long "e", as in pail
i = "i" as in it
í = "i" as in exceeding
o = "o" as in obvious
ó = "o" as in boring
ö = as in hurt
u = as in who
ú = as in pool
ü = like a monophthongal few
y = (at the end of family names) see "i"

Consonants:
c = "ts" as in patsy
cs = "ch" as in chapter
gy (doubles as ggy) = combination of
   "d" and "yuh"
j = y as in yell
ly (doubled as lly) = "y" as in
   yell (emphatically pronounced)
ny (doubled as nny) = the "ni"
   as in onion
s (doubled as ss) = "sh" as in shoot
sz (doubled as ssz) = "s" as in sissy
ty (doubled as tty) = a hissing "ti" as
   in tiara
z = "z" as in zee
zs = dungeon without the "d" sound

Note that mispronouncing the letters
can result in misunderstandings. *ágy*
means bed, *agy* means brain. Be especially careful about differentiating e and é
and s and sz! It is best to practice the toast
egészségedre (to your health) very dil-
igently to avoid embarrassing faux-pas.
The emphasis in Hungarian words is always on the first syllable.

General words

ár . . . . price
áruház . department store/supermarket
bejárat . . entrance (highways, houses)
benzinkút . . . . gasoline station
bolt . . . . store
bor, borozó . . . . wine, wine bar
cipö (csipész) . . . . . shoe (shoemaker)
csárda . . . . inn
csatorna . . . . canal
csemege . . . . delicatessen
dohány . . . tobacco (slang for money)
emlékmü . . . . memorial
étterem . . . . restaurant
férfi . . . . man, i.e., men's room
foglalt . . . . occupied
fodrász . . . . hairdresser
folyó . . . . river
földalatti . . . . underground
fogorvos . . . . dentist
fürdö . . . . bath

gyár . . . . factory
gyümölcs . . . . fruit
határ . . . . border
hentesáru . . . . . butcher (for sausages)
híd . . . . bridge
huzni . . . . pull
hús . . . . butcher
jávitás . . . . repair
kijárat . . . . . exit (highways, houses)
komp . . . . ferry
könyv . . . . book
kórház . . . . hospital
Magyarország . . . . Hungary
nö, nöi . . women, women's (i.e. room)
ólommentes . . . . lead-free
orvos . . . . doctor
pályaudvar . . . . terminal train station
patika . . . . . . pharmacy, drugstore
pince . . . . cellar
rendörség . . . . police
rév . . . . harbor, ferry
rom . . . . ruin
sör, sörözö . . . . beer, beer bar
szabad . . . . free
szálloda . . . . hotel
szoba . . . . room
tilos . . . . forbidden
üzlet . . . . shop, business
vám . . . . customs
vár . . . . fortress
vasútállomás . . . . train station
vendéglö . . . . restaurant
veszélyes . . . . dangerous
viggyázz . . . . watch out !
tolni . . . . push
útépités . . . . road repairs
zárva . . . . closed
zöldség . . . . vegetables

Words in restaurants

alma . . . . apple
ásványvíz . . . . mineral water
bárány . . . . lamb
birka . . . . mutton
borjú . . . . veal
csirke . . . . chicken
cukor . . . . sugar
édes . . . . sweet

elöételek	hors d'oeuvres
dinnye	melon
ebéd	lunch
fagylalt	ice cream
fácán	pheasant
fehér bor	white wine
fejes saláta	lettuce
frissensültek freshly	fried
galuska	dumplings
gomba	mushroom
hagyma	onion
hal	fish
hideg	cold
káposzta	cabbage
kávé	coffee
körte	pear
köret	side-dishes
különlegességek	specialties
leves(ek)	soup(s)
málna	raspberry
marha	beef
meggy	sour cherry
meleg	warm
narancs	orange
nyúl	rabbit
öszibarack	peach
palacsinta thin	Hungarian pancake
paradicsom	tomato
pezsgö	sparkling wine, champagne
reggeli	breakfast
rizs	rice
sajt	cheese
sárgabarack	apricot
sertés	pork
saláták	salads
só	salt
sült	roasted
száraz	dry
szárnyas	foul
szarvas	deer
szölö	grape
tea	tea
tej, tejszin	milk, cream
töltött	stuffed
teszták pastries (incl. noodles and dumplings)	
uborka	cucumber
vacsora	dinner
vad	venison
vaddisznó	boar
vegyes	mixed
velö	brain
vörös bor	red wine

Some expressions:

Good day!	Jó napot kívánok!
Good morning!	Jó reggelt kívánok!
Good evening!	Jó estét kívánok!
Hi! Hello!	Szervusz!
Good bye!	Visszontlátásra!
Bye! See you!	Szia or viszlát!

Frequently heard is the expression (*kezi*) *csókolom*, from a man to a woman or children to adults, it means "I kiss (your hand)".

Bon appetit!	Jó étvágyat kívánok!
Good night	Jó éjszakát kívánok!
Please!	Kérem (szépen)!
Thank you!	Köszönöm (szépen)!
With pleasure!	Szívesen!
Excuse me!	Bocsánat!
yes - no	igen - nem
Do you speak ...?	Beszél ... ?
English	angolul
German	németül
French	franciául
Italian	olaszul
Russian	oroszul
I am very ill	Nagyon beteg vagyok.

I need a doctor (fast)
Nekem kell egy orvos (gyorsan).

I would like to pay	Szeretnék fizetni
Help!	Segitség!
Leave me alone	Hagyj békén!
Where is	Hol ...?

How much does it cost?
Mennyibe kerül?

Finally, a frequently heard word is *tessék*, meaning please when drawing someone's attention to something, or when answering a call for attention or the telephone. Another is *persze*, usually spoken with great emphasis. It means "naturally".

AUTHORS

Amalia Morgenstern, born in Miskolc, was raised in Budapest, where she studied German and Geography. She left Hungary in the 1950s to settle in Toronto. A reluctant exile, she welcomed the changes in Eastern Europe that allowed her to renew her ties to her homeland.

Marton Radkai, a freelance writer, radio reporter, photographer and editor of Hungarian and German descent, has traveled to and through Hungary extensively in the past four years, writing travel articles and reporting on political and cultural events for Radio *Deutsche Welle*. He was born in New York City, raised in France and Great Britain, and now lives near Munich, Germany. He has worked on several Hungary-related books and has appeared in such publications as *House and Garden* and *World of Interiors*.

Erika Bollweg, who lives in Cologne, has entertained a long and fruitful relationship with Hungary over the past decades. She learned Hungarian in the midst of a singing career and has since established a solid reputation as a writer and translator of Hungarian literature.

Lilla Milassin was born in Hungary and spent her childhood in Dresden, (then East) Germany. She is currently living in Budapest but can often be found in Pécs or Leipzig where she is pursuing her studies in German and Art History.

Hans-Horst Skupy, a Hungary connoisseur from way back has written and edited innumerable words on the little country. He was born in Bratislava (Pozsony to the Hungarians) in Czechoslovakia and lives (when he is not traveling somewhere in the world) in Wessling near Munich. His keen pen is matched by a keen eye: Half his time is spent with a camera in hand (see list of photographers).

Judit Szász, a Romanian-born Hungarian with a German passport living in Munich, is a freelance journalist working today on the staff of Otto von Habsburg, a representative in the European Parliament.

Ferenc Bodor lives in Budapest where he runs the *Tölgyfa* gallery which specializes in Hungarian cultural trends.

PHOTOGRAPHERS